VISIONS FROM THE SOUL

Visions from the Soul

Bridging Personality to Spirit

BY

MAURIE D. PRESSMAN, M.D.

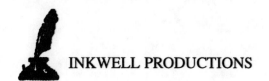

INKWELL PRODUCTIONS

To my wife,
my life companion,
who provides the soft matrix that makes my work and life a joy.

Acknowledgments

My great appreciation to Ann Nunley, who read this manuscript with deep understanding, and gave me the faith and opportunity to bring it forth.

My great appreciation for the devotion of my friend Marylou Auchter whose elegance and care supported this manuscript with her own excellence.

Sculpture on the Cover:
"The Encounter"
by Mirtala
For more information, contact
Maurie D. Pressman, M.D.
200 Locust Street
Philadelphia, PA 19106
Tel: 215-922-0204
E-mail: mauriedavid@spirituali.com

MAURIE D. PRESSMAN, M.D.
Life Fellow American Psychiatric Association
Clinical Professor of Psychiatry, Temple University
Health Sciences Center.

ISBN   0-9658158-2-x

Cover design: Paul Klissas, V-Space Design, Phoenix, AZ
Typesetting: Madalyn Johnson, Type 'n Graphics, Mesa, AZ

Published by Inkwell Productions, Scottsdale, AZ
Developed by Self Publishers Group, www.selfpublishersgroup.com
Printed in the United States of America

Contents

Preface

This is a book about you. It contains stories about the emotional and spiritual quests of ordinary people. The term "ordinary" may be misleading since, although we may lead seemingly unremarkable lives, we are each unique and capable of extraordinary experiences.

In his book, Dr. Pressman celebrates our wholeness of body, mind, and spirit calling upon each of us to claim our unique "extraordinary" or "spiritual" components.

Mainstream medicine and psychology have, for the most part, focused on illness. Following a model that excludes the spiritual dimension, the tendency has been to diagnose what is "wrong" and then use psychological or pharmacological methods in an effort to fix or cure symptoms.

While Dr. Pressman's initial training in medicine and psychotherapy formed a solid foundation from which to go forth, it also served to inspire his curiosity about the limitations of conventional approaches and their missing elements. What followed has been forty years of medicine practice as a psychiatrist and as many years of creative personal and professional exploration and innovation.

In true healing we don't deal with the fragments in order to become whole – but rather we accept our wholeness in order to deal with the fragments. Dr. Pressman points out that if we're honest we come to realize that the only effective therapist is one who helps us liberate our own innate "healer within." This requires us to open up three basic levels of the psyche - levels that include super-conscious, self-conscious, and sub-conscious aspects of ourselves.

The *super-conscious* level links us to a transcendental, universal field of consciousness. As such it both contains and reaches beyond personal awareness, memory and experience. There is no linear time in this field of consciousness and to reach balance and foster true healing without calling upon this higher consciousness is like trying to manufacture a car with no designer and no blueprint.

The *self-conscious* level is our most familiar realm of consciousness. The self-conscious mind has difficulty recognizing and integrating the information made available by the super-conscious and sub-conscious and is our most limited aspect of mind. However, self-consciousness is vital to our survival and provides the mechanism for bringing transformative, spiritual awareness into physical reality. Without the strong foundation of our self-conscious mind we would be "spacey" and ineffectual.

The *sub-conscious* level links us to the unconscious memories and feelings. This aspect of mind communicates symbolically and emotionally, providing feelings, visions, insights, and dreams that can guide our understanding of who we are, where we've been, and where we may be going.

When positively acknowledged, both the sub-conscious and super-conscious support healing by communicating with us during various forms of therapy, meditation, quiet contemplation, and sleep.

Healing and wholeness require us to open doors of awareness between all three of these levels so that the insights and integrative power of spirit can act upon feelings and beliefs locked within our sub-conscious memory, bringing healing to the attitudes and emotions expressed in daily life.

Dr. Pressman's search for approaches and methods that successfully bring forth this healing awareness, his innate core and compassion and his many years of experience with patients are beautifully narrated in this volume. Through personal experiences and touching, human stories about the experiences of his methods of healing, choosing a counselor or therapist, and for launching our own spiritual *self*-healing, *Visions from the Soul* is a "must read" for all those who seek physical, emotional, and spiritual wholeness.

– Ann Nunley, PhD. - Author of the *Inner Counselor*

Introduction

More than anything else, I wish this book to be an adventure in self-help, through self-psychotherapy. I firmly believe that through introspection, meditation, and the courageous willingness to face our resistances to self-knowledge, we can be released from the bonds and restrictions that have been placed upon us by a too-physically oriented society. Once released, there is an inherent buoyancy of the soul, a goodness called divinity that we are at center, a soul that wants to rise up and will rise to express itself in our personalities and will cause us to teach by example.

I have been on the scene, medically and psychiatrically, for more than forty years, and I have come to know that the mind in its broader sense, encompasses the body, and that psychology/psychiatry and self-counseling are bigger than medicine. Why do I say this? The farther I have gone along, the more I know the power of the divinity that we are within, so great that if it can be expressed through the mind, it can conquer any illness, correct any deformity, lead onward to powers which seem by comparison to our Western standards as magic. There have been so many "spontaneous healings" leading to rupture in the rules of American medicine, so many who have been healed and cured of cancer, of lupus erythematosis, of neurological conditions which were not supposed to heal and yet have. American medicine would call this an anomaly, but I would call it the power of the soul expressed through the mind. Not long ago Norman Cousins cured himself of malignancy by watching silent movie comedies to make himself laugh; the power of visualization in the matrix of the calm that comes with prayer and meditation has shown itself to be enormous, again causing remissions in so-called incurable conditions. American medicine and American psychiatry have become so biologically minded; they suffer because they shrink and constrict the soul by concentration on the physical-chemical. I believe that the mind, the expression of the soul, is bigger than Medicine, and can lead to an enormous advance in the healing arts. More than that, it can lead to an advancement of the personality on up to soul levels, so that we can realize and we can sponsor the advance toward the next race of men/women. As such we will honor, as we are beginning to do, the power of the mind in conjunction with the soul, the heart of love, and we will communicate more and more through empathy, intuition and telepathy.

It is for this reason that I want to bring before you this book written out of the experiences of a conventionally trained psychiatrist and psychoanalyst, with the conviction that if we become familiar with that center of truth called the intuitive heart, and rely upon it, we can become our own best therapist, and we can release that inherent goodness called the soul toward our own ascension into spiritual realms, and engage in the lifting of society out of its all-too-material encumbrance.

PERSONAL JOURNEY:
THE SEARCH FOR THE SOUL IN PSYCHOTHERAPY

My Journey: Guidance From Above Through Surrender To Intuition -- Spiritual Beginnings -- Lack Of Psychology To Say Nothing Of Spirituality In Medical School -- Opening To Adventures With Sigmund Freud -- The Invitation To Intuition From A Psychoanalytic Teacher -- Adventures With Olympic Athletes -- Stanislav Grof And Breathwork -- My Recovering Memories From Birth -- Introduction To Muktananda -- Lessons From The Ascended Masters Of The East -- Readings In Theosophy -- Brazil And The Spiritists And An Expanded Approach To Patients.

It has been well said that when the student is ready the master will appear. I have learned from the journeys of others on a path that I wanted to follow. Since we all are the same, at bottom, there is good reason to believe that we will learn from these descriptions.

I believe that we are creatures of divinity; that we are in our essence, Beings of light, love, wisdom and immortality. I believe these things quite literally. I believe also that these essences are covered by layers of acquired and acculturated creeds that tell us that the physical self and the physical world in which we live are the sole proprietors of reality. Clinging to this acculturation we fail to see the essences of energy, love and wisdom, intuitive knowledge and divine unity that are our natural inheritance. I base this fundamental position upon a number of things: studies of the teachings of the ancient masters that arise largely out of Eastern philosophies; my own introspective adventures; and, more than anything else, the validation of certain of my experiences by my patients. All of these things have helped me to establish a bridge between some seemingly far out beliefs and life as we live it.

Everywhere in life, if we aspire higher, we will touch higher.

We each speak a different language. Language frames the assumptions through which we see the world, hear the world, and speak to the world, often passionately. Republicans and Democrats spend a great deal of time arguing about cures for the country, but neither side listens much to the other. Psychoanalysts are convinced that the behaviorists are superficial. The poor and dispossessed are certain that they will never be heard, and the wealthy feel put upon because people think that no one with money should ever have problems. All of these factions, schools of thought, and economic groups exist in a world that cries out for understanding, and inwardly longs for communion.

I have learned from the experiences of respected teachers and authors that biography, telling the story of one's own journey and seasoning, is a good way to share one's worldview, and concepts of the spiritual. Hopefully, through the stories I share in these pages, a new and clearer meaning of spirituality will emerge, moving us both, reader and writer, forward and upward.

My Jewish heritage had a deep effect upon my journey to manhood. As a son I was much attached to my very loving, nurturing Jewish mother and her desire for a child who was a doctor or a rabbi guided and inspired me. While I was happy to follow the path of the physician, I never lost the priestly half of my calling. My mother was the first human being to teach me how wonderful it was to help people, and she was profoundly right in this insight. In the giving spiritual atmosphere of our household, my connections with what I now call spiritual psychotherapy were foreshadowed. Later, the inspiration my mother gave me for service was confirmed by the teachings of the Ascended Masters who taught, "Strive for the Universal Fellowship; ascend in yourself through service to others."

At the age of twenty I applied to medical school, but it was hard to penetrate the quota for Jewish students that existed at the time. I was refused by many universities, but finally experienced an almost overwhelming gratitude when the Bowman Gray School of Medicine at Wake Forest University accepted me. As a student who was on his way at last, I was eager to learn about how the mind and personality functioned. Sadly, however, I found that psychiatry had been relegated to a half day of the entire medical school curriculum, and was taught by someone who believed only in the neurological hard wiring of the mind.

Internship proved a fascinating time of discovery, giving me my first taste of the inspired pleasure of healing others. Even then, however, I saw that medicine did not always work the way I had been taught that it did. I was amazed to see the difference between the woman of eighty-two who needed emergency gallbladder surgery and the forty-year-old who was physically well prepared for the same surgery. The eighty-two-year-old was calm and serene; the forty-year-old full of dreadful expectations.

To my great surprise, the older woman sailed through the postoperative period, while the forty-year-old suffered numerous complications.

Now, years later, I have come to understand the serenity that can come with advanced years. The greater perspective of the elderly and their inner knowing about immortality yields immense protection in the field of medicine. Now I know the profound effect that such inner peace, hard-won through the struggles of life, has upon the immune system--how peace can protect the body from assault. When I was young, however, such things were a mystery.

My residency in psychiatry in 1947 and 1948 was a gloomy time for me. The locked doors in the mental hospitals opened to callous staff members, whom the inmates nicknamed "the Chiefs," who shook their fists at patients. Staff and doctors alike shared an almost inhuman view of the "mad patient." Occasionally, however, I saw brief flashes of kindness. I will never forget watching one of the younger Assistant Chiefs who sat at a patient's bedside and communicated with him, heart-to-heart. This understanding without words stood in stark contrast to the other "instructions" that I had received. At that time there was no treatment for mental illness except hot and cold baths, Phenobarbital given in large doses, and the new wonder treatment, electroshock therapy. For the most part my residency seemed like a visit to hell: gloom surrounded by mystery and helplessness.

At this time a fortunate and transformative event transpired in my life: the writings of Sigmund Freud began to appear in English. I absorbed these teachings with great fascination, walked through the outer vestments of the inner mind and began to travel to the interior--into the great heartland of the unconscious mind. The unconscious mind! Nowadays, this seems like a well-worn concept, but it surely was news then, and a far cry from what I had been taught before. Suddenly patient behaviors that I had not been able to explain within the context of traditional psychiatry began to make sense, and there was a promise of better things to come. Freud offered me the chance to touch the inner humanity of my patients, my fellow human beings, and to find a way out of my own feelings of unhappiness and inferiority. Through his theory of sublimation, that wonderful concept whereby one could have all kinds of reprehensible instincts, and yet redeem them by making them useful to society and to the self, Freud freed us from the debilitating burden of self-hatred and guilt. The man who as a child was unnaturally curious and cut open small animals and birds to see what was inside, could turn this curiosity into the profession of surgery, using it to heal. The individual who was overly inquisitive about the thoughts and inner motivations of others could become a psychiatrist, satisfying his or her curiosity in a socially useful way. Freud offered the promise that the cure for those things we struggled with was also the road to fulfillment, service and happiness. His humanistic way of treating patients was a promise that foreshadowed my later journey onto the spiritual path.

Although Freud's ideas were new to the West, I later discovered that they had been practiced by those in the east for thousands of years. The path to introspection had been followed for millennia through the traditions of the Eastern Masters through the art of meditation. The penetration into the deeper mind, its secrets and powers, had been studied and transmitted to countless generations of aspirants. Psychoanalysis might be a late arrival on the scene, but it was a pioneering arrival as far as the West was concerned.

Having learned about psychoanalysis, I decided that this, indeed, was what I needed, and I entered into training. Despite the painful trial of working with my training analyst, someone who was highly authoritative, and whom I realized, in retrospect, didn't like me--a warning to everyone to pay close attention to the counselor-patient fit--I had an important realization. I saw clearly through reading and experiences with other supervisors, that the essence of mental and physical health is to find the inner wellsprings of desire and talent and then to let them flow through avenues that are approved and rewarded by Society. This implies service to others, a concept that is, again, parallel to the teachings of the Eastern Masters of Wisdom. They teach that we should live to create a universal fellowship of man/woman, and thus ascend by service.[1]

I was undergoing another kind of struggle at the time, at least the priestly portion of me was. Where was religion in my life? Did it exist? I had started out as a devout person, but where was my faith now? I had attended Hebrew College, but gradually relinquished my beliefs when I was challenged by agnostics and confronted with questions I couldn't answer. Medical school, with its secular explanations for every human ill, was no help; and psychoanalytic training embodied Freud's teachings that religion was society's soporific, or worse, an obsessional neurosis. I wasn't

---

[1] Someone has argued that to comply with and be rewarded by a society that has become increasingly materialistic is not an advance but a retreat from spirit. While that is true, I believe that it is better to work courageously from within, pushing the envelope toward expansion. This can also be a lesson by example.

satisfied with either explanation.

I began inquiring of rabbis, priests and other members of the cloth, "How do you remain religious?" Unfortunately, their answers returned always as if by rote, rather than through inspired belief. One day, however, I had a different kind of response while I was talking to a senior psycho-analyst who had, to my great surprise, remained an Orthodox Jew. "How do you remain religious?" I asked him.

He answered, "Some things you know with your mind, and some things you know with your heart." That statement rang true, resonating within me, and for the first time I felt a certain satisfaction. For me, this conversation represented the initial opening of my gates of intuition, at least a bit. It led me to the insight that intuition was at the heart of knowing. When this gentleman answered me, it was my intuition that had resonated.

In spite of this profound experience, I knew very well that intuition is disparaged, even scorned in Western science, including that science that should be the most introspective of all, psychoanalysis.

Much later, after I had learned about the teachings of the Eastern Masters, I found that they not only recognized intuition, but identified it as a higher perception than reason. In my current practice, I have found that the more I trust intuition--always in the context of grounded common sense--the more available it becomes.. The more available it becomes, the more reason there is to trust in it, because it does not lead us astray in our search for answers.

My journey, my doubts and seeking continued throughout the years that I was developing my private practice. Then came another mile-stone in my understanding of the human mind. I discovered the marvelous effectiveness of hypnosis in reaching the unconscious mind and unleashing its powers. This came about because two of my sons were figure skating competitors. At one of the advanced competitions, I met two Olympic coaches who, to my surprise, were interested in me as a psychiatrist. I was surely interested in them since I was a father. This encounter marked the beginning of my work with Olympic skaters, coaching them psychologically.

At first, I tried to encourage them with conventional psychoanalytic wisdom, "Face your anxiety, and all will be well!" I exhorted. With that, they fairly threw me out of the room. In the heat of the moment, and in fear of losing the job, which I needed, I sought more direct means. I began to use hypnosis on the skaters, borrowing some guidelines from behavior modification, then an emerging science, and adding the injunction that they visualize a perfect performance. The results were sudden and dramatic. In fact, they seemed too good to be true. Could it really be this easy to invoke a better performance, I wondered? My scientific training cast all sorts of doubts in my mind, but the improvements in the skaters were there.

Later, I discovered that a celebrated authority and early researcher into the effects of relaxation on the body, Edmund Jacobson, had long before discovered that visualization is reflected in the muscular movements. In his book, *Modern Treatments of Tense Patients,* he described the effectiveness of progressive relaxation. This technique involved alternately tensing and relaxing muscles, thereby inducing a state of mental relaxation.

Today we have learned much more about the power of visualization. For example, studies in psycho-neuro-immunology show the response of the immune system to visualization and to emotional peaks and valleys. In his book *The Holographic Universe,* Michael Talbot suggests that when we visualize we may be dipping into the actual creative substratum that comprises the basis for the development of all physical manifestation. David Bohm has described this substrate as part of the implicate order, that place from whence the material world manifests. Thus, when I asked the Olympic skaters under hypnosis and subsequent autohypnosis to visualize the perfect performance, this suggestion had a training effect upon the body as well as the mind.

Accordingly, I learned that the mind, the mental energy body, creates things in the material world. In effect, a new skater had emerged as the mind reached into itself through hypnosis-meditation (all hypnosis is akin to meditation); and a new person, the more nearly perfect skater, appeared. What does this tell us? It reveals that our essential being, our essential divinity, resides deeply within and can be reached and employed to guide us and empower us toward perfection.

As a result of my work with the athletes, which was seen as a pioneering effort, I was invited to speak at an International Sports Congress. There, I had an encounter that was to change my entire life. I met a psychologist who represented the Esalen Institute in California, and he told me about the work of Stanislav Grof, a psychiatrist who was conducting workshops at the Esalen Institute about consciousness at birth. I had never heard of such a thing, but I decided to visit him and take the workshop.

This was a very strange decision for me to make. Travelling to Esalen on the trail of someone whom I thought was probably not well integrated scientifically was both inconvenient and expensive, but I was compelled to do so by a force outside of myself. This was the first of a

compelled to do so by a force outside of myself. This was the first of a series of compulsions, or "calls" as I came to think of them, that would come upon me at various times in my life.

I visited Grof and took his birthing workshop, which combined breathwork and select powerful music. The experience was remarkable, and my own curtain of doubt was penetrated as I discovered something I had not known about my own birth. During the experience, I was lying on the floor and began to burrow beneath some very large pillows. The facilitators began to pull me back by my legs to make room for others. As they pulled, I suddenly had the distinct impression of being breech birthed. This was strange, because I had always known that I had been delivered by forceps. I'd had so many marks on my face that the doctors wouldn't show me to my mother for days. I returned home and asked my father if he knew anything about my birth. I couldn't ask my mother since she had already died. He replied, "Do I! You had a hell of a time. You came out feet first." His remark was provocative to say the least, and certainly gave credence to the awareness I had undergone in the workshop.

Breathwork in combination with music is a mighty instrument. It produces an altered state of mind, releasing repressed feelings and memories, often transporting people to transpersonal realms. It is a mind-altering technique, yet during it one remains fully conscious and in charge. It is a commanding technique that we use in our clinic to release clients from the anchors of old conditioning, allowing them to move into transpersonal and spiritual realms.

My meeting with Grof was transformative in another way. For some reason the Grofs decided to arrange a personal meeting for me with Swami Muktananda who was the most recent in an ancient lineage of Siddha Masters. At that time, Muktananda was carrying out his assigned mission of bringing the teachings of Kasmir Shaivism to the West. A part of this teaching was the awakening of the Kundalini, the Divine Energy, by the imparting of Shaktipat, the transfer of his own divine energy to kindle the Kundalini fire within the other.

My experience with Muktananda was startling. In spite of the fact that I was then a reserved and highly skeptical man in his mid-fifties, I felt a tremendous outflow and inflow of love in the presence of this stranger-- and an inflammation of my desire to serve humanity through my profession of psychiatry. Though not yet on the spiritual path, strictly speaking, I was certainly being prepared. It is said that when the student is ready, the teacher appears. Muktananda was one of a series of teachers who began to appear to me at this time. As my spiritual education progressed, his teachings were followed by the writings of Madam Blavatsky and the Himalayan Masters with whom she had studied, Morya and Koot Hoomi.

Madame Blavatsky was a Russian aristocrat who, from her earliest years, was of an independent and almost reckless temperament. She searched throughout the world for knowledge and eventually found herself in Egypt, the Near East and then Tibet. While in the mountain reaches of the Himalayas, she was taken under the tutelage of the Masters Morya and Koot Hoomi. There, for the next four years, she was trained as a "chela" or disciple. Afterward, they sent her on her mission to teach the philosophies of these Masters in the West, where she later organized the teachings under the name of the Theosophical Society. The mission of the Society was not only to teach but also to advocate a universal fellowship of men and women; to encourage the study of comparative religion, philosophy and science; and to investigate the unexplained laws of nature and the powers latent within humanity. I was strongly drawn to Theosophical teachings, clearly understanding that these principles certainly parallel the worthy mission of the physician, and all the more of the "Physician-Priest."

An intimate view of these ancient masters was published in *The Mahatma Letters,* the correspondence between Morya and Koot Hoomi and A.P. Sinnett, an influential Englishman and publisher of the important Anglo-Indian Newspaper. Sinnett was interested in both the teachings of Madame Blavatsky and her extraordinary, almost magical performances in which she was able to produce material objects, such as gemstones, out of thin air. Sinnett believed that these abilities indicated that she had been taught secrets of nature that were not known to the world of science.

The Mahatma Letters, which were never intended to be published, discussed the advanced philosophy of the Masters, their inherent world-altruism, and their command of unusual powers, including the power to project their thoughts as well as their astral presence. Their thought projections even took on a material form, and they told Sinnett that their letters were inscribed by mental power alone. It was unfortunate, however, that Sinnett was interested primarily in these paranormal powers. In his search to understand them, he forgot the essential message, which was to honor and teach the equality of all human beings. Because of this, and after a considerable correspondence, the Masters put an end to their communication with him.

Sinnett's lack of perception caused him to throw away a great opportunity. Even though Madame Blavatsky herself was able to perform many of these sorts of "miracles," materializing rings and precious jewels from thin air, and creating the sounds of bells and the movement of objects, she did not make much of these abilities. Her primary interest was in teaching her fellow men and women how to be better people and how to make a better world. Even today, there are teachers who have the ability to manifest material objects. Sai Baba, a realized master in India, is one of them; but he too uses these manifestations to evoke interest in the higher teachings.

The real significance of such feats is that they teach us that there is more to Nature than is known to our Western science. This is true of the powers of the mind as well, as indicated by our more recent studies in such phenomena as fire-walking, spontaneous healing and the power of prayer. The basic point is that we all acquire unusual powers as we ascend to the point where we are more focussed on love and the community of our fellowship than on power or personal gain. Knowledge and power follow upon such service. These powers are latent within all of us, but they are screened out, so to speak, by the worldview we are taught from childhood and the great curtain of doubt that modern science places in front of everything that is not material.

It might seem a surprising result, but my experience of Muktananda and his teachings restored me to my own religion, Judaism. Now, however, I no longer perceived my religion in a separate way, as embodying the only truth, but rather as a part of an ecumenical realization that God is within me and that I am within God--as are we all. Each of us is a molecule in the sea of God and, collectively, we become and comprise that sea. This realization is the echo of what lies ahead: that day when we shall all have ascended enough to live, serve and practice in the context of a Universal Fellowship. I believe that herein lies the real, and only, answer to the many and perilous problems that beset our society. And I believe that the day will come when we will take greater pleasure in our love of community than in individual power.

All of these events came into my life in 1978, which I now think of as the year of my opening. That year I also had my first contact with *A Course in Miracles,* a modern-day bible written in the Christian idiom. Its central tenet is that love is what we are; love is the fundamental reality. All else is illusion; an illusion often called fear. This belief may seem unrealistic in view of our usual cultural assumptions, but the workbook that accompanies "The Course" gradually brings one into the practical applications of these teachings. A good source for anyone interested in reading about The Course can be found in Dr. Gerry Jampolsky's concise summary entitled *Love is Letting Go of Fear.*[2] Fate, and I suspect hidden guidance, brought me into contact with some of the original players who brought *A Course in Miracles* on the scene; and it later became an important facet of the therapy that we offer people at my clinic, the Pressman Center For Mind/Body Wellness.

A year later another major event took place in my life when I was invited to Council Grove. I was quite excited about the invitation for I had read about this gathering in Grof's book *Realms of the Human Unconscious,* and I longed to be a part of this high-minded and progressive group who had dedicated themselves to learning about the new field of brain/mind research.

The Council Grove convocation was begun around 1960 by Elmer Green, one of the fathers of biofeedback and recent head of the Voluntary Controls department at the Menninger Clinic. The meeting takes place each year outside of Topeka, Kansas, the home of the Menninger Clinic. At that time, about a hundred scientists, teachers and philosophers gather for a weeklong retreat to speak freely about new domains of the mind, science and spirit. The seclusion of the meeting place frees them from the threat of ridicule or loss of academic status they would encounter if they met and discussed these things at their own universities or places of business.

---

[2]   Jampolsky was a successful pediatrician, wealthy, well-known, and full of ennui. He became an alcoholic, lost his family and remained an addict - until he came in contact with *A Course in Miracles.* Then his life changed. Jampolsky was one of the earliest adherents to the Course and a good friend of Judy Skutch, who was central to the arrival and early distribution of the manuscript.

The Course has an interesting history. It arrived on the scene in the early 1970's, through the mind of an academic psychologist at Columbia-Presbyterian University. Helen Schuchman was a Jewish agnostic, working with her boss and friend, Bill Thetford. One day they commiserated over the academic "rat race" and wished that there might be a better way to live. That night she heard a message, "This is a course in miracles, take notes." She was alarmed and thought that she was going crazy. Bill comforted her and advised that she write down the thoughts that she was "hearing." She did so, and he was able to see and tell her that what she wrote was compellingly beautiful.

She continued to hear the "voice" and the messages to be transcribed every night for seven years. Then they ceased. After that Thetford and Schuchman put the three volumes of manuscript away where they couldn't be seen, for fear that they would lose their academic standing if anyone found out that they

During the first week that I attended, the Theosophical concepts of Alice Bailey and her teachers came repeatedly to the fore.

Soon certain books which had acquired a familiar ring began to fall into my hands, Sinnett's *The Mahatma Letters* and Charles J. Ryan's *H.P. Blavatsky*. I was compelled to read about Madame Blavatsky in spite of the fact that the book by Ryan was poorly written and loosely assembled. Why was I so gripped by it? It was as if I were surrendering to a guiding force, and I was reminded again and again of the adage that when the student is ready, the Master will appear. We often miss such guidance in life, because it does not appear in the usual manner, but rather through subtle hints, synchronicities and intuitive messages.

The Mahatma Letters seemed too much for me at first, but when I called this volume to the attention of a fellow seeker, Patricia Joudry, a Canadian author with whom I was destined to write the book-- *Twin Souls: A Guide to Finding Your True Spiritual Partner,* she re-kindled my interest. I took a second look and the teachings unfolded. From there I went on to read Blavatsky's later writings, *Isis Unveiled* and *The Secret Doctrine.*

What is there in these teachings that fired my interest and inspiration, despite the fact that, at the time, I was still a relatively conservative academic psychiatrist? Perhaps it was that they contained the message that is core to all religions, the simple, yet profound message of unconditional love through service. Through these teachings, the spirit of God called me, the

---

that they existed. Fate would have it that Judy Skutch, a spiritual networker, was also looking for a better way to live at that time. Almost immediately she was introduced to Thetford and Schuchman. When she heard about the manuscripts, she had to have them. She stayed up night after night until she had read them all, and then, characteristically shared them, and created a discussion circle.

The time came when the manuscripts could no longer be reproduced by mimeograph because the demand was too great, yet there wasn't money enough for printing. The circle decided to meditate and pray. In a few days a letter arrived from Mexico, with a check enclosed, and a message as well. They were to print the "Course" and enclosed money was just enough for the first five thousand copies. The check had come from a man who had originally participated in the circle. He said he had felt led to sell a piece of land, and send them the enclosed money, which was just enough to answer the group's prayer.

A Course in Miracles has now spread throughout the world and has recently even been translated into Chinese. Its message that love is the universal energy, our divine core is the essence of all true spiritual teachings.

physician, to my role as physician-priest; to become again the healer who calls upon the power of devotion, and heals the hearts of others through the example of loving care.

Theosophical teachings also exhort us to investigate the powers of the mind, which expand as one goes deeper inward to the core. There the Divine Essence is met, revealing the unlimited power of the mind to live, to love and to heal. This message was balm to the ears of one who had dedicated his life to healing the mind and the soul.

I admired the fact that Madame Blavatsky taught these things by example, revealing that one does well to immerse oneself in truth. Her life demonstrated that an absolute commitment to honesty leads to humility and loving devotion. In this way, one gains personal power, even though the acquisition of power is far from one's goal.

I was thrilled when I learned this, for I recognized that just such a powerful commitment to honesty was inherent in Freud's early teachings. Psychoanalysis with its rule of "free association" bespoke it. Only honesty and the truth could make one free in mind, body and soul. Free association, which demands that everything be spoken, regardless of inhibition, also requires of the analyst that he/she be fully committed to the pursuit of truth, even to the point of being willing to recognize his or her own foibles. Although this exercise is not always easy, the rewards are great. When an analyst is willing to drop his or her self-centeredness and devote the self to others, supernormal powers of healing and prescience are often the result; for the greatest teaching we convey is through the teaching of what we are.

A psychiatrist may find, much to his or her surprise, that patients have a much greater readiness to accept these parapsychological and spiritual ideas than had been suspected. When the physician can allow these concepts he or she too will be lifted upward. I have been, I am being--and I look forward to more.

In my travels to other cultures, I have seen ample proof of the empowerment that follows upon one's surrendering to service. In 1982 my wife and I visited Brazil and Macchu Picchu on a spiritual journey. There are a great many "spiritists" in Sao Paulo who follow the work of Alain Kardec. These individuals believe in possession by dark spirits and devote themselves, without pay and without stint, to relieving such influences through their administrations and good deeds. While there, I met a psycho-therapist who had formerly been very "academic" and intellectually bound. By performing this selfless work, she had discovered that her intuition had grown to the point where she could hear what her patient was about to say before it was even said. I have never forgotten that conversation, and find that now, I too am having such experiences. Through them, my ability to help others has grown immensely.

We also met Brother Macedo, a former professional man who was called to leave his business and devote himself to spiritual and charitable work. He had a tremendous power which I, as well as those twelve others who were present with me that evening, felt deeply. Although I have always been fully identified with my Jewish faith, I had a vision of Jesus lifting me in His arms, calling to me and enfolding me. This was a tremendously moving and inspirational experience and, though I remain Jewish, I believe in the life and teachings of Jesus. After all, Jesus was a rabbi.

Experiences such as this have given me a more ecumenical approach to my patients and to people in general. We can all share in the inspired messages that come from on high, understanding that such visions and visualizations are a part of another world that is just as real as the one in which we are living now. Knowing this, I can share the message of our immortality with my patients, helping them to visit and hold close their dear departed ones. Such actions are comforting and elevating to both of us. I can now approach people I might have felt helpless to help before, with an assurance that God and the God within can create an upward spiral of healing in anyone or any situation.

Through such spiritual teachings all physicians may again become the true physician, the physician-priest. And it may be that this spiritual expansion will come soon to all men and women, healing this chaotic, separatist world.

Exercises and Guidelines:

Examine your own life for the beginnings of your interest in spiritual ascension. Look for the intuitions and seek guidelines for your path to finding the interests which won't leave you alone. Read biographies of teachers such as Aurobindo, Steiner, Helen Blavatsky (especially *HPB* by Sylvia Cranston).

CHAPTER I:

The Return to the Physician Priest and
The Emergence of the Spiritual Self

Physician "Heal Thyself" But No Need To Be A Physician To Be A Spiritual Healer -- Wise Women Healers And Shamans -- A Case History Of A Young Woman Who Was Despoiled By The Non-Humanistic Approach Of Modern Biological Psychiatry -- The Return Of The Spiritual -- Tools For Self-Exploration -- Guidelines For Transformation And Spiritual Growth -- Cautionary Signals About Following False Teachers ((Physician Teachers-Spiritual Teachers) -- The Limitations Of The Current Psychological Paradigm -- Realms Of The Mind -- The Energy Bodies -- The Physician Priest And The Divine Self -- Case History Of Enlightenment In A Physician -- Opening The Gates To Our Essential Power.

In the beginning, the priestly function was also the healing function; the physician and the priest were one. The shaman was the great religious spirit, the healer, the foreteller, the one who allied with and contended with the Devas and forces of nature. He/she was the channel between the flock and higher forces, connecting them with the Divine, and their power was acquired from both above and below.

Every culture has had its physician priests from time immemorial. The god-descended pharaohs of ancient Egypt exercised the authority, power and healing of both roles. Jesus was the supreme physician, who called upon the healing power of the almighty Father; but he was the rabbi as well. Moses too derived his power to heal from the divine source. He was the high priest who met with God's Presence on the mountaintop and carried His message to His people. He functioned as miracle worker, messenger of God and healer of humankind's soul. Sigmund Freud attributed the creation of Monotheism to Moses, and believed that he was actually the Pharaoh Akhnaton who brought Monotheism to Egypt and was sorely persecuted for it.

There have also always been wise women healers and shamans; and in recent times, there have been many great physician-priestesses. Sometimes these women are the partners of holy men. "The Mother," the life partner to Sri Aurobindo, was a healer in her own right and the teacher-adviser who succeeded him. Aurobindo considered The Mother to be his

Shakti, the great creative female power, the nurturer, and the one who brings forth. Indeed she protected him and nurtured him, while he continued to infuse her and his disciples with the wisdom received from his own meditative inspirations and from his studies, which he transmitted in voluminous written and oral teachings.

In India Mother Theresa lived the life of a saint while yet incarnate. An exemplary healer of souls, she ministered to the desperately poor and to babies who were victims of the AIDS virus. A recent avatar, Madame Blavatsky, dedicated her strength and energy to healing the world through the dissemination of ageless wisdom from the Masters of the East. Maria Von Sievers was companion and perhaps twin soul to the great genius of the nineteenth and twentieth century, Rudolph Steiner. Von Sievers created healing through Eurythmy, a type of dance and movement used for spiritual therapy, and through spiritually oriented drama. Other advanced women healers include Jean Houston, the highly intuitive Patricia Joudry, and Elizabeth Kubler-Ross.

Elizabeth Kubler-Ross is a supreme example of the physician-priestess. Renowned for her work, she brought the science of helping the dying patient to the attention of the medical community worldwide. She went on to discover the meaning of life after death, and brought comfort not only to the dying but to their families as well. I had the privilege of meeting her once, and she told me that when a person went far enough into meditation or heightened awareness, "they," the spiritual guides, met you and allowed you to visit the other side, and then return. Her work has been part of an emerging series of adventures into the world beyond this body, and is parallel to that of Raymond Moody, author of *Life After Death,* and Kenneth Ring, author of *Going to Omega.*

Although the medical community has lost its understanding of the priestly side of healing, many of us can still remember times when this was not so. Even in the early twentieth century, the physician was still viewed almost as a priest, revered and called upon in times of spiritual as well as physical need. In turn he exercised the powers generated through idealism and self-sacrificing concern for his patient with no concern for money. When I was a child Dr. Rubin was always ready to be at my bedside when we needed him. All that was necessary was for him to be there, and all would be well with the world. I would know that I was protected and healed. I remember what an idealistic profession medicine was when I went to medical school, and, in turn, with how much reverence the physician was treated.

Sadly, the physician's calling has become degraded, contaminated by over-organization, materialism, and business-like bottom-line. Today we are faced with a gerrymandered outline of physician-function, which has grown like Topsy until it has almost burst the bounds of the house that created it. Insurance, originally a creative ideal designed to share the cost of catastrophic expense, has now become the giant who devours its own children, suffocating the energy of the physician while creating more and more degeneration of health care. Medicare, once a great idealistic adventure, has almost destroyed the home of its birth, threatening the very existence of the system it was designed to serve. Medicine has become big business, and sadly, all too often the doctor has become the consummate business-man. Reverence for the physician-priest has given way to distrust, distance, misanthropy and separatism. And why not? Even in psychiatry the quick fix by drugs is preferred to the more strenuous, but really more rewarding, treatment by understanding. Biological psychiatry is in the ascendancy, often leading to tragedy.

This tragedy can be seen in the case of a twenty-six-year-old woman who came to me after being treated elsewhere for "depression." Her so-called "disorder" was only ordinary human sadness that was caused by a failed marriage into which she had allowed herself to be precipitated, and an exaggerated sense of self-criticism that relentlessly pursued her when she failed at anything. Another psychiatrist had diagnosed her as having a major disorder, manic-depression or schizophrenia, the latter because she had spoken to him about certain spiritual experiences. In search of a "cure," she was transferred from one pharmacological specialist to another, filled with powerful medications and, when each one failed, she was given another and yet another. Nowhere in her treatment scheme was there the kind of psychological investigation that would lead to compas-sionate understanding. Worse yet, when she wanted to stop the medications, she was confronted with dire predictions of what would happen to her because she had a "serious chemical imbalance."

Heroically, she took a chance, stopped all medication--and felt better. When she was referred to me, I found her to be a woman who had a great introspective capacity along with a strong ego and personality; therefore, someone who could expand into health through therapeutic understanding--someone who very much wanted to. She made rapid progress within a drug-free treatment that helped her to understand her feelings and what had caused them.

This story illustrates the destructive effects of the unspoken but active alliance between the pharmaceutical industry and the physician, and in truth society itself. The fact is that doctors are looking for a way to deliver a fast cure, patients are looking for the magical and easy way, and pharmaceutical companies are looking to enlarge the figures on the much-worshipped bottom line. This is a powerful combination, an unconscious collusion, which cements us into a materialistic approach to medicine. It shuts the door on humanistic, person-to-person understanding and help.

There is an amazing amount of ignorance in clinical medicine of the ordinary psychology of the patient. Doctors are unwilling to acknowledge that psychological stresses express themselves in psychosomatic disorders and psychosomatic prolongation of organic disturbance. This leads to the high cost of suffering and the high cost of medical care, for if the patient is not fully diagnosed the treatment will at best be partial, and sometimes it is far off center.

This collusion is hard to break but, fortunately, a counterforce is now at work in the field of alternative medicine. There is an increasing demand among patients for alternative therapies, and we are currently riding the leading edge of a demand for spiritual medicine, and spiritual psychotherapy.

It is heartening to learn that a new organization has been established called the National Institute for Healthcare Research In its national convocations, it assembled the most celebrated and careful researchers in the country. They have brought indisputable evidence to show the power of prayer in medical healing. For example, Dr. Larry Dossey, author of *Space, Time and Medicine* and *Recovering the Soul: A Scientific and Spiritual Search*, has produced hard evidence of the power of prayer in speeding recovery from a heart attack, or from surgery.

A significant sign of the times can be seen in the decision of the founder of the prestigious publication *Psychology Today* to establish a new magazine, *Spirituality and Healing*. In the book world, the hot topic of publishers, as acknowledged at the 1996 Writer's Conference in Maui, was spirituality.

The Decline of Professional Ethics

The failures in medicine are not medical misfortunes alone. They are part of the disease and decline of our society, reflections of a similar debasement in business, law, politics, and even in religious organizations themselves.

Lawyers, like so many doctors, are retiring from a profession that was once a practice field for their ideals. They are retiring because of a kind of disillusionment, even disgust, with the conduct of their colleagues. One senior partner in a prestigious law firm told me that, when he went into practice, law was an honorable profession, "There was hardly any litigation." He smiled in recognition when I told him that I thought that the change in the practice of law was part and parcel of a moral decline in society.

Business has become heartless in its treatment of employees. In the midst of all the mergers and the "efficiencies" that follow them, there is little consideration for the fate of the long-affiliated employees who are sacrificed to the relentless search for yet more efficiency. And what has happened to the warm person-to-person contact that we used to experience in shops and department stores during the time when "the customer was always right"?

All too often our religious institutions have lost the spirit and messages of their God-instructed avatars, and have become ruled by ritual and the self-serving, self-sustaining power of the organization. Though Jesus taught that the poor would inherit the earth, it is the rich who are sought by congregational and pastoral leaders. The secular demands of large congregations leave little time for their spiritual leader to engage in religious and meditative studies.

I remember visiting Kasmir in 1982 and having the privilege of meeting Laksmandu, the reputed authority on Kasmir Shaivism. He could be found in the mountains, surrounded by a small group of disciples, living simply, and dispensing knowledge. Once a week he was incommunicado, for he spent a full day in retreat and meditation. I thought, "What a splendid example! What a splendid life. What a pure demonstration of what spiritual living and teaching could be."

The Return of the Spiritual

In the midst of this alienation from humanistic and spiritual values, there is also a "return" taking place. More and more people are turning to spirituality rather than to organized religion. More and more are finding, within their own hearts, the Christ message, the God-infused spirit, the conjunction with all humankind, with all nature and with the omnipotent All, Itself. Small groups are springing up all over the country and the world: *A Course in Miracles* groups; self-help groups; addiction groups practicing the Twelve Steps, (themselves of spiritual origin). More and more individuals in the West are becoming interested in and practicing

Buddhism, Sufism and Zen. There is a growing respect for the wisdom of the Native American traditions, the Irish Wiccan tradition, and even the mystery traditions of Christianity. An example of the latter can be seen in the work of Reverend Doctor Lauren Artress who wrote *Walking a Sacred Path: Rediscovering the Labyrinth as a Spiritual Tool.* Working at Grace Cathedral in San Francisco and in workshops all over the country, Artress has introduced thousands of men and women to the image of the ancient labyrinth in the Cathedral of Chartres as a walking meditation that introduces one to the stillness, cyclic rather than linear time, and an openness in the soul to a feeling of healing and wholeness. To quote Artress: "When we walk into the path of the labyrinth, a new world greets us. This world is not riddled with the splits and division between mind and body. Woven into this experience is a new vision of reality, an evolutionary step..."

All of these paths are pursued as a way out of existential despair into something more and more meaningful. All of these groups are rising; and as they rise, they draw toward each other. One day, not too distantly, they will aggregate and will create a critical mass, and then the message of God will be spread to all.

Hopefully, at this time, the physician will have become a priest once more and will spread the message through his/her example. The message begins with the return of the physician to the priestly functions, to administering to those who seek out him or her for healing with compassion and whole vision in a way that honors the soul as well as the body. This kind of healing will extend far beyond the physico-chemical, laboratory-minded principles that now dehumanize both the caretaker and the cared-for.

Tools for the Spiritual Transformation of the Doctor

The essence of the transformation of the doctor in the return to the physician-priest will be the personal transformational experience. This introspective change was inaugurated by Freud who instructed that the basis for understanding psychoanalysis was the personal analysis of the aspiring analyst. Jung brought out the same thing in his biography, *Memories, Dreams, Reflections:*

"The psychotherapist, however, must understand not only the patient; it is equally important that he should understand himself. For that reason the sine qua non is the analysis of the analyst, what is called the training analysis. The patient's treatment begins with the doctor, so to speak. Only if the doctor knows how to cope with himself and his own problems will he be able to teach the patient to do the same." [3] The transformational experience of the doctor, psychiatrist, family practitioner, or counselor can only be achieved through a courageous self-exploration. This exploration will be much enlarged if the psychiatrist/psychologist can employ some of the newer techniques of self-realization such as transpersonal breathwork. [4]

Another tool that I have found to be important for self-transformation is meditation. When I met the great spiritual leader Muktananda, I asked him how I could learn more about the Self. He said, "Meditate, meditate, meditate!" I didn't know the value of that teaching at the time, but I do now. Great spiritual teachers make meditation a necessary, even central, part of their lives. For someone seeking to walk a spiritual path, it soon becomes a necessity, one that is richly rewarded with closeness to the soul, a view of life in the spiritual realms, and inspired messages.

Guidelines for Transformation and Spiritual Growth

In my own life, I have found that the following guidelines have been useful in self-transformation and development, both in the spiritual realm and in my work. These guidelines are helpful not only to the physician who wants to become a physician priest, but to anyone who is looking for a way to walk upon a spiritual path.

1. Meditate. Set a time aside each day for meditation.

2. Read. Books enable one to open the mind to new and undreamed of realms. A good place to start is with the great spiritual teachers. There is a rich store in the writings of the great yogis such as Yogananda, and in Ghandi, Martin Buber, Blavatsky and the great masters who taught her, and the great Western spiritual master, Rudolph Steiner. Many books have been

---

[3]   Carl Jung, *Memories, Dreams, Reflections;* (New York: Vintage Books 1965), page 132.

[4]   Transpersonal breathwork is a combination of powerful, select music, and controlled, deep breathing. It is an instrument that washes out stored-up emotions, and emotional adhesions, often releasing the experiencer to beatific and transpersonal realms. We employ transpersonal breathwork at the Pressman Center for Mind/Body Wellness, using a modification of a technique devised by psychiatrist Stanislov Grof.

written about *A Course in Miracles,* and there is also an official workbook with lessons that lead one into the new and higher realms.

Other books of interest that deal with matters of the soul and aid in personal transformation are Larry Dossey's *Space, Time, and Medicine* and *The Healing Power of Words;* Gary Zukav's *The Seat of the Soul;* Scott Peck's *The Road Less Traveled;* Joan Borysenko's *Fire in the Soul: A New Psychology of Spiritual Optimism;* James Hillman's *The Soul's Code: In Search of Character and Calling;* and Thomas Moore's *Care of the Soul: A Guide for Cultivating Sacredness in Everyday Life.*

Such reading sets seeds in the mind that will grow over time. When certain books resonate within you, what follows is an inner recognition of a great truth that allows the mind to open. The information then becomes personal, and can be lived through one's experience.

3. Attend seminars and workshops on spiritual and humanistic subjects. I learned a great deal when I entered group therapy as a patient, including many new techniques for healing. When I laid aside my professional mask and began to work with individuals such as Grof and Muktananda, I was both humbled and enlightened. Exposure to new experiences always sets the stage for learning and absorption of new ideas. Immersion in workshops allows for a cognitive re-orientation that expands the mind. For example, I was lucky to have been invited to the Council Grove Retreat for a number of years. The new knowledge and dialogue I shared with good minds that were pursuing spiritual and scientific information provided a thrilling immersion into a world of new possibilities.

4. Cultivate intuition. Our intuitive receptive apparatus is a high one, and receives much wisdom, both from within and from above. Socialization, self-doubt and scientific training tend to suppress it. It is very important that we overcome this conditioning and get back in touch with our intuition. We cannot bootstrap our way out of our socialized conditioning, but our intuition, which comes from our higher self, can cut through our confusion and our limitations, showing us answers that we cannot arrive at by conventional means, such as intellectual reasoning.

5. Give service. Nowhere is there a greater opportunity for meaningful spiritual service than in the practice of healing; and nowhere is there a more empowered and acknowledged opportunity than that which lies ready at hand to the physician. When a physician sees him- or herself as one who gives service, the result is a different and more all-encompassing kind of transaction between the physician and the patient-seeker. What I am speaking of is a soul-to-soul contract, born out of the patient's surrender

to discovering personal truth when it is met by the absolute, unconditional dedication of the physician to the welfare of the patient. This approach implies a deep respect for the other human being, and commits both to a deep searching and a knowing of the other in a way that recognizes his/her unlimited capacity for healing and growth. The integrity and humility that follows such service opens a resonance of communication between physician and patient that leads to a healing empathy that is very similar to what is experienced in any love communion. Love is a powerful healer, the most powerful.

Cautionary Signals about following Spiritual Teachers

When one is looking for a spiritual path, it is often helpful to work with a teacher, someone who has been down that road before. Whereas this sort of work is often rewarding, one must never forget to be cautious and discerning about who he or she chooses as a mentor. The glamour and excitement that a person feels when the powerful possibilities of the spiritual mind are opened can lead to a kind of enthusiasm that sometimes impairs common sense, making the seeker highly susceptible and vulnerable to charlatans who have more invested in monetary gain and their own personal egos than in selfless teaching. Therefore, I'd like to offer some guidelines to help one avoid the false guru or the teacher who is a poor fit.

1. Respect your intuition about the fit between you and a teacher, as well as your resonance with what he/she says.

2. Avoid anyone who is pompous and self-convinced that his or her way is the only true way. Truly enlightened teachers know that they are only a conduit and that there are many paths that will take one to God and God's realms.

3. Make sure that you feel comfortable in the presence of the teacher and feel a respect coming toward you from him/her.

4. A genuine teacher is not overly obsessed with money and charging astronomical fees for their workshops and weekend seminars, but treats money as a modest necessity.

Whether you are a physician longing to be a physician-priest or an ordinary spiritual seeker, these tools will help guide you to find the right teacher for you. Most important, remember that one cannot be a questionable person and a good teacher. We teach what we are.

The Limitations of the Current Psychological Paradigm

For us to truly embrace the concept of the physician-priest and the development of the spiritual self as the highest, most productive, and most fulfilling goal, we must find a way to move beyond the current psychological paradigm that we are trapped in and develop a new vision, new definitions of the human body, mind and soul.

Psychotherapy, as it is practiced today, is still caught in the web of our present societal beliefs. Medicine is still focussed upon a materialistic worldview that sees the body and the mind as machines--chemical factories that can be repaired by the ingestion of more chemicals. When we are faced with a human being who is seriously depressed or may not be acting in a way that we define as "normal," psychiatric diagnosis and treatment is still largely confined within the net of so-called scientific objectivity, what we can perceive with our five senses. The only way that we can change this limited, materialistic view of human nature and human dysfunction is to elevate beyond this matrix, to take a view from above.

Modern medicine's most limiting belief is that the body is all, and that spirit is somewhere else and not particularly relevant. This viewpoint keeps us looking straight ahead, fitted with blinders that deny the great body of evidence all around us that shows us that the mechanistic view of the body and the mind cannot possibly explain all of human experience. Claiming that if we cannot measure a phenomenon with our instruments, then it is not worthy of notice, also denies the important messages that come to us through intuition. It eliminates the "feeling life," the subjective life of the healer, making a sterility of a science that would otherwise serve its fellow human beings. And woe to the professional who advocates an open mind toward such things.

I saw this attitude at work in the case of a twenty-six-year-old woman named Jane who had sought help because of an unusual and frightening recurring experience. She had been sent from one psychopharmacologist to another in search of relief, but no one had been able to help her; in fact, she seemed to be getting worse and was now fighting with bouts of depression. When Jane finally was referred to me, she told the following story. In the middle of the night she would find herself much oppressed by a presence that entered the room. It enveloped her face and created great pressure by sitting on her chest. At such times, she was sure that she would die, and tried desperately to call out to her roommate, but found that she could make no sounds. The experience was terrifying to her, and she desperately sought relief from it.

When Jane had related this experience to each of the psychiatrists she had worked with, in search of an explanation for this strange and very frightening phenomenon, she was promptly labeled as a borderline psychotic, and was warned that she must stay on various powerful medications to keep her "symptoms" under control. Unfortunately, these same medicines were having a deleterious effect upon her, causing her to feel deeper and deeper feelings of depression. She finally found some measure of relief when, against advice, she stopped all medicine.

When I interviewed her, I did not feel that I was talking to a woman who was borderline psychotic. I found her to have a very stable ego, and a strong attachment to reality. Because I did not ascribe to a narrow, traditional theory of human behavior, I was also able to accurately identify and explain her experience to her. When I heard her story, I was immediately able to say, "That was the Old Hag!" She had not heard this expression before, and neither had her doctors; but I knew that David Hufford, a professor of anthropology at the University of Pennsylvania, had written about these kinds of experiences in his book, *The Terror That Comes in the Night.* He had done very extensive research on this phenomenon and had collected many such experiences from mythology and from modern men and women who were all very stable and rational individuals. One such account, written about a twenty-seven-year-old woman, sounded almost exactly like Jane's. This woman described feeling a mass coming towards her as she lay in bed sleeping. It would partially envelop her whole chest area, creating a sensation of weight, giving her the feeling that she was dying and causing her to call someone for help. She would find relief by morning.

I was able to share these stories with Jane, showing her that her experience was not some kind of psychotic episode, but one of the mysteries of the human experience, something that had happened to many stable men and women all over the world. Jane reacted with considerable relief, and began to regain confidence in her stablity, a confidence that had been severely eroded by the dire implications of her needing the powerful medications, "or else." She experienced great relief from her depression, and though she is still in treatment with me, she continues to show the strength of ego and character, which will see her through to a successful result.

This study, with its many supporting accounts, illustrates Hufford's open-minded scientific approach, which stands in sharp contrast to the "sticking-to-your-training" mind-set that my patient Jane had encountered.

If Jane had continued to accept the consensus diagnosis that she was psychotic and needed to be filled with medications, the stability and reality orientation that was so apparent to me when I interviewed her probably would have deteriorated to the point where she was seriously unstable. This Procrustean bed [5] of attachment to consensus confines our medical practitioners, so that they too must fit in the bed of traditional scientific doctrine, just right. It is all the sadder that these same practitioners start out as curious, idealistically minded medical students, who later are taught to conform.

There are many limiting forces that are active in our medical community at this time, forces that are motivated more by political expediency than by humanistic goals. One of the most insidious is the fact that medical research is largely funded by the pharmaceutical companies. Medical schools depend on this source of grant money. In this way, a continuous feedback loop is formed, propagating the worship of the chemical magic bullet in place of a deeper search for understanding--of our fellow human beings and of the laws of God's universe as they are played out in health and disease. God does not rest on pharmaceuticals alone.

Another highly limiting and damaging force can be seen in the subtle form of materialism that hovers over the scene in academic institutions under the heading of "publish or perish." The idea is to get as many articles into the journals as possible, otherwise you are liable to lose your standing in the institution, and the institution is liable to lose its face. This leads to a worship of recognition by the community, a kind of substitute for money. This jockeying for position and prestige soon replaces the humble dedication to the search for God's laws and the self-sacrificing service that true healing requires.

Small wonder that our society no longer reveres the doctor, that people are disappointed, frustrated and mistrustful of the medical profession as a whole. Small wonder that the doctor who used to encourage his children to enter medical school, is now advising them to go in some other direction.

---

5   Procrustes was a giant who welcomed weary wayfarers, fed them, and put them to bed. It was a special bed, one size fit all. The trouble was that if the occupant was too short, the giant stretched him until the fit was just right. if he was too long, the host chopped off his legs, again for the perfect accommodation.

The Realms of the Mind

My profession, psychiatry, has been defined as a science that makes a study of the mind, yet our cultural definition of the mind is very limited indeed. The mind, especially the thought-mind, is a higher sense organ that cannot be defined using only our five senses. Mind is not limited to thought alone. As knowledge of our spiritual reach grows, we can come to know and appreciate that there are levels of mind, just as there are levels of feeling. There is a mind that is body-concentrated, focused on the body, the one we usually are referring to when we use the expression "mind/body connection" in holistic health. There is also the mind that attends to the concrete and practical necessities of life: "How will I pay this bill on time? Where is that cup of coffee that I need in the morning?"

As we rise to a higher level of the mind, we begin to think and create, to appreciate and love with the mind. At this level, we are able to receive an intuitive inflow, those "hunches" that come from within and from above. Being in touch with our intuition is crucial to the spiritual journey, for it is here that we begin to receive an understanding of who we truly are, and the meaning and purpose of our lives.

Finally, there is a mind that is peacefully blank, in touch with the soul, and ready to receive inspirations from above. This happens in deep meditation, when the mind is open to the knowledge within and the knowledge that surrounds us in the universe. Meditation's aim is to achieve a "blank mind," that state in which we have left our attachment to the body, its emotions, and the material world, and are ready to peer further into a friendly darkness that invites exploration. At that point we have a sense-knowing that there are realms that are not circumscribed by the limitations of our experiences so far, and which are beyond our present capacities. Yet as we perceive this and peer further, our mind and our capacities also increase.

This kind of experience is demonstrated by a meditation that came to me recently. As I moved deeply into trance, I had the realization that I was looking into a dark, but friendly realm. I was drawn to it and wanted to see into it, but could not yet make anything out. At the same time I knew that I would be able to experience what was there -- progressively. It would be much like the sensation of being in a dark room and gradually seeing one's surroundings appear, as if a rheostat were slowly adjusting the light from dim to brighter. I was drawn to this place with the same quietly excited attraction that drew me to spiritual readings, to the desire to know about my death and what happens beyond death; and, more than that, to the desire to know what is going on deep within me and high above me, for they are both the same. These are the spiritual realms that both attend to our needs, and with which we, in the body, exchange energy, feelings, intimations and intuitions.

I recognized the feelings I was having during this meditation as the excitement and the resonant "knowing" that occurs when I am learning something new, especially something that has to do with the spiritual, such as my readings in Steiner, Yogananda, Blavatsky, Freud, Jung or Ghandi. I knew because the resonance I experienced was a sympathetic chord struck between high inspirational knowledge and the recognition of the teaching that was at hand for me. I "knew because I have always known," as we have all always known, about those realms existing just beyond the reach of our everyday perceptions. I felt a sense of "Aha! This is it"--the draw that leads us to intuitional knowing, the thrill of the recognition of knowledge.

The Energy Bodies

Just as there are different types of mind, there are also different types of bodies that surround the physical; energy bodies that operate at higher vibrational levels that are beyond thought in the ordinary sense. The first of these, the astral body, immediately encloses the physical frame. This is the realm of feeling, whose vibrational levels describes the spectrum of emotions from the basest to the most aesthetic and highly enlightened.

Surrounding the astral is the mental body, which has levels of its own, ascending from the basic body-mind which thinks of its physical needs, up to the highest cognitions of generosity, spirituality and aspiration. Beyond the mental body is another, more refined, ineffable and subtle level known as the causal body. The causal is the repository of all of our most elevated and positive spiritual experiences. It is the mediator between the lesser bodies and the highest emanations of inspiration and intuition that flow from the All-High, translating these energies on down into the physical-material body that we inhabit. It is the causal body that collects and retains the positive experiences of a lifetime, and allows for our continuation and growth into the next incarnation. It functions much like a valve which allows a one-way stream upward during this phase. At other times it allows a flow from the On-High to the physical mind. The causal body retains the positive and more spiritual experiences of the living individual and will generate another body in another incarnation. In this way, we are able to continue to learn and evolve more, until we have evolved into a fully developed spiritual being who can then pass on to yet higher realms, closer to God.

The Physician-Priest and the Divine Self

If as therapists, we are willing to open ourselves to these teachings, we can then see them at work in our own lives and in the lives of our patients. We can set them as beacon lights, as goals for higher achievement.

To know that, at center, we are divine--that we contain the divine spark--is to know wisdom. Love and wisdom communicate with a higher form that surrounds us. When we express this love in its highest state, allowing it to flow from within ourselves to our patients, we know God. For the physician priest, the highest form of this love-wisdom is embodied not only in our dedication to our patient's healing, but also in our recognition of his many latent abilities, his greater potential. If we open to this love wisdom, we will also be able to allow patients' love to flow toward us. The result of this openness is not crude physical expression, but the felt beatitude and refined joyous bliss that bursts the bounds of the body to embrace, not only the therapist, but the patient's self, the community, life itself, the planet and all of God's creations.

To allow this expansion of the self is to make room for the Law of Essence. This tells us that love is the essence of God, the force that is beyond psychotherapy. This love hastens the patient's journey upward to rejoin his/her divine essence with the Divine All. As such divine love seeks to express itself; it may feel well nigh intolerable at first, as if it can no longer be contained within the body. But if the patient and the therapist can tolerate this seemingly unbearable feeling without resistance and without carrying it into physical expression, then a breakthrough will occur, a kind of bursting out of the body to enter into the realm beyond the body. In this highly expansive place, the patient will embrace the group, widening his/her expanses of influence and bliss.

I remember a patient who told me, shamefaced, that she didn't know what I was talking about when I asked what she was feeling. She only knew about appearances. No one in her life, either when she was a child or when she was a grown woman, had even shown her what a feeling was. As her treatment went on, she discovered not only her unfulfilled need to be loved, but also her need to express her love and have it acknowledged and received. At times she could hardly stand these feelings of wanting to give love to the world. When they were not accepted by her husband, who had never learned how to express his own feelings, she went on to satisfy them in her great love for spiritual reading, in her devotion to a spiritual teacher in whom she believed, in beautiful expressions of prose, and in a flowering of artistic talent. In meditation, she would burst beyond her body and have adventures in the astral realm, seeing beautiful colors that seemed to exist only on another plane of existence. In times of loneliness, she experienced a closeness of the astral presence of the teacher whose work and life she was following.

Another manifestation of what happens when the soul's power to love is released can be seen in the response to a book that I co-authored called *Twin Souls: A Guide to Finding Your True Spiritual Partner.* After the book's publication, a number of "twin souls" contacted me. In their thrill of finding each other, they experienced joy beyond measure, and a near intolerable sense of excitement and fulfillment. Inevitably, they wanted to share their joy and love with their community through works that would serve to make a better world.

Two Steps Upward, One Step BacK

This manifestation of love is an integral part of our upward journey toward the soul, but it cannot be achieved all at once. Instead, it is really a matter of stepping upward and then stepping back, eventually increasing one's ability to live on the higher plane for longer and longer periods of time.

This process can be seen in the case of Samuel, a twenty-six-year-old physician-healer who came to me because he felt constricted, in spite of the fact that he was much devoted to self-discovery and generous efforts toward others. One day, he admitted that he was having great difficulty coming to our sessions. I was not surprised when he said this, because I knew that it was a natural consequence of his resistance to me, a dislike of having to "lower" himself to accept help from somebody else, even when he had asked for it.

It was difficult for him to admit this to me, and his throat felt tight and constricted while he did so, but this honesty marked the beginning of his true introspective journey onto a higher level of being. As we talked, he began to understand how much he resisted releasing his feelings, and how difficult that made it for him to help his own patients. This resistance to being close also spilled over into his personal life. Because he kept a certain amount of himself emotionally apart from his fiancée, he was having trouble with that relationship as well.

"I feel very far away from you," he said. When I remained silent and accepting, he sat quietly thinking, allowing my compassion, understanding and willingness to accept his feelings penetrate his facade.

The transformation that happened next was remarkable. As I held him in quiet acceptance, his soul began to open suddenly, "I feel closer. I am drawing closer; in fact I am merging with you. I am you. I fill the room. I fill everywhere. I fill the outer expanses and I join with them." He began to laugh ecstatically, enjoying the moment, reveling in this state of Ananda, the place of the bliss of the soul.

I have seen this sudden breakthrough into Ananda a number of times. Initially, it usually does not last very long, but it creates a map, a vision, of a territory that can be inhabited more and more as the work of ascension is accomplished. I've heard people describe the light that burns over everything, of becoming one with the leaves, the wind and the sun-- joined with them and with the All. I have heard them speak of the indescribable bliss that is the accompaniment of such realization. And then, these perceptions will disappear, only to return again and again until the individual has gotten used to living on a new level. Each individual's progress proceeds at a different pace, more often than not because they have to struggle through the many resistances to the bliss-soul that they encounter whenever they return to ordinary life.

Such are the gates to the inner world, gates that open to our essential power, wisdom and divine love. Sigmund Freud opened them for the West. Philosophers and poets had long known about that reality, but it was Freud who built a scientific foundation upon which psychiatrists and psychologists could, if they so chose, explore the inner mind, intuition and the greater knowledge that we all contain.

Sadly, all too few have chosen to follow Freud's inspired lead. It is strange that Western philosophy and, most of all, the philosophy that undergirds psychoanalytic science, has not only ignored but actually disparaged the use of intuition. Psychoanalysis, above all other sciences, should stand for introspection and should respect intuition, for these qualities enhance our knowledge of the patient's inner life. Intuitive exploration of the inner life can lead in turn to revelation, a higher knowledge of the self, of the other, of the world and of nature; in fact of the universe of which we are a part.

I have seen all of these fruits of intuition amply validated by my experiences as a psychotherapist. That the use of intuition causes the soul to rise naturally is a tribute to our essential goodness and divinity. Admittedly, there are contending forces of darkness, evil, selfishness and greed that abound within us and around us; but it is impressive to see that each time we release a patient from an ancient personal fixation, there emerges greater freedom of personality and soul, and also a greater goodness, a greater love of his or her fellow beings and a greater wish to give service. In complementary fashion, the more we dedicate ourselves to service and altruism, the more we become refined and the more does the essential Self and Soul come forth.

Guidelines and Exercises:

A. Tools For Exploration:

1. Introspect, meditate, exchange with a good friend.

2. Find a spiritual group: *A Course in Miracles* group; 12-step groups, (especially Adult Children of Dysfunctional Families); Theosophy Groups; Anthroposophy Groups (Steiner); Siddha Yoga Groups: and many others. See Appendix for a listing of groups.

3. Read: journeys and self-explorations of others e.g. Jung, Blavatsky, Muktnanda, Steiner and others

4. Attend Spiritual Seminars and Workshops - be selective.

B. Guidelines for Growth:

1. Meditate: Set a time and place for meditation each day. Be faithful.

2. Read inspirational books, especially the great spiritual teachers and writings. (See Appendix for recommended reading.)

3. Cultivate Intuition.

4. Give Service; give from the heart in a service which also calls on your talents and your interests, although if nothing else even scrubbing floors can be a meditation as Mother Theresa has shown.

C. Cautionary Signals about Following Spiritual Teachers:

1. Above all, respect your intuition, your own feelings, about the way you fit with the teacher, and about his/her qualities.

2. Avoid anyone who is self-convinced, arrogant, and who does not respect your feelings and you. A true teacher will empower you - not dis-empower.

3. Make sure you feel comfortable with the teacher and that there is due respect coming to you.

4. Be cautious about anyone who charges excessively. In the eyes of a spiritual teacher money is a necessity and an enabler for the work, and nothing more.

D. Knowledge of Our Energy Splendor: The Energy Bodies:

Remember that there are seven planes of vibration and experience, of which the lower four are relevant to us. They are in ascending order:

a. The physical, surrounded by an etheric net;

b. The astral (the emotional body);

c. The mental (the province of thought);

d. The Intuitional (in Sanskrit called Buddhi - or Causal Body) It is the seat of the soul; e., f., and g. are on high and transmit to the soul.

CHAPTER II:

Embracing the Hologram -
Expanding Our Definitions of Consciousness and Reality

Embracing The Hologram, The Vision Of Our Oneness And Infinite Potential -- Sympathies, Empathies, Intuitions, Telepathies -- The Feelings of Our God-Oneness -- Recognizing Our Expanded Selves In An Expanded Consciousness -- Identifying Resistances -- Our Expanded View of Consciousness and Reality.
Making The Soul Understandable -- Spiritual Experiences Are All Around Us -- Understanding Strange Affiliations -- Associations With Past Lives -- God-Experiences That Medicine Would Call "Crazy" -- The Spiritual Emergence Network -- The Observing Self, The Soul That Hovers Over The Scene.

We are at a time in our history when the rationalist, materialistic Western view of reality is being challenged as never before. Western culture is being confronted with the same shocking dilemma that people faced when they learned that the earth was not flat, but round. They were literally hanging on to trees in a desperate attempt to avoid falling. This may sound humorous to us today--but think of the fear and resistance that confronts our scientists, doctors and teachers when they are on the edge of a new realization--that the world and the mind that we see is only a lesser part of a larger world, a larger mind, a larger reality. Everything that has given stability to their worldview is threatened. Their expertise, indeed their ability to make a living, is at risk.

This is the situation that confronted physicists earlier in this century. Until then, everyone was comfortably ensconced in a Newtonian universe in which the ultimate particle, the atom, a kind of billiard ball, was central. And then, following the smashing of the atom came the new physics. No longer did the billiard ball theory reign supreme. Atoms were divisible into smaller and smaller entities. Exotic particles such as quarks and bosuns were the ultimate in smallness. But, physicists soon discovered, there was no ultimate, only infinitely smaller, and infinitely larger, going on forever in an expanding universe that only God could comprehend.

And now the emerging psychology of the mind promises to go on infinitely in its search and revelations, leading also to an infinity of mystery-

-and promise. The new spiritual psychotherapy respects the knowledge that the mind, and we, are basically limitless, infinite in powers, and endless in our relationship to God.

This limitlessness of the mind is beautifully described in *The Holographic Universe* by Michael Talbot. Here the author discusses the discoveries of the neurosurgeon Karl Pribram and the physicist David Bohm. For many years Pribram searched for the specific location in the brain where memory was stored. Failing to find it, and noting that when a part of the brain was damaged the lost function could be recovered using another part of the brain, he postulated that, ultimately, each part of the brain could function as the whole.

Now that was a wonderful discovery, all the more so since it was consistent with the idea of the hologram. The hologram is familiar to us as the three-dimensional images that are seen in Disneyland or on our credit cards. In Disneyland, we might find a three-dimensional ghost seated next to us or another projected image that retains its holographic shape as we walk around it. Holograms are formed by recording the points of intersecting light waves on a photographic plate, and then projecting them. When you break a hologram into pieces, each section is able to recreate the whole.

David Bohm, a protege of Einstein, became interested in the hologram, and related it to the way in which the universe itself behaved. Bohm described what he called an "implicate and explicate order," which presumed that a latent energy exists that unfolds upon demand and manifests as a created product. There is an interesting story connected with this idea, which describes the phenomenon pretty well. While watching British television, Bohm saw a demonstration in which one cylinder was suspended inside another in glycerin. A drop of ink was then inserted between the two cylinders. As one cylinder was rotated inside the other, the ink spread. When the rotation was reversed, however, the ink disappeared. Where did it go? It went into a latent state. The ink could be made to reappear when the rotation was reversed.

Bohm thought that this was similar to the latency in a hologram, which is made up of squiggles recorded on the holographic plate. These squiggles are recordings of the lines of light interference caught by a special photographic setup. In turn, these squiggles could be made to produce a three-dimensional image when a light is shown through them, thus producing the hologram.

Each of the two scientists, working separately, discovered and defined the hologram as the very basis for creation. Talbot aptly describes the hologram as "the all contained in the part and the part contained in the all." He goes on to relate the holographic description of reality to mental functioning, social functioning and to the explanation of many phenomena of the mind that might otherwise be puzzling, including out-of-body experiences, telepathy, remote viewing, the collapse of time, and our absolute and intimate union with each other. These descriptions of the operation of the hologram and the holographic universe are in their way scientific validations of the powers of the mind and ultimately the powers of the soul.

The holographic network refers to the fact that we are all connected as part of each other, that the earth, its constituents, the universe itself all function as part of a progressively larger unit. Since any part of the hologram contains all of the information, if the holographic plate is cut in two, the projected image remains complete. Similarly, if one-quarter of the plate is projected the image remains complete, and so on to one-one-hundred and twenty-eighth. This means that each part contains the whole. Both Pribram and Bohm concluded that the brain and the entire universe function this way. Significantly, this point of view is consistent with the Eastern philosophies and religions, which say that we are part of God, and that God is within each of us. If this is true, and I firmly believe that it is, then it is easy to love one's neighbor as one's self, and to understand many paranormal phenomena such as telepathy, intuition, remote viewing, clairvoyance and clairaudience. If all of this is so, then it is a matter of course that we ascend to these powers through service to mankind, and through our effort to create a Universal Fellowship.

The Holographic Universe in Psychotherapy

I have seen evidence of this holographic universe at work in my practice for many years. One of its manifestations can be seen in the collapse of time. If every event in the universe is connected to every other, then linear time does not exist and all time is now. During a thrilling group therapy session, time has literally flown for everyone in the room to the point where we cannot believe where the time has gone. I have also found that a discreet interval of time can also be both stretched and lengthened during hypnosis. I can suggest to the individual being hypnotised that he or she create an hour out of a minute or a minute from an hour. It is also significant to note that in deep meditation, or any state of absolute absorption, such as the creative state, time disappears.

Clairvoyance, seeing into the future or seeing things at a distance, and clairaudience, hearing things that are not spoken, are also manifestations of a holographic universe. Lately, I have found that I can often hear what my patients are about to say before they say it, attesting to our innate interconnectedness. This is a new phenomenon for me. An example of clairvoyance was demonstrated to us all during a recent group therapy session. During breathwork, one of my patients was able to enter into the dream state of another, accurately describing what she had experienced in her dream. I have also read that researchers at Stanford University and Princeton are conducting research on "remote viewing," viewing at a distance. Their data also points compellingly to the holographic nature of reality.

I consistently see the holographic phenomenon at work each and every time a new group enters therapy together. It inevitably happens that the group forms a kind of family in which each member feels deeply connected with the rest. Each person wants to help the other, and each intuitively enters into the needs of the other.

Contemporary science also has its share of evidence that we do indeed live in an interconnected holographic reality. Some of this evidence can be seen in the work of British botanist and researcher, Rupert Sheldrake. Sheldrake has discovered waves of interaction that he calls morphogenic fields, which transmit behavioral information within species. For example, if rats in London are trained to perform a certain task, and their new behavior is then transmitted/taught to their offspring, that same behavior will suddenly show up in the progeny of rats of the same species across the ocean, at Duke University in North Carolina.

New ideas and new discoveries appear rapidly across the world, without any communication between the scientists. Different investigators discover them in parallel, so to speak. For example, as my friend Joy Parker was preparing to sit down with her writing partner, biographer Linda Schele, to write *Maya Cosmos,* a book on the spiritual practices and world view of the Maya Indians, Linda made a major breakthrough in the translation of a very important hieroglyph. This glyph, which meant "sorcery, to sleep, to dream" became central to the ideas of the new book. What was extraordinary, however, was that within ten days of Linda's discovery, two other linguists in other parts of the world contacted her with great excitement--each of them had independently broken through to the translation of this glyph.

We get a view of this deeply interconnected higher realm, with its holographic influences, as we develop our personalities and approach the place of the higher self where the soul resides. It is then possible to discard selfish and self-limiting goals, such as the drive to fill material, sensate and power-driven desires. We go beyond ourselves, beyond even family, to recognition that we serve the group. We understand not only that we must, but that our interest and greatest fulfillment, our most exalted joy, comes from being a part of the group around us; and the larger the group, the greater the fulfillment. When we realize the importance and relevance of the holographic theory, we approach closer to the magical divinity and all-encompassing creativity that we all possess.

After one has had the experience of fire walking or of reading a book at 25,000 words a minute, one begins to have a new belief system. One of my colleagues said after he had taken the course in Photo-reading, "I think I have always had this capacity, but I didn't have the belief system." When we acquire a new belief system, and manifest these seemingly impossible results, we are dipping into the implicate order of the mind, the latent powers that we possess in our divinity.

All that is really absent from our lives is the courageous willingness to face our inner selves. In our society, even in our professional psychiatric circles, which are focussed on the "chemical imbalance" theory of mental and emotional illnesses, we have failed to teach people how to do that. That inside "stuff" from which we run, keeps running us, and our minds. That inside stuff includes the most base within us as well as roof-brain-chatter. But it also embraces the highest and finest, including our High Self. In both cases, that "inside stuff" runs us, not we it.

This unwillingness to look within is illustrated by two of my most admired and brilliant colleagues. Their dedication to helping people is immense. Their hunger for more and more knowledge and desire to create more helpful approaches to their patients' cures are unfailing. Yet they are the victims of that very thing that keeps them on the surface when it comes to exploring their own depth, and therefore the depths of their patients. The one wishes he could communicate better with his patients, and no wonder. His rapid staccato speech is not only a measure of his brilliance, but an indication that he is compelled by his need to get away from his emotions, especially his need to confront some very painful realizations about his failed relationship with his father. The other colleague is equally brilliant, yet he too runs away from self-realization, from knowing himself inside as well as out. He is compelled by inner forces to be "on top" at all times. He generously pours his help upon his patients; but it is evident that he cannot let himself receive help, and I am sure that this is due to the very terrible start he had in life when his family failed him. Although this limits him, as he began to realize in one of our discussions, he refuses to look further. As long as these relentless defenses against painful memories are in the drivers' seat of our lives, we cannot be fully authentic. They keep us chained to a certain level and prevent ascent to higher levels of self-realization and spiritual development. I believe that authenticity (unfailing truthfulness in a loving context) is godliness, and therefore soulfulness.

Identifying Resistances

The focus of the work that I try to do with my patients begins with spotting their resistances against looking within. These resistances were usually created to fend off painful feelings, but developed into burdens when they became automatic. They are at the root of the social superficiality that we so often meet. Once I can see what those painful feelings are, I try vigorously to help the patient to see them, knowing that these defenses lead to constrictions of the personality and obstructions to harmonious flow. Obstructions are the layers of defense that conceal our divine center, the soul, the love essence that we are.

Overcoming resistance is another idea for which we are indebted to Sigmund Freud, and it is of paramount importance to any real practice of psychoanalysis. With enormous courage, Freud faced a world of psychiatry that was fully convinced that the only mind was the one we were aware of, the conscious mind--really its most superficial portion. He was the first in the West to define the unconscious, that larger structure of which we are unaware, but which, nevertheless, runs us. Against great opposition, Freud was the first individual to advocate introspection within the scientific circles of his day, because he saw it as the key that opens the gate to the interior of the mind.

In like fashion, the Eastern Masters obtained higher knowledge from meditation, and then transmitted it to their apprentices. These masters teach us that the initiations into higher consciousness rest upon acquired wisdom and a consciousness of the soul, which resides in the subtle realms. Their initiations of disciples were not ritualistic performances, but rather knowledge-achievements, leading to sudden expansions--much like quantum leaps--into new areas of consciousness, realization and insight. Once their disciples arrived in these new areas, they acquired a more expansive view, a view of their unity with everything.

Freud's work represents a path in the West that runs parallel to many of the most important teachings of the East. Beginning with his studies in hypnosis, Freud's view of the mind deepened progressively until he understood that even the earliest experiences, those in the first year of life, placed their stamp of influence upon adult life.

Freud's view was expanded by Carl Jung who, not surprisingly, was himself a student of Eastern philosophy. Jung explored and defined what he called the "archetypes," those overarching forces that surround us with their influences and with which we join as we ascend in personality and spirit. Tragically, Freud rejected Jung's concepts, notwithstanding the fact that Jung had been his most intimate and beloved pupil. He felt that Jung's work was too mysterious, too religious, and would dilute the "pure gold of psychoanalysis" that was struggling for its own survival at the time. Jung's psychology has survived, nevertheless, and is flowering today.

Freud's initial discoveries were followed by a burgeoning interest in the mind, its depths and possibilities and the ways to release hidden human potential. Prominent among the new breed of humanistic psychologists who came after him were Abraham Maslow and David Reisman, who advocated looking for the best, not the worst, in a human being. Instead of concentrating on the repressed material, which contained all that we are ashamed of, these individuals looked to the peak experiences and hidden latencies. In recognizing and releasing these capacities, Maslow and Reisman were knocking on the door of soul-recognition.

Other humanistic psychologists who created an appreciation of our higher capacities were Fritz Perls, who developed Gestalt therapy, and Alan Watts. In 1961 psychoanalysis was in its greatest ascendancy, yet Watts instructed us that psychoanalytic doctrine fell short when it claimed that only the individual was responsible for what became of his or her life. Watts pointed out that we were a part of our culture, and insofar as we were embedded in the culture, we could not be seen in isolation.

The teachings of psychologists and psychiatrists who became interested in the Eastern Masters, such as Watts, Stanislav Grof, Richard Alpert (Ram Dass) and Roberto Assagioli, led to an increased appreciation of the deep unconscious mind, its potential, and its relation to the immortality of the human soul.[6] In fact, the recently created specialties of pre- and perinatal psychology grew from clinical experiences that indicated that an individual has consciousness even in the uterus. This knowledge coordinated with the larger understanding that consciousness is the immortal quintessence of the human being, and the immortal essence, indeed, of the cosmos itself.

Einstein, among others, shared this belief; in fact, it was the physicists who led the way to the understanding that consciousness is not an emanation from the cortex, but a form of the universal "mind stuff," a state of consciousness that goes far beyond the human brain. This mind stuff is shared by every element of the universe, and represents a universal mind into which we human beings can enter. Elizabeth Kubler-Ross, in her pioneer studies of life after death, has revealed the immortal essence of the human being. This essence, which exists far beyond the physical vehicle, is defined not only by the soul, but also by that still higher power known as the spirit.

Expanding Our Definitions of Consciousness and Reality

Since then, many others have understood that consciousness is far beyond the brain and the body, as we know them. The ranks of those who discovered greater abilities of the mind, life after death, and evidence of karma and past-life influences include men and women with impressive credentials and training.

For example, there have been studies done on psychokinesis at Princeton University in the Department of Engineering by Dean Robert Jahn and Brenda Dunne. Their research has resulted in evidence of the power of the mind to move objects. With scrupulous detail Jahn and Dunne have validated that small balls will fall in a changed pattern when influenced by mental energy. The effect of these mental influences is increased

---

[6]   The Indian schools (the Vedas, the Upanishads, the Hindu scriptures) speak of the immortality of the human being, the soul essence. The introspective gateways have been developed more nearly perfectly in the deepest reaches of India and in Tibet, than anywhere else.

The secret and ancient teachings of the Eastern masters were brought into the open after millennia of secrecy and transmission only to disciples, through Helen Blavatsky. In this way Theosophy was created. Theosophy swept the world from 1875 onward and continues today as an expression of the introspective discoveries of these masters of ancient wisdom. They lead directly to an awareness of soul-essence and of spirit.

Recently there has been an even greater infusion of Eastern philosophy to the West. This has been met by a progressively open and excited acceptance by our Western culture. The arrival in the West of such great teachers as Swami Muktananda, Swami Rama, Krishnamurti and Yogananda has been greeted by enthusiastic seekers including psychologists such as Ken Wilber, Stan Krippner, June Singer, Frances Vaughan and Jean Houston.

sevenfold when generated by bonded lovers.

Another example of the power of the mind can be seen in fire walking, in which ordinary individuals walk on coals heated to 1200 degrees Centigrade without harm to their bodies or their clothes. Workshops in fire walking are becoming commonplace and are being given all over the United States. Furthermore, those who have attended these workshops experience both an expansion of their view of life and a beneficial change in personality. They develop a greater confidence, and a new view of the possibilities of the world as seen through the "whole mind."

Seminars in Superlearning and Photo-reading indicate the vast processing capacity of the mind. Those who practice Superlearning have found that if one surrenders, setting aside doubt, the mind can absorb phenomenal amounts of information. Allegedly, Photo-reading students can read meaningfully at 25,000 words per minute.

These experiences in Superlearning are not entirely different from those that a psychoanalyst may have. Freud enjoined his students to listen to their inner voice with "evenly hovering attention,"--attention without effort. I myself have experienced this kind of ability to recall what I have learned when the need for it is triggered. In one session I remember how material from a patient's first session was still available to me, even two years later. I also remember how amazed I was at the results when I took speed-reading classes with Evelyn Wood. After practicing assiduously, I

---

6 (cont.)

With the synthesis and melding of East and West, new psychological treatments have been born. Some moderns such as Werner Erhardt (EST and

6 (cont.) Landmark Education), John Rogers (Insight), Eva Pierrokos (Pathwork) have created popularized alloys of Eastern philosophies and Western psychology. This is a sign of the times, wherein islands of interest in the "mind of things" stands sharply in contrast to the simultaneous burgeoning of technological medicine, in a technological society. Such interest signals a greater appreciation of the human part of the human being - a greater interest in personality and personal needs.

What is the contribution of Eastern philosophy to the West? The East pays tribute to the power of intuition, and ascribes reality to the power of thought. When they speak of this world as "illusion," they do not deny the consensual reality in which we live and love and work, but they do insist that we are surrounded by other planes which have as great a reality as the one we live in day to day. These planes are of an ascending order, plane upon plane, as we enlarge both vision and knowledge.

had the experience of reading a novel at 15,000 words per minute--at which point the very pages turned into a motion picture. No one was more surprised than I was; and though I have lost that capacity, it nevertheless demonstrated to me the untapped power of the mind, a power that is available to everyone.

Studies in hypnosis have also shown that the innate capacities of the mind are greater than we have believed. Charles Tart, an eminent West Coast psychologist and professor, hypnotized one subject who in turn hypnotized another. They then created a new reality, very different from the one that directs our everyday life. It was very real indeed to those two highly disciplined scientists who were the research subjects, -- just as real as the one we accept as normal.

Ian Stevenson, a professor at Eastern Virginia University, and Brian Weiss, a medical doctor, have both carried on meticulous research in the area of reincarnation, producing convincing evidence of its existence. Weiss has written two excellent books on the subject, *Many Lives, Many Masters* and *Though Time Into Healing.* The latter describes his own conflicted adventures with the past-life memories of many patients. These experiences transformed him from a very conservative academic psychiatrist noted for his work in psychopharmacology, to a believer in reincarnation. I have found that the knowledge of past lives is both important and meaningful in psychotherapy, especially when we find that the residue of a past life experience is still active--supporting a neurotic symptom, or behavior, in this life.

Many researchers, including Charles Tart, have produced much evidence for the existence of out-of-body experiences and near-death experiences, giving rise to an association for the study of these phenomena. The stories of those who have these experiences are quite uniform. They speak of approaching a light which is bright, safe and beautiful. Filled with beatific feelings of peace and love, they delight in meeting their dear departed whom they find in their prime. These experiences coordinate well with Eastern teachings of the immortality of the essential Self, and the advance toward the universal essence of love.

I would like to share one of my own stories of a near-death experience. Thirty-eight years ago, when my son was being born, my wife had an exceedingly difficult and prolonged labor, thirty-two hours. When an emergency Caesarian section was performed to rescue the baby, my wife's blood pressure dropped so low that it couldn't be recorded. She knew she was at the point of death and remembered being on the ceiling, hearing someone say anxiously, "I can't get a blood pressure." By her side was a spiritual being who gave her great comfort. She could look at the sky, through the ceiling of the operating room, and felt joined with the stars. Looking below, she thought, *Why don't they leave the body alone, she is so tired.* The room filled with light, and was occupied by her mother and many relatives, people she longed to see and speak with again. When she remembered me, however, she felt sorry that I would have to raise our child alone without its mother. At that point, the light in the room dimmed, and she returned to her body. She lived.

When she told me the story afterwards, I told her that she had experienced a chemical psychosis because of the drugs that had been administered to her. Such was the thinking of the day. But now, thirty-eight years later, I have learned that hers was a very typical near-death experience. Significantly, my wife has a great deal of access to intuitive realms. Furthermore, I have discovered that many of my patients have been through life-threatening traumas and have experienced similar out-of-body events. So have I, on two occasions.

In light of all this evidence, and the call of our own intuition, we have many reasons to pursue the soul-seeking, soul-searching drive that exists in all of us. If we open ourselves to this capacity, both we and society will be led to higher realms of beneficence, happiness, and enlightened service, to each other, to the planet and to all its inhabitants.

Recognizing the holographic plan of which we are a part, we can also recognize infinite ability, intuitive capacity, limitless creativity, and the realization that we are all one.

Guidelines and Exercises:

1. Most of all practice moving through resistances. Study them. Are you afraid you will be considered gullible, even crazy if you entertain these ideas and experiences about ESP, clairvoyance, seeing auras, feeling at one with the world, with nature, with insects, with the fact that, like Will Rogers you never met a man you didn't like: Practice all these things.

2. Practice suspending doubt about the experiences you are having.

3. When you engage with someone, notice how you feel. Perhaps you can anticipate what he/she will say. Through empathy (becoming him/her), see if you can feel with the other. Especially look into the eyes. Practice with someone you know and with whom you are comfortable.

4. Become quiet, and see if you feel the presence of your guide. Any visions that come to mind, take seriously.

5. When you are in a close family situation, see if you do not feel the joining of souls, or again when you are very close to someone.

6. Have faith -- the more you do, the more you will manifest that which is in your mind, wishes, and visualizations.

7. Visualize a perfect something; perfect performance or whatever is your thing. Visualize it repeatedly, but in a state of quietude as in meditation. Don't be surprised when it manifests. The more you practice this experience, the more it will happen. The more it happens, the more you will have faith.

CHAPTER III:

Spiritual Psychotherapy:
What Is It and How Does It Differ from Classical Psychotherapy?

The Uses And Misuses Of The Transference -- The Janus-Faced Soul That We Carry -- The Transference In Everyday Life -- Using The Transference To Release Our Love Capacities -- The Misuse Of Transference -- Avoiding The Pitfalls Of Uncontrolled Transference -- Two Examples Of The Release Of The Soul (The Sacred Heart) Through The Transference -- From Transference To Transcendence -- Visitations In The Astral Realm -- Spiritual Psychotherapy And The Corrective Emotional Experience -- Integrity In The Face Of Transference -- Recognizing Out Of Body Experiences -- Out Of Body Experiences In Everyday Life, Removal And Dissociation -- The Miracles Of Jesus As They Relate To Spiritual Psychotherapy -- Astral Visits And Dreaming -- More About Intuition.

Spiritual psychotherapy recognizes that the soul is a guiding principle in the inborn search for meaning, for identity and for our spiritual essence. It identifies the soul as the higher essence of the human being and acknowledges union with it as the supreme aim.

The Nature of the Soul

What are the conventional goals of psychotherapy? For Freudians they are to establish the ability to love another human being and to work well. For Maslow, they are the opening of our capacities for the peak experience; for Assagioli and his psychosynthesis, the uniting of spirit and psychoanalysis. For Jung, they are the understanding of the surrounding forces with which we are joined, called archetypes.

Ancient mysteries instruct that in the beginning there was God, the Divine Essence. Modern physics united with spiritual themes would call this Light-Consciousness. We are taught that the vibrations of the Divine, and the downwardly gradient vibrations of Light-Consciousness are so potent that the power of their energy would be intolerable on this plane. Divine creation manifested gradually through the reduction of vibrations, and these diminished vibrations developed into the Monadic, Atmic and Buddhic realms, as described in Sanskrit literature. These are the highest realms, closest to the Divine, and far too potent for us to experience or even comprehend.

As vibrations diminished in intensity and descended, a great inter-face between the highest dominions and the material human kingdom was created. This was called the "soul," or, in Sanskrit, the "causal body." The causal body, in turn, is much like a step-down transformer, receiving ener-gy from above and reducing it to levels that are endurable in the lower realms of near-manifestation and manifestation itself. Below the level of the causal body is the mental body, the emotional (or astral) body and the physical body of manifestation. This last is surrounded by an etheric network, a kind of template from which the physical form is laid down.

Thus, we find that we are descended from the highest vibrations, the highest Divinity. To put it another way, the divine spark, the spirit, is the kernel that, in order to manifest, acquires serial step-down planes of reality until the soul arrives. The soul then, in order to acquire experience on the physical level, manifests, weaves if you will, several bodies in step-down fashion. The mathematician and inventor/philosopher Arthur Young in his seminal work, *The Reflexive Universe*, elaborated a similar scheme. In convincing fashion he described a V-shaped descent-ascent pattern, beginning with the ubiquitous energy, Light, and descending to the nadir point of material manifestation. Thereafter, there was an upturn, travelling through ascending levels of manifestation from the most dense, the mineral, through the plant realm, the animal realm, the human realm and then upward still. This scheme of upward evolution, upward striving, represents a pull toward something higher and yet higher, as described in the Vedic and Buddhic traditions of the Far East.

How does all of this manifest in the material realm? The soul is not only a step-down transformer, it is also a kind of satellite dish that has its sensory, Janus-faced apparatus directed toward the On-High in one direction, and toward the lower levels of manifestation in the other. The soul being the high self, represents a realm of high aspiration. Such high aspirations manifest by attending and obeying the call toward joining the All. As we ascend in our spiritual development, we also rise in our perceptions, and then recognize that we are all part of the holographic network, the network of all living beings, of all manifestation.

How does this relate to soul seeking and soul-searching in spiritual psychotherapy? Roberto Assagioli, distinguished psychiatrist and psycho-analyst, speaks about this in his book, *Psychosynthesis,* informing us of the esoteric crises that precede a spiritual awakening:

"One may say of him [the person who exists nowadays in our social environment] that he `lets himself live' rather than that he lives. He takes life as it comes and does not worry about the problems of its meaning, its worth or its purpose; he devotes himself to the satisfaction of his personal desires; he seeks enjoyment of the senses and endeavors to become rich and satisfy his ambitions. If he is more mature, he subordinates his personal satisfaction to the fulfillment of the various family and social duties assigned to him, without taking the trouble to understand on what basis those duties rest or from what source they spring. Possibly he regards himself as `religious' and as a believer in God....and when he has conformed to the injunctions of his church and shared in its rites he feels that he has done all that is required of him. In short, he believes implicitly that the only reality is that of the physical world which he can see and touch and therefore he is strongly attached to earthly goods, to which he attributes a positive value; thus he practically considers this life an end in itself. His belief in a future `heaven,' if he conceives of one, is altogether theoretical and academic, as is proved by the fact that he takes greatest pains to postpone as long as possible his departure for its joys."[7]

Assagioli goes on to say that when crises, disappointments, the loss of a loved one, or the loss of a loved goal arrive, the individual is left with a sense of emptiness, even though there is no lack of anything material or definite. What is missing from a person's life then is a vague something, elusive and unable to be described. This sense of emptiness in life and in his personal affairs drives the individual to a kind of frenetic activity in which he tries to fill the hole. But he cannot do so through the material pursuit of more power, more sexual pleasure, more sensate experience, or more profit-motivated contact with other people. At that point, Assagioli says, the crises may be followed by a spiritual awakening:

"The opening of the channel between the conscious and the super-conscious levels, between the ego and the Self, and the flood of light, joy and energy which follows, often produce a wonderful release. The... conflicts and sufferings, with psychological and physical symptoms which they generated, vanish sometimes with amazing suddenness, thus confirming the fact that they were not due to any physical cause but were the direct

---

[7]   Roberto Assagioli, *Psychosynthesis Psychosynethesis; A Manual of Principles and Techniques.* New York, Hobbs, Dorman 1965, pages 40-41, 43.

outcome of the inner strife. In such cases the spiritual awakening amounts to a real cure." [8]

A spiritual psychotherapist knows that there is a High Self inherent within each individual, and that this Self is to be recognized, searched for and acknowledged. When the therapist can recognize this inherent value within the patient, then he/she can release it, guiding the patient on his road to fulfillment of the soul.

Spiritual psychotherapy is the tool and agency of the soul-seeking individual. It rests upon the belief and knowledge that the soul is the high essence of the individual, which only needs to be released to carry the individual on to higher and higher realms.

There are several essential differences between spiritual and conventional psychotherapy. They are:

1. The use of transference to allow and encourage transcendence.

2. The recognition of transmutation and transcendence, which describe the change of personality as one enters higher realms.

3. The allowing of the emotional experiences of therapy to become corrective emotional experiences.

4. The recognition and validation of the non-ordinary experiences and perceptions, such as out-of-body experiences, astral visits, energetic fields and the release of energy, the immortality of the soul, and the power of the intuitive mind.

The Uses and Misuses of Transference

Transference was the central concept of psychoanalysis as originally described by Sigmund Freud. It is defined as projecting onto people in one's present life the attitudes, feelings and expectations from important figures in the past, such as the mother or father. For example, the transfer of the fearful image of an all-powerful father may be cast onto the current employer, or the nurturing love-expectations of the mother of childhood onto the present-day wife. Nowhere is transference more commanding than in the therapeutic situation, given time and the tolerant skill of the psychotherapist.

The keystone tool of insight-psychotherapy is to observe the transference, and then to hand it back to the patient. This allows the patient to see that his/her feelings and expectations of the therapist are anachronistic, unnecessary and limiting. In this way, the patient can see how the trans-

---

[8]   Assagioli, page 43.

ference is operative in his or her life, limiting natural potential and energies.

The use of transference in a therapeutic situation can be very liberating, but it can also be misused--employed by the therapist to protect him or her from a fear of intimacy. It is a little-known fact that Freud began to use the couch because he didn't like his patients to be looking him in the face all day. The fear of the intimacy of transference can also be seen in the historical account of the one of the first psychoanalytic patients, Anna O., published in *Studies on Hysteria* by Freud and Joseph Breuer. This monograph described the psychoanalytic cure of an hysterical paralysis through hypnosis and the release of traumatic memories. Later it was revealed that Joseph Breuer, who was Freud's mentor and Anna O.'s first therapist, fled the scene because he was afraid of his patient's passionate love for him. When Breuer's wife had become jealous, he escaped by turning the patient over to Freud. Not infrequently, a doctor or psychotherapist's husband or wife will become jealous, knowing and sensing the adulation of the intense love transference that builds in patients. These love-longings pour out onto the therapist because they have long been aborted, stuffed into the unconscious, and must be fully experienced to enable the patient's release. It is important for the therapist to take a lesson from Breuer's panic and to rely instead on his or her integrity, sticking to the job in the interest of the treatment.

I remember with some sadness a failure that I created in the inexperience of my earlier years of practice. This was during the period when psychoanalysis was the only show in town, and I was intent on becoming trained as an analyst. I had been taught that we must not accept any gifts from a patient, and that everything the patient expresses must be put into words, and not action. In my zeal and fear I carried things too far. I had a beautiful young woman in analysis, and, true to form, she developed strong feelings of love for me. These were transferred from a very romantic father on whom she had remained fixated in spite of her recent marriage. I wanted to help her, but I was stiff. One day she wanted to give me a present, a poem that she had written about me. I refused to accept it, admonishing her to read it instead. She took that as a serious rejection and soon left the treatment, going on to become rather promiscuous despite her elegant background and personality. I had avoided receiving her love, and my avoidance had harmed her.

The real art of psychotherapy is to strike a balance between the allowing of the transference and the setting of boundaries. Such feelings must be put in context. On the one hand, the psychotherapist must be careful not to take the patient's love expressions too personally, as a temptation to the ego. On the other, an insistent interpretation that "this is only a transference, therefore the feelings are not real" can lead to sealing off, suppression, another inhibition of the love capacity of the patient. If indeed the love of the patient is interpreted as only "imaginary," belonging only to the past and not to the present, such an interpretation can be very constraining. A better description of this process can be seen in my experience with Muktananda, a Siddha master who was mandated by his own guru to come to the West and teach ancient wisdom to Western seekers. When I met Muktananda, I felt an indescribable love for him, one that was quite   mystifying to me since I felt that his ashram (retreat center) was very foreign to me. When these feelings persisted with a high intensity over the retreat weekend, I asked, by anonymous note, "Why is it that I feel so much love for you?" His reply was, "This describes your own capacity to love."

This was a powerful demonstration that validating the released love capacity of an individual is both affirming and soul-identifying. Therefore, it is very important that the patient's love be allowed full expression. If his or her love is respected, even to the extent of admitting that there may be qualities in the therapist that actually do appeal to the patient, then the individual's self-respect is honored and maintained. Those things that have kept that love capacity suppressed, such as early training or marriage to a cold partner, can be at least partly neutralized and remedied.

A therapist must always accept these love feelings with absolute ethical integrity. It is vitally important to respect the patient's love and capacity for love, without any acting out on the part of the therapist. Under these conditions allowing the patient's love to flow will also allow it to spread over a larger portion of humanity. To release one's love capacity is to release the Soul, the agency of Love-Wisdom, a transmission from the On-High. Love is the transmission from the inherent divine spark, which nurtures our intrinsic ability to join magnetically with one person, and then with other people, and, finally, with other realms of creation. It is the evidence of our natural capacity to serve the group and creation at large; of our inborn capacity to ascend higher and higher and closer to the Almighty. Gary Zukav expressed this concept in *The Seat of the Soul* when he points out that secular love is exclusive and possessive, whereas soul love is inclusive and expansive. This is a very important concept and certainly a description of a higher, finer and more divine quality of love.

It is also true that this recognition of the love capacity of the patient is a "being-cognition" of the patient. As described by Abraham Maslow, this term defines a loving kind of scrutiny of an individual, like the mother's love for her child, a lover's regard for his beloved, or a scientist's love and focussed inspection of his/her work. Under these conditions the mother, the lover and the scientist discover, through intense and caring scrutiny, new agencies within the object of their love, new latencies and new capacities that can be nourished and released. This kind of scrutiny is different from what takes place in conventional psychotherapy, which, as I was told by my training analyst, "takes the good for granted." As long as the good is taken for granted, its opposite, those qualities that are repressed and criticized by the patient, become nourished by repetition. Meanwhile, the good that is taken for granted atrophies through malnutrition. Therefore, I would encourage that we use the transference to recognize the patient's latent love capacity. In this way, through allowance and release, we will witness an efflorescence of love and wisdom from within the patient, and his or her ascent toward the soul.

The next two cases illustrate many of the principles I have been discussing. Each of these patients tells her own story in her own words. You will no doubt find their narratives singularly eloquent and their psychological adventures unusual; but I believe that these histories reveal the new reaches of the personality that emerge in spiritual psychotherapy. They disclose the enormous potential that we all could express were we released from self-doubt to rise into the high reaches of the soul-self that we essentially are.

Paula: The Body as the Mirror of the Mind

Paula was a remarkable woman but only in retrospect. Her inner beauty, poetry, channeling insights and heights of soul-reach became evident only after three years of psychotherapy and intensive challenge. The "ugly duckling" finally turned into a swan, showing that, under the surface, lay an essential sweetness, beauty and spirituality.

Paula had searched the world for a cure for her "environmental allergy," and help for a shame-producing problem with muscular distortions. She was fifty-eight years old when she came to see me, elegantly attractive despite her disfigurement, queenly in her bearing. At the same time she was boring. Her social etiquette was finely tuned, but it consumed her personality in such a way that the authentic inner person was concealed. In the beginning of her treatment, she related her story emotionlessly and colorlessly. It was not surprising, therefore, that when I asked her what she was feeling, she had to ask me to tell her about emotions and what they were!

Paula was born into a well-to-do and aristocratic family. She had been raised largely by the household maid who functioned as a governess because her mother, a high socialite, was out of the house much of the time. Notwithstanding, Paula remembers all the times she excitedly attended the opening of the door, sure that it was her mother, only to find that it was the maid who would be taking care of her after school. When the patient was sick and ran to the toilet to vomit, it was the maid who took care of her. Yet she had to make the best of things, and adopted an approach to people, both beloved and less loved, which was adaptive, pleasant, superficially friendly -- and empty. This reflected the emptiness of her life.

Paula married a man who was very successful financially and also from a "good family." Together the two lived a life devoted to their children that, by all appearances, was almost the ideal American family. The four children were very obedient and well bred. No one in this highly cultivated and controlled family--no one ever rebelled.

In 1975 Paula's symptoms of spasms and environmental allergy began. Although she thought she wasn't very smart, she showed her highly developed intelligence by learning almost everything there was to know about environmental energy, Candidiasis and dystonias (spasms), demonstrating courage and tenacity as she pursued one cure after another after another in her determination to become normal. Unbeknownst to her at the time, becoming normal meant becoming herself. You will see in her description of the vast numbers of treatments that Paula sought and practiced how her entire household became the victim of her environmental treatment needs.

Paula will tell the story for herself at this point. As you can see, she expresses herself beautifully and has tapped into that poetic part of herself that is so high in spirit and so close to the soul. This narrative is truly a channeling from the high self within her, which in turn is receptive to the greater wisdom and greater poetry that surrounds all of us.

"In the Spring of 1975, I injured my neck while playing tennis and was told to use cervical traction through the summer. Instead of the expected relief, I began to experience painful and uncontrollable spasms. I could have marked the date on the calendar. At that time the uncontrolled movement felt like a hand levitation in hypnosis.

"The summer when the spasms began, I was aware of several occurrences. Our seashore house was treated with chlordane as termite prevention. I clearly remember the piping hot day when the technicians crawled into the space below the house to spray. They drilled holes in the cement porch and poured chlordane inside to prevent invasion. How could that chemical intrusion on one's body not affect one's immune system?

"I spent that summer at the seashore with my children. I was lonely -- oh, so lonely for my husband. He was hard at work and able to visit only on weekends. I felt that I was pushed out of my winter home -- forced out -- forced away from him, forced to go to the seashore. He did not want me, did not want to be with me. I felt unloved. About this time my husband had high blood pressure and the prescribed medication caused further withdrawal.[9] My hurt and disappointment were absorbed back into my body.

"My husband, Jack, was dining and wining well at lunch, and we both indulged at dinner. Our enjoyment of wine, the marriage of wine and food, the preparation of fine cuisine, added to the alcohol consumption that must have been deleterious to my immune system as well.

"My orthopedist suggested that I see a neurologist, who proceeded to ply me with a variety of pills. After extensive tests, he prescribed Haldol. Every inch of my body suffered with itching and scratching due to a poison-ivy-like rash from the medication.

"The neurologist next suggested Sinemet. I felt terrible, constantly nauseous. My spasms were worse, but I continued with the medication because I was told that the missing dopamine would take six months to get to the proper place in my brain in order to be effective. I shook, I was anxious. I was getting worse.

"In June my son was to graduate from college. It was a hot, damp day out on the lawn where the ceremony was taking place. Another son had done so poorly at the school he attended, that they would not even accept him for summer school. As I sat at the graduation, my leg muscles began to involuntarily spasm. I was scared because it felt so weird -- I felt as if I ought to. be hospitalized. My husband drove me to the neurologist who stopped the Sinemet.

"Valium was the next medication recommended. I began slowly with small amounts and increased the quantity as time went on, eventually taking six 'blue-bombers' a day. I forgot whole weekends, gifts I bought, etc.

---

9   Many high blood pressure medications cause a decrease of sexual functioning.

"I then met a doctor who suggested I dispense with the Valium and try hypnosis with him. The day of his treatment, I felt better, well enough to shop, but there was no cure after a year, so I discontinued treatment.

"By now I felt terrible all the time with flu-like symptoms: hangoverish, achy, hazy, cold. I would lay on the sofa all day and shake. My mind was so unclear that I was unable to balance my checkbook. The spasms were increasingly torturous, and my hands would go into spasm as well. I would wonder if a spasm was strong enough to break the glass I was holding; eating and drinking were difficult without spilling food or drink, and applying make-up almost impossible. I discontinued every activity in which I participated. In addition to having this horrendous debilitation, I was embarrassed and retreated from communication with others.

"Next on my agenda was a medical nutritionist in New York who after a thorough `work-up' said that the spasms were due to an allergy/chemical sensitivity. In addition to a multitude of supplements, I began a special all-beef diet program.

"The medical nutritionist prescribed that I enter a `clean unit,' a clinical ecology unit in Texas, for a more complete diagnosis. After fasting for eight days, I was subjected to foods one at a time, and later to chemicals. I reacted to everything, either with spasms, dizziness, or other symptoms. After six weeks I returned home, cleaned house, replaced oil heat with electric, took out the bedroom carpet, and went on a rotation diet with the less reactive organic foods. At this point I was known as a `Universal Reactor,' sensitive to every food, to water, to chemicals and to people."

At this point Paula tried a therapist who balanced her meridians, several chiropractors who used applied kinesiology, and a doctor in Illinois who tested her for food allergies sublingually. When none of these treatments worked, someone finally suggested that she seek out services at my Center for Mind/Body Wellness.

"In 1989 someone suggested that I see a very special, specific psychiatrist, Dr. Maurie D. Pressman. Neither you, your name, nor psychiatry particularly appealed to me. I reluctantly made an appointment with you because I was desperately searching for a solution to my spasms. I now understand that my spasms were a means to the end -- and not a 'thing' unto themselves. Yes, I would love to have a total healing, but the real lesson was within myself ... a lesson of learning who I was, recognizing the me of me, and relating the all of me to God and the Universe. I did not know me, I did not know love, and God was 'up there' -- not a part of me. I lacked spontaneity, vitality and a reality of who I was. I had no ambitions or goals, only an existence -- no true understanding of who I was. There was no truth, no reality.

"I first met you in Dr. B's office as you fumbled unsuccessfully through your briefcase for patient fill-out forms, commenting you were used to having a secretary. The twinkle in your eye was lost as I began treatment in your Philadelphia office.

"In 1989, you were strict, you were stern with an emotionless countenance. As I looked at you, I saw my husband in 1975 at the end of our dining table without emotion, without care, without conversation. Then I hated our dinner hour; I disliked my confrontation with you. I pictured your face mentally on an ice cube and used to melt it down to rid my mind of the experience with you. I also mentally used a peashooter directed your way.

"You asked me to talk of -- to feel -- emotion. I did not know what emotion was and you WERE NO EXAMPLE. I asked you a number of times to list the emotions. It seems stupid to me now -- my not knowing -- but I did not know.

"You commented upon how I scrutinized you. I did so because I could not understand you. You appeared so fractured to me. The front, the back and the profile did not appear to be part of the same person. Each area would have a different personality, yet I saw no personality.

"You stated that you were only a clothes hook upon which to hang my problems. I thought I was living a rather placid and serene life and was not quite sure what my problems were -- except for the spasms. It took many, many months to comprehend that underneath what appeared to be peace was fear, loneliness, lack of love, insecurity. Only the best therapist could dig so deeply and be that intuitive in discovering the turmoil beneath the calm.

"I first realized you were a man, not simply a stone-faced dummy when I attended a retreat. I saw the caring; the love as you worked with your assistants in communicating with patients. You and your staff all respected each other's talents to achieve the best result for the patient.

"As time went on, you softened and I matured. Our meetings became less stagnant.

"You recommended rather elusively that I visit R in Baltimore, a psychologist who specialized in deep muscle therapy and breathing in conjunction with selected powerful music. I took the train weekly to Baltimore and could hardly believe the pent-up emotions that exploded from within as a result of his treatment: fear, anger, hurt. It was exhausting.

It was torture! And it was healing! I saw and talked with R once a week and had sessions with you twice a week. I began having difficulty with a complete allegiance and commitment to two people. R was good. R was excellent. He knew more about me, about the book-learning part of me and my emotions, than you did, but this kind of knowledge meant very little to me. When I saw you, I felt a deep wisdom, an intuitive knowing -- as if Jesus were speaking to me. At the depth at which I felt the wisdom was love. As you spoke I could hardly hear the words because of the joy I felt. I terminated my trips to Baltimore and increased the number of sessions with you.

"When seeing you twice weekly, I felt as if I had to 'perform' each visit. I had to let out my emotions for forty-five minutes, then calmly return home to my husband. I felt as if I was on a stage giving a performance. When I saw you on a daily basis, the performances gave way to more of a state of being me. I let go -- surrendered, rather than trying 'to do.' I became more of a reality of who I was.

"I would visually picture a sore spot at the bottom of a hollow tube in me -- way down deep. The depth was where I felt your love and wisdom. I had exuded anger, hurt and fear but had not dealt with love. You allowed me to communicate all emotions. It was difficult for me to believe that you accepted my anger -- let it flow through you. There was no rebuttal, no consequence, only a freedom of expression. As important as hurt and anger is, so is love. You permitted me to express love and joy, express it to its fullest extent. When one gives love, one receives and the sore spot within me, the spot devoid of love is now fulfilled, a completed soul -- a soul full of love that knows the love of God.

"Through you I have found the essence of me, the very being of me, the God within me. You have installed a vitality never known to me. I believe this original lack of vital essence prohibited my living a natural goal setting way of life. What more can a man offer a person than his/her whole vital essence? To say 'thank you,' or to say that I am grateful, is insufficient.

"As time elapses, the love I express is not limited to the here, the now, but transcends time and space. The love is a merging of our souls -- with all souls to be a part of the All -- the All That Is."

It is easy both to see and to deeply appreciate the insight, and wisdom-capacity of this woman who was formerly, and all of her life, deaf to the call of the inner person, of the poet, of the one who is full of feeling. Reading her story, it is easy to appreciate the release of love-wisdom and the expansion that followed the gradual disappearance of the encrusted bonds that she carried, that had been thrust upon her soul by societal upbringing.

Eloquently describing her newfound experiences of love, Paula further states, "My muscles twist because they hold in all emotions. If I am overly excited, anxious, worried, whatever, the excess seems to collect in my spasms. This is true of love as well. If my feelings of love are so intense that they are greater than my body -- If they are blocked and locked within my physical being, my muscles are in an extremely tight spasm, only relieved by the expression of love.

"One significant contribution that I make to the world is love -- the love I speak of is far beyond the physical body, beyond the here and the now. It is the love of the past, love of the future, a love that travels through the eternity and infinity of time and space. It is not romantic love; it is God's love within me that merges with other souls who expand as I do to the realms of what is, with love.

"When one throws a pebble into the water, ripples form and continue as far as one can see -- so it is with the energy of love. Once can feel the energy of love within a group of people, just as one can sense anger. That love is not confined to the room in which those people sit. There are no boundaries. It flows beyond the room, beyond the building, the town, eventually encompassing the universe. The spreading of such love can heal the world."

Vera: The Poet Emerges

Vera was forty years old, and had found her way to our office after promising herself that she was done with psychiatrists. Having just emerged from a frightening and esteem-damaging experience in a psychiatric hospital, she had foresworn any connection with mental health professionals. She had always been inherently spiritual. Although a devout Catholic, she was unsatisfied with her religious experiences, seeking something more soul-fulfilling. She wandered into our office because of a previous experience with one of our staff who was lecturing on *A Course in Miracles* and because she had heard that our office was one in which spiritual principles were acknowledged. What follows is her experience in her own words.

"If you really want my 'story,' here it is, in the only form I know how to give it ... as if in a letter to you.

"I've told you before that I had a sense about the day that I walked into your clinic for the first time. I was nervous as hell. After all, I had decided that I was through with shrinks. (I was angry that I hadn't become a psychologist myself.) I knew there was a better way but didn't believe that there was anyone else who felt the way I did about the psychological/spiritual connection. I had just SPENT two long years with a psychiatrist who seemed to shrink (himself) at the thought of anything spiritual. I longed to share this part of myself. My psychiatrist sent me to my pastor who bounced me back to my psychiatrist. I finally decided it just wasn't going to happen. Things had never looked darker. Every day was one anxiety attack after the other. Fear loomed in my face.

"Finally, I read an article about fear that George, who works in your office, had written for the newspaper. It really spoke loudly to me. I couldn't believe your office was so near that I passed it often. At the same time I started to read *A Course in Miracles* on my own. The second astounding coincidence was that George was 'into' 'The Course.' Could we connect spiritually? When I called to make an appointment, I was told that I needed an intake appointment with you first. I was scared because I thought you looked so stern. I remember thinking, 'Let me just get past this one, then I'll get to make an appointment with the one I want.'

"At the hour of my appointment, there was a woman there whose husband was dying of cancer. You called me into your office and softly asked if it were okay with me if you spoke to her for just a short time before we were to meet. Your compassion for your other patient overwhelmed me, and I relaxed completely. I don't know that I can truly express to you the hope that filled me that day. Thoughts of having come home were resounding in my head. I know I told you of my need to connect with a professional who could understand my spiritual side. I remember that you said, ever so gently, 'George and I believe in these things.' My heart soared. I was scared to death, but willing as anything to face my fears.

"I think my sessions with you were perfect but at the time I was extremely critical. I also started attending group therapy. If you forgot something, I was all over you. If you said you wanted to do something and didn't follow through with it, I was angry. And you allowed it ... it felt incredible to trust you enough to feel that anger. It was the first time ever that I believed that I could get angry and not be turned away. I was furious when I told you privately that the group just wasn't moving fast enough for me and then you announced to the group that I felt they were duds. I really felt betrayed, and I think that you felt badly about it.

"This situation reminded me somehow of my dad. What was screaming in my head was a scene with him that had happened two years earlier, a few nights before he took me to the hospital and stuck me in the psychiatric ward. All I had said to him was that, although I was a woman with children and a husband, I still wanted his love, I still needed a dad. He said, simply, 'No, you don't.' It doesn't matter now that I know that my father loves me in the best way that he knows how. It doesn't matter that I now know how afraid he was to love. Those words were among the most hurtful words of my life. Three words that he doesn't even remember saying, I am sure..."

The Hospital

"I couldn't believe the depth of despair I was feeling at that time. It had started a few months before when I began to experience a buzzing sensation in my body that would wake me up from my sleep, and make me feel as though I were floating above my bed. I had experienced a trauma a short time before, of a boy coming to my door with his face cut almost off and hanging. I didn't know where to turn so I went to my father. He started me on Xanax as soon as I told him about my symptoms. Soon afterwards, when I wasn't improving, he sent me to Dr. R. Notably, Dr. R was associated with a hospital that my father was NOT affiliated with. I knew that my father had chosen this place on purpose, because he was ashamed of me.

Dr. R was eager to medicate me as well, first with Ativan, then with a 'new, safe, benign' drug called Buspar. I reacted to this drug like I was drinking ten gallons of coffee, but I didn't make the connection that this feeling was coming from the medicine. I assumed it was my anxiety. I had become so bad that my husband withdrew from me and slept in the guestroom. Three days went by where I felt totally terrified, couldn't sleep and could barely move from my bed. That Saturday night, I begged my father to take me to his house so that my children wouldn't see me in the state I was in. He agreed. My parents put me in their guestroom, told me at what hour I could take another Ativan and then quickly fell asleep. I didn't. I crawled into their room, sat in the corner and watched them sleeping. At 8:30 a.m. I started to cry out loud.

"By 9:30 my husband came over. I don't remember any conversation between the two of us. He just gave me a toothbrush and toothpaste and drove me to the hospital. Dad was with us. We parked blocks away ... I was scared we would be mugged. In the emergency room when Dr. C spoke to me, Dad wouldn't let me talk. He told her about my traumatic experience and said that I was feeling badly about this boy. My husband stood way back in the corner and never spoke. Dr. C. introduced me to another doctor and I was immediately admitted. I felt relief to be away from my husband, the kids, and the rest of the family. I remember, however, so very clearly, the words PSYCHIATRIC WARD printed on a place card in the hallway as I was being wheeled into the unit. There was a feeling inside of me of final resignation ... as if I were telling myself that I had just totally and completely bought into their whole story. I was giving up my own truth in order to make them right, because if I were right, I would be alone. I was choosing to be crazy for them. If I chose otherwise I would be totally alone with a self that was scared to death.

"The weeks that followed played like One Flew Over the Cuckoo's Nest in my head: standing in line for meds, being spoken to and treated like an idiot. Every evening I was given another tranquilizer to try and help me sleep, but so far I hadn't. As soon as my eyes closed, I would jerk awake. I cried and moaned. I bled. Dr. R only spoke to me about medication. Interns came in and asked me if I heard voices, asked me questions in sequence and then asked me to repeat them. I seemed too lucid to be of interest even to them. Only Dr. C was a light in my life. We would talk about Jesus (with the door closed). I had to promise that I wouldn't let anyone know that we had these conversations.

"Once Dr. C asked me to engage in a psychodrama with her. She played the part of my father. I remember screaming and yelling and crying at her (him). She then took me into a room with a punching bag and asked me to hit it. Dr. R called her out of the room. I could tell he didn't like what she was doing. I really got into hitting that bag. I went out the other door, went to my room, and started yelling that I didn't belong there. Six or seven people came in to restrain me. When I saw the straightjacket coming at me, I felt a part of me die. After that, I didn't feel like I had put myself in there to get away from it all. I felt as if I had been tricked into going to hell and that there was no way out, not ever.

"My father visited once. My mother, never. My husband would stop often on his way home from work. I can't remember what our conversations involved other than talk about the kids. I do remember saying over and over again that I was sorry.

"After I was released, it was very difficult to go back to my community. My mother had told anyone who asked about my whereabouts that I had cracked up and that she didn't know when I would be coming home.

I've sure spent a lot of time trying to overcome the shame attached to the stigma of having been in a nut house. But out of that came an incredible amount of energy that started me on the road of this glorious spiritual journey ... launched by you and George."

Learning to Love George: The Power of Transference

"The first time I really got to observe George was at a Grof breathing workshop that you invited me to attend. I was so intrigued by him and the way that you two worked together. It was soon after that I started to go to his workshops on *A Course in Miracles*. I couldn't quite believe what I was learning there, how incredibly talented George was in bringing out my pain ever so gently, or how much I loved him. I never actually voiced that feeling to myself for months.

"For years I had carried around an intense hatred for my mother. But in one evening, under the gentle guidance of George's voice and with the biggest trust I ever gave to anyone, I truly got to see my mother as she really is--just scared and lonely. George encouraged me to bring all those years up to the surface. After I had beat the daylights out of a pillow, totally unaware of anything but my rage, he asked me a simple question, `Now do you see your mother?' ...She's never been able to push my buttons since, I have such compassion for her now. It was probably very soon after this that I wrote the first poem I had written in years. It was for George and I felt comfortable enough to give it to him. I had shown the last one I had written, at about age seventeen, to my father, and he had attempted to correct it.

"In November of 1992, I realized that I had to face what I was feeling for George. I knew all about transference and the like, but what I hadn't understood was the incredible dedication he displayed, not just to me, but to everyone I saw him with. His love felt so incredible. I imagined that it had to be the next best thing to experiencing God.

"Even though I felt totally embarrassed by my emotions, I told George anyway. He didn't run and he didn't seem the least bit uncomfortable with it; in fact, he encouraged me to be with those feelings of intense love and desire. I never doubted his ethics or his commitment. My love just grew more and more intense. He told me that eventually it wouldn't hurt, and I believed him. I've never trusted anyone so deeply in my life. He was right. The pain got worse, long before it got better.

"At one point George got really tough with me, when I was refusing to look inside of my self for my own affirmation. He told me, in front of a large group, that I should stop enjoying him so much. He said that he had momentarily gotten hooked into my charm and that he wasn't going to fall for it anymore, because instead of getting to what was really bothering me, I was flirting and kibitzing around with him.

"When he said that he was no longer going to play Mr. Nice Guy, I thought that he was withdrawing all that tenderness he had shown forever. I looked at him, and all I could feel was the love that I wanted him to accept, but there were a lot of people around. So I told him instead that I hated him, and he said `good.' There it was. One of those mini-deaths again. I felt shriveled and dying as I there sat on the floor, sobbing and feeling that I was getting smaller and smaller until the floor would swallow me up. I was totally humiliated and alone.

"When I couldn't feel any smaller, there arose from somewhere deep inside of me a giggle. I don't know to this day exactly how to put it into words, but it felt somehow as if I knew that I was God and that God was me. I started to laugh and a feeling of joy returned to me at that moment. George's face finally softened and he said, `You got it, didn't you!'

"In spite of this joy, I began to be frustrated by my feelings for him. The joy of it was oftentimes overshadowed by deep longing. I know that he wanted me to see the patterns of my past in these feelings, and I could, but I felt that he really couldn't understand that I truly loved him because of who he is, not just what he represents. I would become upset when he would refer to my feelings only as transference. My anxiety got worse, and when I started to think about the scores of women that he had to go through this process with. I felt like a number in a line.

"Christmas time was so difficult. I wanted to share all its enchantment only with him. On New Years' Eve I felt like my heart was breaking, especially since he was away with a lot of people from the group. Every ounce of me was unsatisfied. I studied hard and long about Special Relationships vs. Holy Relationships in 'The Course' and in the book *Seat of the Soul* by Gary Zukav, but the harder I tried to put things into perspective, the worse I felt. As always, George was reassuring, promising over and over again that he would be there for me, that it was okay, that I should just be with the feeling. Ugh!!

"Finally, I began giving up my attachment to needing George, simply loving him without the pain of tomorrows and what ifs. It happened suddenly in moments that felt out of time, like epiphanies. I was learning how to be at peace, in awe of his knowing how to allow this new understanding to unfold for me.

"It feels great now to be able to love him without the pain, frustration, longing and awkwardness. I am free. Somehow in this process I learned to really love myself, to love solitude, to look at the parts of myself that I really don't like and to be okay with them, and to know that many people live a lifetime without ever being able to experience this kind of love. My feelings about George have not really changed, only my attachment to those feelings has.

"I had to be sure that I was feeling what I was feeling. The reason this was important is that spiritual transformation is profound and can set your heart and soul reeling. It would be rather ironic if, after all the dedication you and George put into your `different' approach to therapy, you didn't expect to see the results in your patients as being different as well. I am grateful that you do, that you understand. In all honesty, I believe there is a big difference between the way that women understand themselves and the way that men understand women. Men's views of women are often so socialized, so pop culture. I know that Paula has felt the same way, and I really wish to share this admonition with you.

"I am quoting Marianne Williamson in *A Woman's Worth* when I say:

'The growth of a girl into a woman, a princess into a queen, is not a liberal transition. Like any true creative flow, it is radical. That is not to say it is angry or harsh. But it is radical, the way truth is radical -- and birth and art and real love and death. It changes things. It represents a shift in core beliefs, a belly-up of dominant paradigms. Without this shift, a woman seesaws between the brink of disaster and the brink of salvation. She goes from moments of bliss to terror. And then the children, and the world, begin to seesaw with her.'

"There is an ancient trick to telling a woman to be less than blissful when we are blissful, to inadvertently tell her that when she is in her glory, that this is her weakness. I say this with love, with a deep trust that you and George are of a new breed, thank God, and that you can understand that I have reclaimed who I am and have found that my power is in my joy.

"Maurie, you have called me a 'force.' I appreciate that. It has made me feel simply wonderful. Please know always that I am so honored to have traveled along this path with you. You have been the biggest inspiration in my life, and I am forever grateful for your trust and caring and faith. And know that I love you."

There is occasion to rejoice in the release of this poetic soul from the constrictions of her upbringing and the opinions of conventional psychiatry. We can be warmed by Vera's expansive love. Although it was focused on George, it expanded to embrace an ever widening circle.

Vera spoke of having writer's block that she felt could only be released by writing to someone she loved. What follows illustrates the beauty of her release into poetry:

"To George"
"When you gentle me to see the truth
of all that waits to be awakened
     (no matter how you cut it,
         Freud, transference, whatever analysis ...)
there is a simple truth to it.

So simple that it's the biggest thing I've ever felt
So simple that I know
     that
(wo)man has never invented any bromide
or written erotically enough
     to erase the excitement
of just your hand upon my shoulder ...

Ah -- to sigh in the light of it
to feel the power as it pierces deeply
     to reconcile with God as I bathe in it
So simple is it to feel the joy

     even as I stand alone in its truth
       knowing it's a gift
waiting to be found knowing that you won't

     not really

And so I offer it again and again
     in gestures great and small
stepping into your circle
     and stepping out
to watch up close
     or from afar

As you unfold before me
>   Such beauty in a face I've never seen before
>   taking my breath away

I will be called away
Even now I feel the universe waiting patiently
>   I don't want to go
>   not ever
Even divine harmony is beckoning me to let go
>   to use her lessons and move on
>   but please, don't ever think for a moment
>   that it wasn't really very simple
>   that I will love you for all eternity

even as my feet once again touch the ground
>   as I mother,
>   as I return to give all I know needs to be given
>   to the vows I've made in this life time

that my soul bears how you have graced me

>   and how I've been reborn
>   in loving you"

What Do These Two Women Teach Us?

These two case histories epitomize the transcendence that attends upon the feeling of love toward the psychotherapist. They also demonstrate what happens when the psychotherapist allows the dignity of the feeling, encouraging the patient to tolerate the love without suppression or acting out. When love transference is allowed to follow its course, it ascends from the realm of personal love into the broader, all-embracing realms of humanity.

The ebullient expressions of joy communicated by these two patients also express, albeit in a quieter way, the gratitude of the spiritual psychotherapist for being allowed to participate, and even risk his/her own feelings, in a healing and soul release such as this.

But it is not easy to withstand the onslaught of feelings, not only from the patient, but from the inner self. It is necessary, of course, to be true to the treatment and therapeutic integrity. In so doing, the therapist builds strength and psychological muscle, elevating himself/herself to a higher position in pursuit of a higher purpose. I remember, very early in practice, how hard pressed I was in the face of the loving admiration of an extremely beautiful woman. It is hard to withstand such invitations to the ego to a secular and forbidden love. But the soul whispers to the therapist that yielding would damage another human being and tarnish all dedication to the healing profession. In listening and heeding, I grew in strength and purpose, and the patient also continued to grow. She learned to express herself in safety and could increase her trust in both herself and in me.

Not all feelings of transference are pleasant ones. Some can be very angry, hateful and distressing. I well remember other times when the bitter criticism of a patient would make me feel like retaliating in kind. By biting my lip and exploring the reason for my feeling, however, I grew and learned more about the sources of my own sensitivity. Using the feelings I had tolerated for reflection upon what was going on within the patient, I could now know him better, and better serve our common purpose in coming together. This encounter was, and remains, a growth process.

In all of this the therapist is healed and elevated as well as the patient. I believe that this is always so if the therapy succeeds, and if the therapist is open. In my work, I often end the group session with the following prayer from *A Course in Miracles:*

> "I'm here only to be truly helpful.
> I'm here to represent Him Who sent me.
> I don't have to worry about what to say or what to do, for He Who
> sent me will direct me.
> I am content to be wherever He wishes, knowing He goes there
> with me.
> I will be healed as I let Him teach me to heal."

Tolerance and Transcendence: Breaking Loose into Higher Realms of Human Capacity

The experiences that Paula and Vera have just described tell us that when we allow the love capacity to flow toward the therapist, it will, if rightly handled, expand beyond the therapist. At the same time the therapist will feel enlarged. Relieved of any self-conscious sense of responsibility, he/she will feel the reward of having enabled a flowing and fulfilled patient. This feeling is much like the pride and fulfillment of a parent.

Concomitantly, the therapist learns and is healed as the experiences of the expanded life of the patient course into him/her. Such are the wonderful rewards of this work.

The love permission that the therapist has granted provides validation and recognition of an inner soul capacity within the patient. It also allows for its augmentation. As Gary Zukav has related in *Seat of the Soul,* soul love is expansive and increasingly encompassing. These now liberated love forces have been described by patients repeatedly as "intolerable." At that point the patient tries to escape these forces by distraction, denial or inhibition of feeling. Here, it is a good idea to remember again that the forces and energies of the soul--of the higher agencies--are so intense, so powerful that they would destroy the material self, were they not toned down. This reality finds expression on the clinical level in statements such as, "What am I going to do with these feelings?" They are akin to the intolerance of sexual excitement that occurs during foreplay and just before the explosion of orgasmic release. If the love feelings, and the sexual feelings, are tolerated instead of denied and repressed, then the sensation of incipient explosion will fade, and the patient will break through into higher realms of bliss, of joining, of union with the All.

I would like to offer a case history from my practice that illustrates this dynamic. The matter of tolerance and transcendence is an intrinsic principle in the human being and will allow for transcendence into higher realms in a kind of emergence from the physical body. It is much like breaking loose into the higher realms of capacity wherein the soul resides.

From Transference to Transcendence: A Case History

Alexandra was a highly spiritual person, so dedicated to soul-ascendance in the latter part of her life that she became a near hermit. She lived in nature and restricted her human contacts to only a few. She immersed herself in literature and dedicated herself to serving the human community through her creative literary works. These were labors that taught the messages of the soul, of love and reincarnation.

She had been through a series of traumatic relationships with men, including a marriage to a man who was both physically and verbally abusive. Through these experiences, she had become sensitive to the presence of both high and dark forces. She endured a terrible period in her life when she was almost overcome by gloom. In the middle of the night, she would feel a heavy presence on her chest and suffered actual choking episodes, bringing her near to death. She had struggled with the Dark Forces and had emerged informed and enlightened. After that, she continued her journey with greater awareness.

Despite her unhappy experiences, she continued to need to be loved and to express love. She met a man who was very much like her. He had similar soul-aspirations, shared her love of music and literature, and had a strong desire to help humanity. When she met him she felt an instant recognition, and was strongly drawn to him. Throughout the next year or more they met infrequently, but had a strong connection by phone. During this time her feelings blossomed, and she became aware of new possibilities within herself. She also became conscious of her sharpness, which she had used as a shield to protect herself from the hurt and disappointment she always anticipated from others.

As the interchange continued between Alexandra and Roy, each recognized and supported the inner talents of the other. Such appreciation strengthened both the relationship and each individual personality. In the beginning she expected what had been true of other relationships, that he would want a physical consummation, but this was not possible for a variety of reasons. Roy was well married and a devoted family man and did not really desire this consummation. Instead, they shared higher meetings on the astral plane, which were signaled when Alexandra felt a passing breeze on her face. This indicated the presence of Roy's soul, which, in traditional sacred literature, is often felt as a passing breeze.

These astral visits caused Alexandra to see an inner purple light, and to feel strong vibrations, which she experienced as a source of powerful energy that filled her with well-being. Purple is the color of spirit, and so it felt to Alexandra. She did not at first recognize her longings and sadness for what they were, but soon became acutely aware of them. As she was able to tolerate them, a breakthrough followed, taking her into ever higher realms accompanied by astral meetings with her soul-partner. Characteristically, during these meetings, an all-pervading peace and bliss surrounded her, a joy-quietude signalling the presence of the soul. Her elevation to these higher realms replaced her physical longing, so that she soon began to feel that the material satisfaction of a physical consummation was no longer desired or desirable.

This is an ongoing story. The communion and collaboration between Alexandra and Roy continues. She has become more and more outgoing, and her writing too has transcended itself. Formerly, she wrote in a rather frivolous, though entertaining, style. Now her writing soars to high poetry and beautiful descriptions of nature. Once a recluse, she has become surrounded by a small group of admirers who want to learn from her, and take care of her. At one time she would have bristled at their approach. Now she radiates warmth as well as teaching. High souls emanate a magnetic force that is a part of the love that is so representative of an elevate personality, and this is certainly true of Alexandra. While she remains covetous of her time, so that she may meditate in nature and write, she has blossomed through the things she has learned from her relationship with Roy. In so blossoming, she is influencing others through example, teaching, love.

Her writing, deriving from her visions and meditations, has carried a powerful message to the world. The freeing of her personality, which had become so constricted by her unhappy experiences, brings its message to all of us. Confined within the walls of her defenses and her need to push others away was a huge store of unconditional love and desire for service. It was not easy for her to learn the new lessons of a love experience through Roy, but she was willing and courageous -- and rewarded. This is a lesson for all of us, to remain open to ourselves and to overcome the anxieties that have walled our essential self within.

Visitations on the Astral Plane

I believe that astral visits, such as Alexandra experienced, are the counterpart of out-of-body experiences. We are surrounded by other more subtle bodies of which the astral body is one. The subtle energies that comprise these bodies can be felt and seen by sensitives, but they can also be recorded by Kirlian photography for anyone's viewing. We ourselves can feel them if we relax and suspend doubt. In this state, when the palms of the hands are brought close to each other, we can feel a tingling and a kind of ball of pressure between them. Astral visits have been described in *The Mahatma Letters*. In these letters the masters often spoke of making visits to their pupils by projecting their astral bodies over long distances. Madame Blavatsky herself, it was said, was able to astrally visit the Vatican archives, retrieving material that was hidden from all others on the outside, which she was then able to incorporate into her writings. Such is the power of the soul, such is the power achieved when the personality is elevated through continual discipline and aspiration. Such power is inherent to the planes of existence that lie closer to love.

The Unbearable Lightness of Being

I want to relate one more vignette illustrating the rewards that follow upon tolerating the so-called intolerable. To do so, I will return to Paula, the woman who recovered from her spasms and environmental allergies.

"I felt absolutely desperate - distraught in your office at the thought of not always and forever being with you in a complete connection of love. I felt the loss and the separation as it came close to the time for me to depart, and felt teary-eyed when faced with the fact I had to leave.

"I was in a somewhat altered, pensive state as I awakened at 4:30 the next morning thinking how distraught I had felt the previous day. How could I satisfactorily and effectively explain to you the depth of those feelings? One analogy that came into my mind was the desperation that the Iraqi women must have had felt when being bombed during the Gulf War. How hopeless! How desperate! How alone! How helplessly tormented!

"I contemplated, `What is on the other side of those feelings?' And rapidly I determined that it was a total body, mind and soul union with you. At that thought, I spontaneously saw a white ball of light, our joined-togetherness with God. As the white light expanded, it came closer to enfold and entirely fill me with its glow. This experience wasn't intentionally thought out or directed, it just happened -- pure bliss to be joined with you, with the All, with God. Tears of joy came with the merging. I was at peace.

"When I separated from God and came back to earth into my limiting human body, I realized that for me there had always been a lack of full love, a lack of mother-bonding and God-love bonding. I had never felt whole - not complete. I also realized that somehow this recent experience had been part of my completion. It's another step, perhaps an initiation into my ascension to the Oneness of the Universe, the Cosmos. I am thankful to God. I am thankful to you for helping."

What Have We Learned?

All three of these women, Paula, Vera and Alexandra, were highly constricted before entering therapy. To the world at large, they appeared "lucky," because they had all the necessary material possessions, but they were miserable, without knowing why. As they were released by their therapy, and as their considerable love was allowed to flow, their personalities rose and these women were elevated to the level of soul, to realms of joy and joyous living that are beyond this plane. The spontaneous poetry of their language described the higher planes upon which we can all dwell. In our journey to get there, every one of us can recognize more and more, and teach more and more, the beauty of authenticity. We can live our lives in such a way that we invite our own personality and those of others to flow and to rise to these soul levels.

Spiritual Psychotherapy and the Corrective Emotional Experience

In the 1940's and 1950's the well-known Chicago psychoanalysts, French and Alexander, advocated a therapy that employed what they called the "corrective emotional experience." Their theories were not popular at the time, but later were endorsed by Anna Freud, who was then the acknowledged leader in psychoanalytic circles. The corrective emotional experience is one in which the patient relives, in a more favorable way, those traumatic or deprivation experiences of childhood that have been carried in the unconscious mind since their inception. By having a new and more fulfilling experience in the therapeutic situation, the old cravings and the old inhibitions can be released, either to be satisfied or to fade. In this light, we can see how the allowance of the expression of love feelings in the psychotherapeutic situation is corrective and allows the patient to progress and to express his or her love capacities in a larger sense.

Life itself constantly provides experiences that cause change. In enlightened therapy, the healing environment is purposely set up to correct, in a meaningful and honest way, the mistakes of the past that the patient may have encountered. Therefore, if a person has become too timid because of an overwhelmingly critical father, the therapist will quite naturally act in a noncritical way, accepting with respect whatever the patient brings forth. This is a new experience, and if all goes well, the patient will then try to bring out his or her honest criticisms of the therapist, with a sense of increasing security. Then, when faced with a new experience, the person can try out the new feelings of honesty and security in life, thus enlarging both experience and person.

This is what happened to Alexandra. She had been terribly bruised by her former marriage to an abusive husband. She protected herself with bristles on her personality, and withdrew from people generally. Then, to her surprise, she was attracted to Roy, and again, to her surprise, reached toward him. He reacted to her overtures of friendship in a manner that was accepting and even encouraging. There was a strained moment when she was expecting physical intimacy and he withdrew from that. Such an occurrence could have sent her back to her defenses, but with considerable grit, she stayed with her feelings. He, on the other hand, was tender, and continually acknowledged her high level of intuition and unstinting support of him. In this context, new experiences came into her life. She gradually generalized her love feelings, and began to accept overtures from women who wanted be her friends.

Alexandra was very reserved, to say the least, but with considerable discrimination, she developed a circle of admirers who surrounded her with support and loving care. This nourished her more and more and, at last report, she was the star of a convocation in which she presented her original work. This acknowledgement by a sizeable audience caused her, at last, to realize who she was, and to move forward into her work of writing and teaching. Her experience with Roy began a series of new corrective emotional experiences through which she could now continue as she opened herself to her considerable talent, and to life itself.

The same is true, and even more so, of Paula. Paula had been so constricted, and so assaulted with feelings of inferiority, even unworthiness, that she could hardly express herself, her intelligence and her considerable artistic talent. During therapy, I offered interpretations of her situation, which she accepted, but interpretations are never enough. They are simply invitations to rearrange one's thinking, and then to set about trying a new way. This is exactly what Paula did, under the auspices of her therapist's recognition of her true self, through the new experience of receiving acknowledgement, and finding confidence in her own expressions of love and lovingness. Now, she is a woman who is ascending to God, so full of love that these feelings become well nigh intolerable to her. At such times, she breaks forth into rhapsodies of poetry, painting, photographic enchantments and service. In Paula, we see unconditional lovingness set free; the soul has been released.

The Integrity of the Therapist During Transference

It is vitally important that the spiritual psychotherapist walk the fine line in reference to the transference. On the one hand he or she must not be excessively humble, taking the patient's accolades as transference only; on the other hand he or she must avoid becoming inflated by the patient's love, admiration and idealization. The honest therapist is always modestly aware of his/her positive attributes and also of his or her limitations.

In this respect personal treatment experience for the healer is very valuable. What is essential is to keep up a constant self-awareness and a continuous and courageous self-exploration. This is all the more true when we realize that we have the patient's life in our hands, as surely as does a surgeon. We are extremely lucky as therapists to have the opportunity to grow in our own dimensions, through experiences with our clients. Some patients will tell us about ourselves, "like it is really is." It would be twice harmful if we were to dismiss these accurate observations of ourselves as only "transference." We have been enjoined, and rightly so, to stand for reality first. When we are told something about ourselves, we must first look in the mirror, at the reality of what we are. Then if we find that something said by the patient is exaggerated or distorted, we can interpret it as such. This takes courage, but the honesty and humility of the therapist stand as a valuable model for the patient. We can only teach what we are. It takes strength to listen to the accolades and love of the patient without running away with ourselves. It takes courage to tolerate the stings of criticism, and to use all of this with one thing in mind: to think of how can this be used to help the patient.

But the reward for the therapist is great. There is an extension and expansion of one's own personality, and a boost toward higher soul levels. There is the gratification of spreading love through our work in a most meaningful way.

Recognizing and Validating the Experiences of an Expanded Paradigm

A new paradigm has arisen since the smashing of the atom and the coming to the West of Eastern thought and spirituality. The experiences within this paradigm have been studied by a new breed of psychologists, bringing clinical evidence to bear on experiences that classical Western psychology had formerly called "psychosis."

It is extremely important to recognize that these paranormal experiences often arise in a well-integrated personality, and therefore one that has not "broken with reality." That personality has simply expanded into a new and greater awareness. Sadly, too many people who have sought professional help in order to understand these events have been diagnosed as "sick" and subdued with in-patient hospitalization or with major tranquilizers. This misdiagnosis becomes all the more potent because of the tremendous power invested in the therapist, and all the more so because of the power of the transference.

Recognizing Out of Body Experiences

There is a large body of experience now that has been incorporated into the literature concerning the frequency of out-of-body experiences. This phenomenon has been examined and described by several well-respected individuals including Robert Munroe, an engineer, seeker and philanthropist who wrote *Journeys Out of the Body;* respected clinician and researcher Charles Tart, who wrote *States of Consciousness;* and psychoanalysts Dr. Glenn Gabbard and Stuart Twemlow, who correlated out-of-the-body experiences with the commonly known states of dissociation, derealization and depersonalization. My patient with the muscular spasms commonly turned her head from introspection to social propriety. By doing this, she was living in her head as if her real self were elsewhere, out-of-body.

All too often the search for the soul leads to a too seclusive life that fails to make a bridge to the material world. This is a mistake, an escape from the world. It is a failure of our assignment to express the soul's mission by uniting our higher self to service to our fellow beings on this planet. This bridging of the material in-body with the higher aspects of out-of-body is of prime importance. This concept has been well described by the Indian master, Sri Aurobindo, who advocated that we express the soul's purpose in this body in this lifetime, through service to humankind.

I had always retained the memory of my wife's out-of-body experience, which, sadly, I had derided at the time. For this reason, I was struck later when I read Robert Monroe's book, which described experiences identical with my wife's. Since then, I have come to recognize that many of my patients have had out-of-body experiences, and I too have had at least partial OBE's. These occurred during two near-death ventures. In one I was scuba diving and had run out of air. My life vest wouldn't inflate, and the sea was rough enough that I couldn't blow it up. I remember adding up my insurance for my family's welfare, and feeling, to my surprise, very calm--I had always expected that I would be terrified of dying.

When I told my diving buddy that I was in trouble, he dove down and released my weight belt, which I had forgotten to do. All was well after that, but I have never forgotten the feeling of calm security. On another occasion, I had a gall bladder attack in the airport as we were embarking for Copenhagen and a cruise. I didn't want to forgo the trip, and insisted on travelling. I can remember lying on the floor in the airport in a darkened conference room that they let me use for seclusion. I was in intense pain, and Rosalie, my wife, was rubbing my back in loving sympathy. I was crying, and she asked me if it hurt so much. I told her that I was not crying in pain, but in gratitude and love for the life and the children that she had given me. I was calm, despite the pain; that was unusual for me.

On the ship I went from bad to worse, and was taken off in Germany (fortunately not Latvia, our next stop). By the time the German doctors released the stone, I was yellow with jaundice and my pancreas was affected. The surgeon told me that he didn't know which way it would go with the pancreas. I knew as a physician that one couldn't live without this important organ, but again I was calm and optimistic. I'll never forget the patience and serenity that surrounded me all through that time. While neither episode is typical of a near-death experience, I was close to death in both of them--and I was surrounded by peace.

Removal and Dissociation

I believe that out-of-body experiences are closely related to the emotional defenses of removal and dissociation that we erect against anxiety. To illustrate this, I will relate some examples from my personal experience that I feel are consistent with the fact that NDEs (near-death experiences) and the defensive maneuver of dissociation are related.

My Experience with the Cadaver

On my first day of medical school, the other freshmen students and I were taken to the anatomy laboratory by our professor, a former army major with a sadistic bent. When he told us to turn the cadaver over, unwrap it and make a "bold stroke down the back, ha-ha-ha-ha!" I felt that I couldn't do it. I looked around at the other students and saw them proceeding. After a considerable struggle, I decided to pretend that it wasn't me doing this, but that I was outside the building looking in on the actions of another person. At that point, having dissociated myself, I could get my fear and revulsion under control and move ahead. I believe that this "looking through the window from the outside" was a kind of out-of-body experience, related to dissociation. It was also related to the presence of the Witness.

The Witness is the self-observing self. We commonly experience it as the agent that watches us from within and without at the same time. It is consciousness beyond the body, and related to a higher essence. The Witness is spoken of in different terms in Eastern literature. Aurobindo speaks of it as "Supermind." The closest that Theosophy comes to this idea is what it calls "Atma" (high spirit) and "Buddhi" (soul). Rudolph Steiner in the West comes closer to my idea of the Witness when he defines it as the "I" that is infused with the highest portion, the Divine Spark.

I believe that the Witness is the soul, related to the Holy Spirit within, the Divine Agency, which is the seat of self-observation. The Witness is the portion of us that is pure consciousness, and into this we withdraw more and more as we ascend in personality toward enlightenment. This self-observing self is an out-of-body self and arises as a state of pure consciousness when one is near death, in a coma, or floating on the ceiling.

Are there not thrilling implications in all of this? If we are not that consciousness that emanates from the cerebral cortex, confined to the skull--if we are beyond that, then we are something more, something beyond our bodies, something immortal.

Healing Energy

It should not be thought that spiritual psychotherapy is something new. Two thousand years ago, Jesus was doing something very similar. What follows is a commentary of the healings of Jesus taken from a book by Stephen Mitchell entitled *The Gospel According to Jesus.* [10] In this book, Mitchell asked his friend Laura, a modern-day healer whose insights he deeply respected, to comment on Jesus' healings. Laura made some very interesting observations about both Christ's work and her own approach to healing that I feel relate directly to spiritual psychotherapy as I practice it.

Remarking on how Jesus performed his healings, Laura says, "I feel that Jesus touched people from a place of great presence and love. He was in contact with the essence of these sick people, and they recognized that. And if they were open to him, they could receive that love and use it to heal themselves."

I have found that love is the essence of healing. The best moments in psychotherapy happen when the patient and I have a soul-to-soul contact. This is felt as a total communication, and demands that there be complete commitment on both parts. The patient knows of my concern, feels it, and is made secure by it.

Laura goes on to say, "The people he [Jesus] healed were ready to let go of something. There was an opening in them which was probably

---

[10]   Stephen Mitchell, *The Gospel According to Jesus* (New York; Harper Collins, 1991), pages 295-300.

there before they saw him, but when they saw him there was a deeper opening that allowed them to move through pain or suffering in order to be healed. These healings are described as instantaneous, but they weren't necessarily instantaneous. There were probably many steps along the way which led to the healing. If someone is completely ready to be healed, and if the healer can hold the space of wholeness and love for her, then it's possible at that moment for her to open up and heal herself through the healer. But with some of my patients, most of what I do is lay groundwork. Every moment of laying groundwork is just as important as that one moment when everything opens up. That seems more miraculous because you can see and feel the cure. But actually every moment along the way is just as miraculous."

I couldn't agree more with what Laura is saying here. In spiritual psychotherapy, the groundwork for healing is laid by the successive meetings that test the therapist's love and commitment. This is followed by a progression of interpretations, and an increasing detachment of the patient from his or her previous beliefs and attachments to the body. At the right moment he or she will realize how the symptom, pain or illness has served a purpose. The entire process involves and creates an openness of the patient to the healer and the healer to the patient.

"But healing can be deeper than that," she continues. "It can be a transformation of the whole person: not just a physical healing but an emotional and spiritual opening as well. When you embrace an illness, and really learn what it's trying to communicate to you, your whole life can be transformed, from the inside out."

One thing that spiritual psychotherapy stresses is that there is no separation of body from emotions, psyche or soul. Any change that is real involves all these areas. For that reason, the essential goodness of the person, the soul, arises as a result of the new insights and change.

"When I'm doing a healing with someone," Laura continues, "I don't try to direct the energy out through my hands. I allow it to flow out. Basically, what happens is that the energy which is connected to everything else, the energy of the Tao, or `source energy,' as I sometimes call it, fills my whole body, and it moves my hands also, and the person I'm working with remembers that energy in her body."

This is true of all authentic healers, and it proves that the much vaunted powers of "interpretation" are beside the point. In spite of what the patient may "realize" about him- or herself, the real healing takes place because the patient is basking in a context of loving concern, experiencing a transfer of love energy. This fills the patient's subtle bodies with wellbeing and builds their self-esteem in that material body.

On the Healing of the Woman with the Flow of Blood

Laura goes on to describe what happened between Jesus and the woman who had been ill for many years with a flow of blood. "The flow of Jesus' healing force, when he `felt in himself that power had gone forth from him,' seems to be a response he had to the woman without consciously knowing it. When the energy flows, it's not as if it somehow goes out of me and leaves me drained, it flows through me. It feels like it's more present for me as well."

Again, I think that this is right to the point. The energetic flow does not deplete the healer. On the contrary, both healer and patient are elevated and energized. After a good session, I feel stimulated, refreshed, elevated, even holy. This is God's energy working through us, His servants.

On the Healing of the Blind Man

"I like this story a lot. I like the blind man's description of 'men like trees walking,' because it sounds so real, like it wasn't made up by some editor. Only someone who had been blind would say that. And I also like the fact that Jesus did the healing in two parts: he did a first healing and the man got partly better, and then he did another, and the man could see clearly. So it happened in steps. Most healing does. Usually the instantaneous healing is glorified, but most growth in life, most changes, happen gradually. We take in as much light as we can, and we digest it and assimilate it, and then we go on to the next step and then the next; and there's something very beautiful about that. Whenever people transform their lives and do really deep healing, that's a miracle. It's not any more miraculous to get rid of physical symptoms all in one step."

I like Laura's description of this healing, because it demonstrates the same steps that we take in good psychotherapy, which is more a "process" than a "miracle." Her comments also demonstrate that if a we are committed through love, we all, as therapists, have the Christ within us, ready to heal. All we need do is to surrender to it. This is different from the classical psychotherapeutic point of view, which is quite ego-filled in its own way and thinks that its interpretations, or gestalt evocations of feeling, are curative. The traditional approach would have us think that we DO something, instead of simply participating with our hearts in a process. This step-by-step process results in the miracles of healing, miracles which are not acknowledged by traditional medicine.

Concerning Immortality

Trained as a hard-nosed academic, I could only look upon the idea of immortality as a bit of religious fluff. Secretly, however, I wanted to believe it. This is the story of my own conversion to the spiritual path.

Like most people, I longed to be immortal, but was trained to believe that I was NOT. As a doctor, I had to accept that I was a body and that was that.

I saw too much of death and of the end of things when I was in medical school, first by working on a cadaver, and subsequently in the hospitals watching people take their last breaths. It was also very hard for me to witness the death of my mother, even though it was a peaceful one.

All of this seemed to me like the end of things. Death was accompanied by a great fear, more than that, a hopelessness, helplessness and despair as I attended those with chronic and incurable diseases. Cancer wasted away the body, and there was nothing left toward the end. What could I do? Give false hope? Deny the oncoming death of the body? Give my patients morphine both physically and mentally? All I could do was to attend to their bodies and ease their suffering as much as I could, but their suffering was very great, and I felt that I was ultimately unable to do anything to alleviate it.

I could pray, but I could not believe at that time that prayer meant anything, if there was such a thing as a God Who could intervene in the affairs of men. The body was the body and religion was religion and ne'er the two would meet.

About twenty years ago, however, beginning with my encounters with Grof and Muktananda, I began to explore other possibilities. I learned about Eastern psychologies and their beliefs in re-incarnation, the immortality of the soul who we are. At first these things seemed strange to me, but I felt a strong call to religion when I heard the expression, "I am God and God is within me. I am part of God." This seemed somehow to make sense; I was a molecule in the great ocean of life.

But which, I began to ask myself as I progressed through my studies, is the ocean and which the molecule? Each is total, and each is in the other. The one in the All and the All in the one. It seemed to me that if we were all one and all eternal, then we were both separate and together in our identities.

I began to learn about and remember the essential "I" within me. I realized that the "I" who I am today is not so very different from the "I" that I was when I was four years old, six years, eleven, thirteen, twenty-one or thirty-five. Student, father, grandfather--it didn't matter what role I assumed in life, the eternal "I" remained the same. Whether I was dreaming or meditating, the "I" was out there, hovering above me as I watched myself in self-seeking contemplation. As the Witness who watches over everything that exists, now and forever, the "I" is who I truly am, even when my body changes.

Slowly within my life, the experiences and evidences for the reality of this essential "I" began to add up. Once I treated a triple amputee. He had been run over by a train in his car, and had survived. He was unhappy, handicapped and brave. He was trying and he was sad, but his inner self had not changed, neither in his basic self-concept and his hopes for the future, nor in the person he dreamed himself to be at night. I treated quadriplegics, paraplegics and those who had become dwarfed in the body through old-age. Yet, no matter what happened to the body all of these people remained, they remained as they were.

A poem that I read at this time made a deep impression on me. It was entitled "Nurse Look At Me" and described the life of a ninety-year-old woman who had been found dead on the floor of an Israeli nursing home. This poem recounted who she was--not the doddering, slobbering old thing who had existed just before she was found, but rather the young girl, the blooming adolescent, the woman graced by love, the joyful mother in full bloom and the fulfilled grandmother. Always the same "I" remaining, hovering over the scene, deep within her core, always eternal within the body.

I also began to explore the discoveries and the literature that dealt with immortality. There have been many life-after-death stories gathered by Raymond Moody, stories of those who beckon from the other realm, stories of those who have died and been brought back by electro-shock applied to the heart, stories of those who lay in a deathlike coma but nevertheless knew everything that was going on around them. All of these experiences bespeak an eternal consciousness that hovers above us, different from the body and even from the brain.

The studies that I read at this time about reincarnation also strengthened my belief in the immortality of the soul. These were not accounts written by wild-eyed new agers, but by very reputable scientists who evaluated their data with merciless scrutiny. I found great food for thought in Professor Ian Stevenson's exhaustive scientific study of individuals reborn in India who recognized places where they had lived before. The concept of reincarnation is also coming more to the fore in the field of psychology as psychoanalytically trained, psychodynamically thinking clinicians are discovering that the memories of their patients' past lives are deeply affecting their lives now.

All this, taken together, creates a round gem of evidence whose many facets show that we are indeed more than just our bodies. Indeed, we are different from the body and exist beyond it when the body dies. Modern, introspective investigation only bears out the knowledge brought to us by the teachers from the East who have been studying the inner realm for centuries.

It is important for us to be aware that we are immortal. This knowledge implies both a promise and a moral obligation. We might be able to fool our contemporaries, to hide our sins and our selfishness, but we can't hide them from the eternal "I" who will come back to continue our journey onward, but at the cost of our having to make up for the sins and harms we have committed in this lifetime. On the other hand, we know that as we ascend the ladder of karma, we will indeed be rewarded for our good deeds by growing ever closer to love, to our brothers and sisters, and to God Himself, becoming a part of God--the molecule in the ocean containing the God within the All.

More than that, knowing the eternal powers of the "I," we also know the powers of the body and the mind to repair seemingly incurable illness. As I have learned this and transmitted it to my patients, I have seen it bring hope and transformation even to the hopeless.
Love is all, Love is eternal--and so are we.

On Astral Visits and Dreaming

When I first heard stories of astral travel, I felt nonplussed, yet curious. One such account came from a good friend of mine whom I regarded as a very grounded and well-trained clinician. He told me about his adventures astral travelling at night, and how his wife had seen him slip back into his body. I respected him, I didn't doubt him, but I wondered what was wrong with me. I was disappointed that I didn't have the same kinds of experiences.

Since then, however, I have learned that all of us perform a kind of astral travel, even if only when we dream or observe ourselves. I have often asked my patients, and many other people, where their consciousness resides when they are self-observing. Often this question puzzles them. One thing is sure, during those times; we are not in our heads, enclosed in our skulls. Most often people report the sensation as being above and behind ourselves, or somewhere out of body.

This description relates well to our dream "reality." It is said that the soul leaves the body during sleep and travels to higher soul realms, where it is refreshed. Certainly, we are not in our bodies lying on the bed at such times. In dreams, we are able to fly and to move through walls. We are able to actually observe ourselves talking and interacting with other dream figures, for in dreams all the beings that we see are representatives of the self.

In my own dreams, I can often feel the presence of my departed loved ones: my mother, my father, my favorite cousin who was a childhood sweetheart; and surely I am not alone in feeling such things. I am not surprised any longer when a patient who is highly invested in her treatment with me, will feel my presence next to her at night and find this presence fulfilling. Roy visited Alexandra many times and, as the more sensitive of the pair, she was able to reliably perceive these visits. I had the occasion to observe and interact with each of them, geographical distance notwithstanding.

The Release and Exchange of Energy

There have been many experiences both in my life and in my practice that have provided me with convincing evidence of the exchange of energy between individuals. I have long witnessed how powerful the energy is in group therapy, much more so than in each individual taken separately. Another example is the enormous power that is mobilized in mobs.

Hypnosis, which is essentially an altered state of mind, is also based upon energy exchange, assisted by the energy of the hypnotist. Hypnosis is similar to the state into which one retreats when meditating, or when shocked by an overwhelming emotional experience such as a sudden accident. At such times, one becomes removed, cool and distant from the self. Group hypnosis is much easier than individual, because the energy of the members multiplies the effect. A great deal of energy is released back to me at such times and I feel invigorated and enlivened.

The energy release one experiences when one is in love is near boundless, and can be related to the almost infinite energy that we experience in any emotionally elated condition.

The other side of the exchange of energy can be seen when we are around a person who is depressed. There is no doubt that depression is marked by a depletion of energy that can be felt by others who inter-relate with the depressed individual. I certainly feel this energy when I am in a therapy session with such an individual. There are also those who suck energy out of the people they relate to. Such people are exceedingly needy and, in therapy, try to hang on for just one more moment of attention and time. Doubtless, such individuals are the vampires of the energy world.

Another type of energy is boredom, which arises when energy is "stuffed inside," that is, when one is repressing needs and interest. At such times the world seems pale and endlessly empty. Boredom is a deprivation of energy, insofar as energy can no longer flow. Such people seem flat, and the ambience they create is depleted of energy.

More About Intuition

The intuitive sense is our highest sense, the highest type of intelligence that we carry. Unfortunately, it is much disparaged by our contemporary "science." Intuition is a transmission from a higher realm of knowledge, and when properly received grants us remarkable powers of introspection and discovery. Many great inventions and scientific discoveries have come about in a flash of intuition resulting in what we call the "Eureka" experience. While in the bathtub, Archimedes received his inspiration about how to measure the weight of water, and what made objects float.

I believe that I have always been highly intuitive. Such openness has had its cost, for I have been too sensitive in the past. My intuition has been invaluable in my work, however, for it is a way of receiving, empathizing and appreciating what another human being is going through. As this ability is cultivated and preserved against the doubt that often surrounds it, it can lead us to high inspirational knowledge, taking us further on the journey to ascension. I believe that intuition is on the rise and will eventually become commonplace as our civilization, helping us to evolve into the next race of men/women.

Intuition always intensifies with practice. Over the years, the more I have learned to trust my intuition, the more reliable it has become. I can now feel the emotions that are repressed in a client and anticipate when these emotions are on the edge of coming forth. This ability is very useful, and has been very productive in helping me to create a faster moving therapy. What I have learned to do, we can all do, for intuitive knowledge is a talent that is inherent in everyone, if only we can learn to remove our doubt.

Taking the Good for Granted

When I first began practice, I was very eager to be trained as a psychoanalyst. At that time it was the only discipline I knew of that made sense of what was happening within my patients. Furthermore, I wanted to find out what was going on within me. I spent six years with a analyst, only to discover, in retrospect, that he really didn't like me. At the time that we were working together, I couldn't afford to acknowledge his dislike. I needed my credentials, and everything depended upon my having a successful conclusion to my "training analysis." I had no protection from the judgements of this man because there were no constraints placed upon him. He operated in the privacy of "confidentiality." No one was watching him and, at the time, the general belief was that "the training analyst is always right." During that time, I wasn't expanded, - I was shrunk! I had changed all right, but from someone who was perhaps too intuitive to a therapist who was as cold and obsessional as my analyst had been.

Our sessions together were carried on in the atmosphere of "objectivity" in which the therapist was supposed to be a blank screen. Rather than giving me a chance to express myself, however, this approach offered coldness rather than empathy. Misunderstanding must always occur when empathy is absent. For someone who was dedicated to the model of strict abstinence from feeling, as my training analyst was, a lack of empathy was the inevitable result.

As I have emerged from this experience over the last twenty years, I have learned how important it is to encourage my patients, to liberally express my appreciation of their good points, rather than simply "taking the good for granted," as the rule of classical psychotherapy would have it. This doesn't mean that I hesitate to point out to my patients what remains to be improved. It's just that caring and respect are much more powerful when they are expressed.

Far from remaining a blank screen, I always share my own experiences when I believe that they will be helpful and instructive to the patient. This open acknowledgement of the patient's worth and humble admission of the therapist's person, sets an example of truth as a goal to be pursued above all.

I finally noticed a change in my training analyst's attitude when I myself changed toward him. This happened when I broke the rule of making no important decisions while in treatment. When I told him that I had become engaged, I fully expected him to throw me out. He knew, however, that I would not retreat or change my decision, and he actually liked my wife a great deal. This confrontation was a new experience for me and through it I actually became more self-acknowledged. My marriage also opened me up. I had found someone who was quite spiritual and very supportive. A good marriage is a corrective emotional experience of the first order.

When I was in training, the field of traditional psychoanalysis was highly restrictive and, in its own way, full of nepotism. Certain leaders had their favorites, and these were always the obedient ones, hoeing their row strictly along the lines of Freud's teachings. One of my teachers, a renaissance man in his knowledge, proclaimed at a national convention that no further progress could be made in our science until the next genius (meaning the next Freud) came along. In reflection, I can see that these attitudes merely reflect the overly obedient and restrictive attitudes that were prevalent in the culture of that time.

Even today, however, these strict and repressive attitudes are still present in many, many of our therapies. Although there have been pioneers, such as James Hillman and Stanislav Grof, many psychotherapists are still afraid to venture out armed with their own authenticity and challenge the borders of our science in a meaningful way. For this reason, the recognition of the soul in our patients, and its release in psychotherapy, is largely regarded as a declaration of challenge in our medical/psychological societies.

Since I was never obedient enough as a student, I was always at the edge of the bullseye. I was never elevated to the status of a training analyst, the one who instructs and prepares others to become psychoanalysts through a "training analysis." There was always something suspect about me, because I was ready to embrace new ideas. This attitude again defines the difference between spiritual and classical psychotherapy. The spiritual psychotherapist relies on the emergence of a high knowledge from within the patient, and encourages exploration into new areas of belief. Far from being authoritative, he/she appreciates the fact that experience and training have a rightful place, but that the psychiatrist should always remain humble in respect to the patient and the patient's inherent wisdom.

As I matured spiritually and became freer to experiment with the rules, I allowed myself to engage with patients in various ways. One of the things I began to do was to visit their homes, in this way receiving a much fuller picture of who my patients really were. This helped both them and me. As I learned more and more about the spiritual and parapsychological realms, I shared these things with my clients, and found that they were more than ready for them. Many of my patients now felt free to tell me of their own spiritual experiences, which they had formerly withheld, fearing that I would call them psychotic.

When I began to invite my patients to seminars that I gave on personality development and spiritual realms, I found that placing a seed of new knowledge in their minds started new growth within them. This was often expressed as a hunger for more, and an increasing realization of who they were at center.

Above all I became freer to let my patients express their love for me. Formerly, I would have viewed all such feelings as transference. Now I know that there are things about me that might be loveable, and that my patients might actually be grateful to me as a person who is fully committed to them.

I now understand how important these expressions of love are. Insofar as I let my patients experience and express their lovingness they-- and I--are all growing and fulfilling a need. It is not only necessary for us to feel as if we are loved, it is just as necessary for us to be able to express our love in a way that is meaningful and validated by being accepted with gratitude.

To Summarize

Spiritual psychotherapy is psychotherapy that recognizes the existence of the soul as relevant to our efforts and treatment. It helps the patient to make contact with the soul, not only through acknowledging it, and thus validating it as meaningful, but also by removing the obstacles to its release. These impediments are commonly called defenses, or resistances, and while they are constructed to guard against painful feelings, they also hinder the natural buoyancy of the soul.

When the patient is encouraged to tolerate seemingly intolerable feelings, there follows an inevitable breakthrough to higher realms of feeling and personality, with an outflow of love. This love is perhaps first felt in the transference toward the therapist. It is a big mistake to identify such love only as transference. This is as bad as calling it illusory, thus denying the reality of the patient's love capacity. Therefore, it is important for the therapist and the one in therapy to acknowledge its validity, while restraining both parties from acting out. This produces gains for both. After all, the healer is always healed as God allows him/her to heal. In this framework, the experience of the therapy is corrective--repairing the insults of the past, and perhaps the present--and again confirming the love capacity of the person.

Spiritual psychotherapy also acknowledges the legitimacy of para-normal experiences, such as astral visits. Too often the patient's encounter with spiritual realms has been condemned as psychotic, and this often suffocates the emerging spiritual capacities. The spiritual psychotherapist believes that the miracles that were performed by Jesus are ultimately available to us all as we purify ourselves to the soul-level. In a very practical way, this type of psychotherapy allows the therapist to give legitimate hope to those with seemingly hopeless conditions such as terminal illness, or other allegedly incurable disorders. When modern medicine denies the marvelous capacities of the mind and soul, it subjects both the patient and the doctor to a kind of creeping paralysis, an entrapment that comes from believing that we are only the body.

The hope that spiritual psychotherapy offers our culture is long overdue. There is an old Chinese curse that says, "May you live in difficult times," and no one can deny that the problems that we face in our world and in our personal lives are exceedingly difficult. The Chinese symbol for difficulty also means "opportunity," however. By connecting with the trans-formational powers of our soul, we have an opportunity to open the gate-ways not only for our own healing, but for the healing of the world.

Guidelines and Exercises:

1. Remember the sevenfold plane, and the levels from physical to intuitional.

2. Let yourself notice the very peaceful moments of quiet bliss, and know that is contact with the soul.

3. Take a walk in Nature, look at the trees, the squirrels, the insects, even the stones, and let yourself see the consciousness in everything. Watch the joyousness of a new bud, flower or leaf. See the insect carrying out its task. As you do, you may well feel a commonality. Look deeply within a stone and see its structure, molecules organized in just the right way as if the stone had an intelligent plan, and you will know that this is more than just an external law, "just the way it is."

4. Examine your relationships. Look for exaggerated reactions to someone, someone you love extraordinarily though the reason may not be plain. Does he/she remind you of someone you grew up with—parent, sibling, best friend? Are you turned off by someone, unnecessarily afraid of him/her? Maybe you are dealing with a harsh authoritarian figure from the past. Then you are in a better situation to let reason prevail.

5. Use your transference experiences to know yourself better, and to seek corrective experiences, to heal fear, to find a sustained outlet for love or service. Do you need to mother or protect some one? Find a way to do it.

6. Examine your dreams. Do you dream of the dear departed? Consider that a visit. Do you have feelings of a presence of someone dear to you, or a guide? Consider that to be real on the astral plane. Seek these experiences. In your dreams when you fly or move easily through walls, you are experiencing the astral plane.

CHAPTER IV:

Psychotherapy At The Pressman Center For
Mind / Body Wellness

Releasing The Hidden Self -- What We Do At The Center For Mind/Body Wellness Can Be Done At Home; Do Not Be Intimidated By Professional Credentials, You Can Apply Similar Techniques And Insights To Yourself -- Example Of Freud And Wilhelm Fliess, Freud's Monumental Self-Analysis Grew Out Of A Correspondence With A Valued And Intimate Friend, Fliess -- Group Therapy, The Formation Of A Group Soul -- Biofeedback, Simple Instruments To Measure Your Meditation -- Self-Help Through Books And Seminars.

Since we all view the world through the eyes of our assumptions, every psychotherapist practices his/her individual style, no matter what the area of his or her formal training. I have noticed that, as with everything else, the product carries the signature of its creator. Working with Olympic figure skaters, I was surprised to see that the personality flowed through the blade. I should have anticipated this, for we create what we are. This is no less true of psychotherapists than of anyone else. Their style, their understanding of the patient, their interpretations, all are predicated, not only on their learned theories, but also their learned selves.

Creating the Center for Mind/ Body Wellness
I believe that Karma, that invisible scenario that directs us from life to life, also directs us within this lifetime. It is a force that allows, indeed, commands us to profit from the mistakes that we have made--more than that, to redeem them. Karma has certainly had its influence on me, allowing me a painful, but happy, redemption. It has certainly had much to do with the creation of our clinic, the Center for Mind/ BodyWellness. Here is its story.

I had always been an idealist, but a restless one. Not being satisfied with the traditional clinical practice of psychoanalysis, which seemed all to passive to me, I joined the staff of a large hospital, the Albert Einstein Medical Center. In time, and through much turmoil, I became the chairman of the department of psychiatry there. With greater responsibility came even more turmoil. This was a time when the community mental health movement was taking hold. Since this program promised to bring much needed mental health services to the poor and dispossessed, I was happy to support it, even inspired. Unfortunately, like a millet seed caught between the grinding stones of the mill, I was pushed into the center--between the new movement on the one hand and the conservative medical forces on the other. Although I was unprepared for the resulting infighting, and unskilled in this new political arena, my staying power allowed me to create a new kind of department for training the doctors under my care.

From all of this emerged both a redemption and a forward movement. The redemption was my ability to reclaim, from the narrow focus of a single traditional approach, a broader vista of therapeutic techniques. I was hard pressed to learn all of these new techniques so that I could teach them to others, but I was inspired by the possibilities they presented, and by the opportunity to reach out to a larger community--and a neglected one at that.

It wasn't easy to reach the poor in our community, for I was identified as "one of them," one of the establishment, the rich and privileged doctors. The very rejection that I initially experienced, however, taught me about the essential community and fellowship of all human beings. I learned many lessons about humility, honesty, suffering and genuiness before I was finally accepted. Today, many years later, I still do some of my practice in poor and deprived areas and I find great comfort there. The patients are so real, and so appreciative. Their presence feels like a fresh breeze blowing through a profession that is becoming more and more hemmed in by struggles with insurance companies and the unreasonable demands of some of the well-off patients.

In 1980, I left the Albert Einstein Medical Center and traveled to Florida to take over a failing psychiatric hospital there, and to establish a research center from the profits of my new venture. Although the hospital had been failing miserably, I was able to resurrect it and make it profitable. Sadly, the research center never materialized, for the businessman who had led the venture had naively duped me. Fortunately, however, the hospital saved me from financial ruin. It not only grew in profits, but also gave me new hopes and a new learning experiences. My staff members were filled with bright-eyed enthusiasm, and together we established new programs, many of which were the offshoot of the community mental health movement.

At that time, I had become interested in new areas of spiritual growth and had learned much of what is now called parapsychology. Although there wasn't much opportunity to introduce spiritual principles into the treatment of the patients in a highly monitored hospital environment, I was able to bring in spiritual teachers for seminars and instruction. After a time the hospital declined, sad to say, because of political turmoil and the greed of the financial leadership, and I resigned the directorship.

In 1986 I returned to Philadelphia and re-established a practice there. This time I was freer to follow my own inclinations and therapeutic models, and the result was the creation of the Center for Psychiatric Wellness, later to be called the Center for Mind Body Wellness. As I grew more and more spiritually oriented, so did the clinic. My psychologist son, who is an internationally recognized authority on A Course in Miracles psychotherapy, and my wife who is an expert in biofeedback partnered me. Our patients have told us that they are deeply grateful for the adventures we have shared with them in the spiritual realms, and for what all of these experiences promise in the way of peace, meaning and relief from the oppression of their daily lives. As they ascend spiritually, the alleviation of their emotional and physical pain is almost inevitable.

Today, we feel that the Center is at the crest of an advancing wave on which other therapists are travelling. These include, among many others, Deepak Chopra, Brian Weiss, Caroline Myss, Frances Vaughn and Stanislav Grof. Spiritual psychotherapy is just beginning to appear in the programs of some established institutions, and these numbers are growing all the time.

True Wellness: Releasing the Hidden Self

At the Center for Psychiatric Wellness, we try to practice true wellness, and this means not so much prevention but the release of the inner potential of each man and woman. Our goal is to release the hidden personality and latent possibilities in the belief that the greatest happiness, productivity and creativity results when a person is liberated. This liberation implies enabling others to satisfy their instinctual wishes and talents, but in a manner that does no harm to anyone, bringing pleasure and rewards from both society and one's own person. We also teach a belief in the limitless powers of the mind and of the soul. These powers are released as the person is released, to self-fulfillment and even greater fulfillment in service to one's fellow creatures.

In the secular, self-centered and materialistic society in which we live, filled with so much daily violence and violation, one might very well question how we can say that service to our fellow human beings brings about the greatest fulfillment that a person can wish for. I believe the answers are ready at hand.

It is a well-known fact that human beings need to give and receive love, and become emotionally and physically sick when they are deprived of it. Caring behaviors are good for our health. A ten-year study of twenty-seven hundred individuals completed by the University of Michigan Survey Research Center found that volunteer work dramatically increased life expectancy. In another study, seventeen hundred women reported feeling a "helpers high" when involved in nurturing and caring behaviors with family, friends, and even total strangers. Altruistic behaviors trigger the release of endorphins, which make us feel good and help decrease stress and anxiety.[11]

When individuals or groups of people come together in true fellowship and are willing to listen to one another and experience a new way, new worlds open up to both. When people have person-to-person contact and lay their passions and preconceptions aside, a communion of understanding and common feeling is the inevitable result. Were this not so, there would be no opportunity for arbitration between labor and industry or between nations about to go to war.

There is a commonality that all human beings share because we are all a part of a Whole. The desire to serve flows directly from the experience of finding that the essential self is a part of the All of humanity. If my brother or sister or the ecosystem are in distress or pain, then I am in pain as well. If this is so, then perhaps our theory of psychological development, which tells us that the "independent individual" is the highest developmental goal needs revision, or at least expansion.

I see our human development from this perspective. In order to love in a full sense one must indeed become independent, but this is something altogether different from being isolated and separated from our society, and indeed our planet. It means that we must transcend our "neediness" so that we can operate in our lives with a necessary degree of confidence. From within that well of confident concern, we can pour ourselves out into an empathic understanding of the needs of others and of the community

---

[11]   Riane Eisler, *Sacred Pleasures: Sex, Myth and the Politics of the Body* (San Francisco: Harper San Francisco, 1995), page 393.

within which we live, including the community of the entire planet. As we identify with and give to these needs, we feel the glow of love and satisfaction that comes from truly giving. Then we realize from the perspective of a higher mind and a higher sense that we are all brothers and sisters.

Ken Wilber expresses these ideas in an interesting and meaningful way when he describes what he calls the "holon."[12] A holon is an entity that is complete in itself, but cannot exist except as a part of a larger environment. For example, if we think of the heart, we realize that while it is complete in its own function, it could not exist except as a part of a larger organism. This is true of everything from atoms to the great blue whale, from the planet to the universe. This is the way that God has made things.

Therefore, as we achieve independence, we can step forward to a new and larger realization, that we are a part of a larger whole. As we understand this, we will live more intensely, more broadly and more fully. We will glow with a greater satisfaction as we serve such an understanding. The more mature we become, the more truly independent we are; but this is an independence that recognizes our place in the scheme of things. It is an independence that allows us to become truly intimate.

Therapeutic Techniques at the Center for Mind/Body Wellness

Each treatment at our clinic is "custom made" because we employ a view of the patient designed to discover what is "underneath." We assess unconscious fears, motivations, needs, and devise treatment that will help the individual to satisfy their needs in active life--each in his or her own unique style. In this, our clinic follows the belief that we fail or succeed as human beings when we know ourselves authentically and are true to ourselves. This is different from self-centeredness; it is instead a matter of following one's truth. Happily, when the human instrument is attuned this way, the divine spark is released, and the hidden potential and soulfulness rises.

The Initial Interview. Initially, we to try to learn as much as we can about the person in order to individualize his or her treatment. In order to accomplish this, we seek to understand the patient in a deeper way. During the initial interview we explore the person's reason for coming and his or

---

[12]   Ken Wilber, *A Brief History of Everything* (Boston and London: Shamballa Press 1996).

her support resources, both personal and environmental. We explore the vision within the person, his or her hopes and wishes for the future, as well as the grief and anxiety that lie underneath their defenses. This approach leads to a greater, more humane understanding of our patients, setting the stage for treatment, for nothing cements human relationships more than true understanding and the sincere effort that lies behind it.

This effort and its results can be seen in the following illustration. A young adolescent boy was sent to see me because of his aggressive conduct in school. Since he was used to bucking authority figures in his daily life, he expected me to be a disciplinarian. Instead, I quickly saw that he had a great tender side that he was afraid of. He had often been ridiculed by his peers for being a "sissy," and was now out to prove that he was tough. Instead of greeting his aggressive approach to me with authority, I met his expectations with words of understanding, and respectfully recognized his tender side. In the face of this kind of treatment, his anger toward me melted, and we were able to settle into a relationship of mutual respect and forward progress. In a sense, this represents a "turning of the other cheek," but in an educated way. It is so helpful to use this kind of insightful forbearance as we go through life. Such understanding is the beginning of the kind of soul-to-soul contact that deepens in the course of both treatment and human relationships.

Group Therapy. Another therapeutic technique that we use at the Center is group therapy. The advantages of "group" become evident as time goes on. They are as follows:

1. Over the course of time each group unites as if it were a family. The power and influence of this mini-community often surpass the authority of the therapist alone.

2. Many facets of the patient's problem, how he or she relates to people can be seen more clearly within a group interaction, whereas they are often hidden in the individual session.

3. We allow communication between group members in between sessions as long as what transacts between them is brought into the next session. This allows each member to give continued support to one another during the week. This support is often very helpful, although it sometimes backfires to the group's detriment, as the following anecdote illustrates.

One of my patients had a severe fixation on his father, which was negative and very destructive. In individual session he extolled his father but, as I learned too late, outside of group therapy he was trying to discourage the members from coming back to treatment, encouraging them to carry on the group's activities centered around him instead. In this way, he was able to act out his destructive wishes toward his deceased father, after having transferred them onto me. None of this was done consciously, of course, but was acted out unconsciously instead of being explored during the treatment. He did, in fact, prevail upon two of the more fragile members of the group. They quit, and no doubt will have a harder time becoming comfortable in a much needed treatment, no matter who they may see.

At the Center, we also periodically add individual treatment sessions to the group sessions. This allows a place of security for those who are not yet comfortable enough to join a group. In addition, the one-to-one transaction between counsellor and patient allows for greater intimacy that aids with bringing out hidden and feared material.

Rose is an example of someone who benefitted greatly from individual treatment prior to joining group. Rose had enjoyed a happy and productive life as the manager of a successful business until the night she was robbed at gunpoint. The robbers promised over and over that they would blow her face off. For six months afterward, she tried to master the awful memory but made no headway. She remained isolated in her home, afraid to go out, unable to return to work, or to any job for fear that the same thing would happen again.

When, almost against her will, she came to see me, I encouraged her to handle the situation in an entirely different manner. I believe that as long as one tries not to remember, they are preserving the memory with all of its awful emotion. When I asked Rose to relive the memory, at first she could hardly believe me. She held her head high and her throat locked, holding in the fear and the tears. Little by little, she allowed herself to speak, and to open her throat, and even to cry a little. She told me, however, that she could never do such a thing in group because she knew that everyone would think that she was weak.

The time did come, however, when she went to group and saw others letting themselves pour out their emotions. Little by little, through the others' example, she allowed herself the same emotional release. She relived her life-threatening experience, and was finally able to cry. The relief brought about by her acceptance by the members of her group was many times more powerful than what she would have felt in the individual session, yet the individual session had prepared the way.

Biofeedback. Another powerful therapeutic tool we use at the Center is biofeedback. This is designed so that the biofeedback therapist is with the patient at all times. The training in relaxation techniques is done in an atmosphere of a kind of counselling, within which the measurement of physiological activity, which is a part of the biofeedback experience, is used to signal the level of anxiety or relief in the patient. So often anxiety is present without a person's knowing it is there. Using the physiological signals that are followed in biofeedback, the patient can learn about and understand what makes him or her anxious, as well as what makes him feel safe. This training creates a new map in the mind, so that one becomes more inwardly aware.

Biofeedback means exactly what is says--it is the feedback of one's biological signals. Under the skilled hands of the trainer, a person is able to achieve a widened introspection and a new awareness of what is happening inside the mind. Biofeedback training can be carried so far that processes that had always been thought of as uncontrollable, such as the heartbeat and the blood pressure, can be brought under voluntary control. If this is true of the physiology, how much more true it is of the temperament.

Although biofeedback is not designed to influence personality directly, it does so at least indirectly. For example, someone who is very high strung, enough so that he or she has developed dangerously high blood pressure readings, can learn to be more in control of stress-- "mellowed out," so to speak. This change in feelings and response begins a benign spiral in that person's life. As he or she becomes more mellow, those in the environment respond gratefully, creating another kind of positive feedback--namely, a reward for a better personality. The results of this rewarding feedback are a new man or woman.

Biofeedback works its benefits in other ways, as well. With the relaxation of the body and mind comes a relaxation of the very defenses that have held so many memories and feared events in repression. Oftimes, this process assists the psychotherapy by relieving the strain of repression so that the abhorrent events and their consequences can be aired out and relieved.

Biofeedback is a valuable tool from which everyone in our society can benefit. Learning how to reduce stress and its dangerous consequences for the body has positive results for the personality. Anyone who eschews his or her feelings and has no idea of what is happening within his/her mind could benefit from biofeedback.

Hypnosis. Hypnosis, which is not unrelated to biofeedback, is another valuable tool that we use at the Center. All relaxation techniques, including hypnosis, open the mind to greater potential, exploration, and contact with its enormous powers. Contrary to popular belief, hypnosis is a common event. We experience it all the time, during "highway hypnosis" or in the kind of complete absorption in a book that prevents us from hearing someone calling our name. Nevertheless, hypnosis, like meditation, allows greater recall, and greater healing of emotionally traumatic memories.

An example of the beneficial effects of hypnosis can be seen in the following story. A huge, muscled black man was electrocuted when a live wire touched a crane next to which he was standing. He was pulled to it like steel to a magnet, and knew that he was dying. The circuit was finally broken and he was hurled to the wall. From then on he had disabling lower back pain.

At the Center, we use hypnosis for pain control by evacuating the painful emotional memory, which is, more often than not, pouring itself into the damaged portion of the body, maintaining and increasing the pain. When this man was hypnotized, he returned to the memory of the accident automatically and lived through it again. He was unhappy when he did this, but he let himself go through it because of his faith in us. Each time he did so, the memory became less and less compelling, and so did the pain.

Hypnosis lowers the defense barriers of the patient, allowing painful feelings to emerge; hastening the therapy as the emergence of the painful memories allows them to be washed out. The hypnotic state can be very healing as traumatic memories, inadequate feelings and learned inhibitions become relieved, allowing a new self-image, more realistic and realistically positive, to arise.

The hypnotic state also occurs when we experience a sudden emotional shock, a kind of momentary, mini-paralysis state equivalent to fainting, but with our consciousness still retained. In such a state we are "open" and the impressions that are brought in are retained, albeit in the unconscious mind. This openness can also become a very good thing when it expands the mind to release trauma, as we saw in the patient who released the memory of his electrocution.

Hypnosis also opens the mind to higher realms. As relaxation occurs, the body and its material and selfish longings seem to become less urgent, and a kind of peaceful state follows, closer to the soul. People seem to be reluctant to leave this state. Meditation accomplishes the same thing. I believe that hypnosis is one with meditation, biofeedback and prayer.

Breathwork. Another technique we use at our clinic is Transpersonal Breathwork. This was begun by Stanislav Grof, who discovered that the use of breath and select music produces an altered state of mind that is conducive to the washing out of old memories, as well as transporting one to transpersonal realms.

The "breathwork" consists of a prolonged group experience in which the members are at first helped to relax and then taught to breathe in tune to the music in a controlled, deep and rapid fashion. Almost universally, people will go through private experiences that wash out emotional traumas and release them to higher realms. More often than not, each member achieves beatific feelings and insights, and rises closer to the soul domain. There seems to be a biologically determined rhythm that causes people to "awaken" (though a kind of soft awareness remains throughout the experience) after about ninety minutes and most people seem eager to repeat the experience.

We combine transpersonal breathwork with bioenergetic body-work, working on spastic or painful parts of the body to release repressed emotions stored in these areas. Very often people will see the "Light", achieve out-of-body states, or release emotions. After everyone has completed his or her encounter, we then invite him or her to draw the experience. Following this there is group discussion, which leads to a yet greater integration of each individual experience. It is gratifying to see how listening to each other helps members of the group. It is even more interesting to learn that sometimes one member will have participated, silently and unwittingly, in the experience of another during that very experience. In the debriefing that follows, this shared adventure becomes known.

In our clinic we believe that it is important to integrate the breath-work with the total therapeutic experience. Therefore, it is important to have follow-up sessions whenever possible. In this way the breathwork gives impetus to the patient's ascent in development.

Does everyone who passes through our doors do the breathwork? No, but I often wish that they did. Transpersonal Breathwork is such a wonderful instrument. Its ability to gather group energy, to help people to share their experiences, and transport them to higher spiritual realms is inspiring, not only to the patients, but to those of us who are lucky enough to lead it as well.

Retreat Weekends. The centerpiece of these retreats is the breath-work and the evocation of emotional events that this work brings up. These two-and-a-half-day weekends are very powerful affairs where people have a chance to meld even more fully with one other. The group energy and intimacy that is developed brings to awareness the natural lovingness of people. Once the obstructions to this closeness are dissolved, again and again we are greeted with evidence of our natural state, the divinity of humankind.

Reba, a sixty-year-old woman who entered therapy because of depression, is an example of the amazing effectiveness of these retreats. She had been employed at a hotel where there was a robbery and chaotic shooting. Such unexpected violence occurred over and over again until she broke down and could no longer last in the job. Reba had been raised in a neighborhood where everything was looked upon concretely and literally. Though she had been a devout Catholic, adventures into the spiritual world were unknown to her--until she experienced a retreat weekend.

Reba had spent the first fifty-five years of her life in a very parochial neighborhood within a large city. Her boundaries had been defined by the four blocks within which lived her family of origin, her children and grandchildren. This limited locale also defined the periphery of her experience in the intellectual world, though she had a strong and adventuresome intelligence. Her attendance at the retreat was evidence of her courage and inquisitive mind. The breathwork opened her to inner experiences of peace and elation, and contact with her departed husband. This was further enlarged by participation in the experiences of others in the group at the time of debriefing, when each would describe his or her episode. For fifty-five years she had traveled a single track. Now she found that there was another track, running parallel to her world, and open to an entirely new vista. Then her very real intelligence and sense of inquiry welcomed these new adventures and the many new things that she learned, from the group leaders and from the other participants, about the subtle realms. She has continued to learn about spiritual reaches of the mind, with intense reading, and repeated attendance at our clinic and seminars.

Not everyone is able to surrender to the intimacy of these weekend retreats. Patrick was a thirty-two-year-old who came to me for the treatment of a depression severe enough that he was in danger of losing his job. He was very cynical, suspicious and aggressively full of doubt. Under the doubt, however, was a great fear of letting go--of being ridiculed and criticized. His defenses were so strong that he could not let himself surrender to the breathwork. For this reason, his experience was only minor. In individual therapy, however, he moved forward progressively and became a man who was quite warm and willing to seek out new relationships. He also benefited greatly from group therapy, which taught him to relax the distance between himself and others.

Education. Although I was taught as a psychoanalyst that to "educate" was to impair the psychoanalytic process, I have come to know that we educate all the time, and that education is a very important part of learning, living and growing, all of which are a part of anyone's treatment. At our clinic, we believe that the principles of human behavior are applicable everywhere, and that we can help to make a better society if we can educate people about them. For example, recently I co-authored a book called *Twin Souls*. This book is about finding one's true spiritual partner, and blends the knowledge of how we work as personalities with the realization of our participation in the soul realms. People are hungry for this knowledge and for better relationships as a way out of loneliness and separation. The seminars we give at the clinic on "Finding Your True Spiritual Partner" have been well-received, attesting to the deep desire people have for a connection with others on every level. These include "A Course In Miracles" workshops, uniting the principles of the "Course" with psychotherapy and techniques for personal as well as soul advancement; Transpersonal Breathwork day-long and weekend retreats; educational classes in spiritual psychotherapy, again bridging the principles of personality development with the high reaches of the mind as related by some of the great spiritual teachers; classes in meditation; and team building techniques for communities, including the communities of industry.

Accordingly, we have taught policemen, teachers, lawyers, doctors and business leaders, in educational seminars. It is sad that there is such a lack of knowledge about how to truly be a human being in our society, and this is as true in medicine as anywhere else. To be truly human means to be ethical, kind, spiritual, forgiving, giving, and above all working to advance in one's personal life and in service to our community of humankind. To do this one must know oneself deeply and intimately.

If we could only bring to others a knowledge of the deeper and higher portions of the human personality at work, we could contribute greatly to the making of a better society.

We teach what we are. In our work, as we educate in seminars or in individual or group sessions, we often recommend that clients attend lectures or read about the "Course in Miracles." Showing the relationship of the Course to our model of therapy and development helps us to teach clients about the immortality of the essential person.

A Course in Miracles is a channeled modern-day bible. It points out that the teacher and the pupil are one. In our group sessions we repeat together the inductive prayer from the Course, which I have mentioned earlier:

"I am here only to be truly helpful;
I am here to represent Him Who sent me;
I don't have to worry about what to say or what to do, for He Who sent me will direct me;
I am content to be wherever He wishes, knowing He goes there with me;
I will be healed as I let Him teach me to heal."

One of the things I have discovered, and share with my patients, is that the therapist is healed as he/she is allowed to heal. The roles of healing are easily reversed; in fact, they are revolving.

I have learned that both my patient and myself are better off if I am willing to face myself, acknowledging my faults and limitations. I have learned to respect the value of honesty. If I am willing to face myself, others become more willing to follow my example. There are times when I have been angry and hurt during the treatment of a patient and have thought that I was effectively concealing it. Not so--the patient sensed that I was angry or upset, and this intuitive knowledge got in the way of our work together. Admitting to and facing this anger was therapeutic for both me and my patient, allowing us to move forward again.

Through the love I have received from my patients, I have also been able to acknowledge some of the better parts of myself, and have learned to get over my "aw shucks!" attitude. This mirroring of my better points has also healed me of my inferiority complex. It has taught me as well to honor the talents and better parts of my patients and to point out the things that must yet be confronted and healed in them. Working with my patients, I have learned much about the power of intuition, and mine has grown enormously thanks to their validation. I have also been able to transcend my own doubt about our immortality as I listen to the experiences of my clients who have had near death encounters or meetings with angels who were the returned spirits of children who have died. More than anyone else, my patients have taught me about the living reality of the expanded soul realms, and of the healing power of love well administered.

Many of my patients have had near-death experiences, and when they speak of them in group therapy, other members of the group are educated, and become freer to speak of their own experiences. Discussions of the immortality of the soul are coupled with past life explorations and these become relevant when we see how past-life experiences are a still-energized and influential force in our present life.

It is always interesting to observe how past lives affect us now. One client in particular had a fascinating series of past-life experiences during one of his breathwork sessions. In one life he was a lion, in another a wild warrior, in another a court physician to a Chinese empress, and in another a revered wise man in a cave. Interestingly, I have seen him transition from someone with a warlike personality to a person who shows increasing compassion and wisdom in his healing profession. I find it interesting to see how the idea of the influences of past lives parallels Freud's thinking. Freud believed that a symptom or a behavior was maintained until the last buried memory that determined the cause of the symptom was elevated to consciousness. In my own practice, I have found that, for some people, the symptom or behavior is maintained until the past life experience has been brought to consciousness. When this occurs, an "aha," a clicking recognition follows, and thereafter the behavior or symptom is no longer compulsive. These results are good and meaningful evidence not only of reincarnation, but also of the immortality of the soul.

Since I have come to understand how past lives connect with the present one, I have much more to offer suffering human beings. For example, I was called in to see a forty-year-old man who was immobilized by antero-lateral sclerosis, Lou Gehrig's disease. By then the paralysis had involved every part of his body except his head. He was very courageous, and with the help of his family, who were wealthy enough to supply as much support as possible, had been able to continue his existence in some kind of comfort. He was much enlivened by our discussions of the immortality of the essential human being, of life after death, of Theosophy and of our continual ascension as we become better human beings, better souls. He was hungry for these insights and quite peaceful when I left him. He died not much later.

Discussions such as these offer so much to people with incurable diseases such as terminal cancer, AIDS or others illnesses that medical science deems hopeless. These exchanges are often coupled with the conviction that I carry that the whole mind and the soul, in its divinity, are capable of healing anything and everything.

Since it is true that we inevitably express what we are, it is also true that the Center for Mind/ Body Wellness is an expression of what I have been, what I have become and what I am becoming - hopefully someone who can contribute to the making of a better world through the release of human potential. The recognition of the Soul at work within, and our readiness for its release is an important recognition for all of us, especially in these so-trying times of struggle with the Forces of Darkness.

Guidelines and Exercises

1. On the road to your personal wellness: take an inventory:
   a. What are your fears and inhibitions, the things that stand in the way of your releasing your talents and desires?
   b. What are your talents and desires, the things that give you the most satisfaction and pleasure to do and to accomplish?
   c. List a number of ways in which your talents, pleasures and desires can be fulfilled in the world, which will be rewarded.

2. Actualize your inventory in spite of fear and inhibition. Remember that each time you do, it will be less fearful to attempt it the next time. Desensitize yourself to temporary failures when they occur.

3. Practice removing self-consciousness and ego. The more things are done for the beauty and pleasure of them, rather than in the spirit of ego, the more they will flow to accomplishment.

4. Practice service: to others, to the good of what you are creating, to the making of a better society. The more you activate yourself in this way, the more you will elevate yourself, and the more you will be rewarded with love of and from others.

5. Find a support group, a discussion group, or a self-help group. Participate and observe yourself, others, the way the group knits together in fellowship and family, with a desire to help each other. It may happen otherwise if there are dissidents. In that case detach, observe, and find a better group, one that suits your own personality and needs better. There are many groups forming now in our society.

There is a group called "Adult Children of Dysfunctional Families," a category into which almost everyone can fit. It is an outgrowth of Alcoholics Anonymous, but is not about alcoholism. Try it. If one group doesn't suit you, find another.

6. Meditate: At least 5 minutes a day. After a while your desire to enlarge this amount of time will grow. In the meantime, you will have an opportunity to cultivate your sensitivity to yourself, your introspection. When you find peace, know you are in contact with your soul. That provides a map, a goal, to which you can strive, more and more in meditation and in life.

7. Know that you do not have to find a professional "guru" to know yourself and advance yourself. If you find a good, wise, tolerant friend who is also open to knowing himself/herself, counsel with each other. IN EVERY CASE USE YOUR INTUITIVE CENTER OF TRUTH TO KNOW WHEN THINGS "CLICK."

CHAPTER V

The Soul in
Psychotherapy

Definition Of The Soul - The Soul As Distinguished From The Spirit -- The Soul And Spirit As Described In Eastern Philosophy -- The Natural Buoyancy Of The Soul -- A Case History Of The Release Of The Soul -- Soul Honesty -- Our Natural Attraction To Each Other -- Impediments To Soul Ascension -- Soul-To-Soul Contact In Psychotherapy -- Soul Honesty In A Case Of Conjoint Therapy -- Authenticity, The Road To The Soul.

What is the Soul?

In popular descriptions, the soul and the spirit are used interchangeably, but this is incorrect; they are not the same. The spirit is the divine spark, a part of God Himself, infusing every part of creation, most certainly including humankind. Because the Divine is all-powerful, all-knowing, It does not experience. One can only experience, become conscious, and know (in our sense) by having limitations. Accordingly, in order to know His creations, God becomes us and walks among us.

In order to experience existence, bodies were acquired by the high energies of Creation; these were developed by stepping down the unimaginable and unbearably potent energies of the Divine, creating bodies of a lower and lower level. In due course these were known as the causal, the mental and the astral bodies. The causal body is the same as the soul. It functions as if it were a step-down transformer, receiving energy from above and lowering its vibrations to acceptable and tolerable levels. Much like the skin, the soul faces in two directions: above to receive, and below to create and communicate. The soul therefore receives instructions from above and transmits them to what is below, down to the physical body and the human brain. The soul is also a storage house for the high experiences of humanity. It is that agency, that intelligence that decides to reincarnate in order to further complete the job of purifying the human condition so that an individual may experience a further ascent toward a return to God. Human experiences are dissipated if they are of a lower order, but the higher-order experiences are stored in the causal body, where they are saved to incarnate in a later body to further enlightened experience. Thus, the soul is distinguished from the Spirit, the Divine Essence.

The Soul and Spirit as Described by Eastern Philosophy

Remembering that the soul and spirit are different, I want to return to the Eastern philosophies to describe their qualities and functions more fully.

Eastern philosophy recognizes that the spirit is the divine spark, the divine essence, the holy immortal part of everything, and calls it the Atma, the Monad. The soul is the vehicle through which the spirit radiates its light and energy, the agent that transmits downward the high energy of the spirit. These philosophies also refer to the soul as Buddhi-Manas (Intuition-High Mind). It is the Causal body, the high subtle body that surrounds the three lower bodies: mental, emotional, and physical. It further acts on the lower levels to cause, and therefore create, manifestation. Soul is intuition, whereas the spirit is Will-Purpose-Intention.

Will-Purpose-Intention is the descriptive name given by Theosophy to the first outpouring of energy from On-High. When Will-Purpose-Intention (the Spirit) seeds Buddhi-Love-Wisdom (the Soul), the result is Humanity, Creation.

The Rise of the Soul in Psychotherapy: Its Natural Buoyancy

There is an intrinsic buoyancy of the soul, which I have seen manifested by its rising after a correct interpretation of a patient's problem, after each resolution of conflict, after each shedding of the chains of the past as he or she comes more and more into her/his own. I became convinced of this internal rising, this inner push upward, when I noticed that over and over again the release from neurotic inhibitions would lead inevitably to the rising of the personality. A patient never became more selfish, power driven or status seeking; rather he/she always became more giving, loving and able to relate to others. This is surely evidence of the inherent divinity that we all carry in our center. It affords us a glimpse at least of the soul's wanting to be released, and its desire to carry its vehicle, the personality, upward.

The release from the past, or any movement through tremendous anxiety, marks our release to become our true selves, and true to ourselves. This process is not only a matter of remembering, reliving, releasing ourselves from past memories, but from our present conditioning as well. Such acculturations infiltrate the very cells of our bodies, and must be released like toxins from the organism. As this release occurs, one must face anxiety. What then emerges is the True Self, and a great feeling of liberty. This is much like the release from the constraints of the physical body that we experience during meditation, the release to live in the larger bodies that surround us and are closer to the soul. There is a wonderful feeling of liberation that occurs when this release finally happens, a sort of recognition that says, "Now, at last, I can be myself."

Following One's Truth; The Release of the Self :

Mendel, a middle-aged psychologist, had always been overprotective of others. This desire was a manifestation of his big heart, even though his protective nature was somewhat overdone. One day he felt called upon by inner forces to follow his own instincts and his commitment to the truth. Even though this decision entailed the risk of alienating his family and professional colleagues, he took a leap. He abandoned his long-standing career in academia, and followed his need to explore new areas of psychology, parapsychology, and spirituality. Braving the opinions of his professional colleagues, who now looked upon him askance, he traveled to California, learned many of the new techniques and returned to join with others in developing a new alternative medico-psychological center. His concerns for financial welfare had given way to the inner injunction to follow his truth. In so doing he was emulating the example of Arjuna in the Bhagavad Gita. Arjuna listened when Lord Krishna told him he must be a soldier since that was his calling, and in so doing set aside all other considerations in pursuing the ideal of doing the best that he could in his chosen way. Mendel did the same, and in the end found the rewards of fulfillment, of service, of excellence. In the end he was also able to meet his financial responsibilities to his family. Today Mendel is happily serving as a new breed of psychologist. His need to protect others has finally been freed into a larger container.

Suffering from an obligatory need to take care of others and to submit too much to social convention, is akin to being confined to the body. When we find new ways of being, of liberating ourselves from the anachronistic influences of the past, we are always led to a release of our true selves, our spiritual selves, and thus to a greater liberation. This freedom represents not only a deliverance from the body, but an invitation to larger realms of expansion, realms of the soul.

The Over-Soul

To achieve true fulfillment, we must all eventually answer the call to service of the god/goddess within. "The Over-Soul," an essay written by Ralph Waldo Emerson, states: "What is the universal sense of want and ignorance, but the fine innuendo by which the soul makes its enormous claim?" This pregnant and poetic line describes a longing within each of us for something higher, for becoming something better, for joining with the All. This is the essence of the search for the soul, and for the surrender to the soul in spiritual psychotherapy. "Our being is descending into us from we know not whence," Emerson says of this soul connection. This statement points to the fact that the highest and finest within us receives its inspiration from above. He goes on to say :

"I am constrained every moment to acknowledge a higher origin for events than the will that I call mine. As with events, so it is with thoughts. When I watch that flowing river, which, out of regions I see not, pours for a season its streams into me, I see that I am a pensioner, not a cause, but a surprised spectator of this ethereal water; that I desire and look up, and put myself in the attitude of reception, but from some alien energy the visions come.

"We live in succession, in division, in parts, in particles. Meantime within man is the soul of the whole; the wise silence; the universal beauty, to which every part and particle is equally related; the eternal ONE.....We see the world piece by piece, as the sun, the moon, the tree; but the whole, of which these are the shining parts, is the Soul."

In these descriptions, Emerson points out that we are in fact part of both the ONE and of each other. This connection is most intensely felt during our most meaningful moments of contact with each other. This touching of souls denotes a true beginning between the therapist and patient. As the two become one, it is as if they are joined by an invisible channel characterized by an intuitive understanding of one another, and by a surrounding envelope of unity and peace. These are the moments of soul-to-soul connection between true partners. These qualities of true spiritual intimacy are the trademarks of the most meaningful seasons of psychotherapy, the moments when the soul is released within both the patient and therapist.

Marsha Sinetar beautifully describes the transcendent quality within this relationship in her book, *Do What You Love and the Money Will Follow:*[14]

---

[14] Mershe Sinetar, *Do What You Love and the Money Will Follow:* (New York: Paulist Press, 1986).

"In this connection, again I quote Thomas Merton who, in discussing this phrase `experience of love,' made it clear that he was talking about a total awakening of the person, a renunciation of self which is made in order to live functionally in relationship with others: `Such love is beyond ...all restrictions of a desiring and self-centered self. Such love begins only when the ego renounces its claim to absolute autonomy and ceases to live in a little kingdom of desires in which it is its own end and reason for existing.'

"Merton, like Suzuki...is defining love as a condition of a liberated, non-self-conscious self, a self which has so totally entered the moment as to have dissolved in it, disappeared."

This quotation from Sinetar describes the experience of the liberated soul. The disappearance of the self-conscious ego is parallel to the disappearance of the body and self-image from the foreground, allowing for a flow of freedom.

Soul Honesty in Group Therapy

Some of the experiences I have had with therapy groups at the Center illustrate these principles. In group one day, I noticed that, for some reason, the session was starting at a rather slow pace. One of its members, Samuel, had re-entered that day after being away for six weeks. This absence followed an abrupt leave-taking during a previous session in which he had announced that he was through. Later, however, he asked to come back again.

When it was Samuel's turn to speak, he began by talking more slowly and thoughtfully than usual. I was glad to observe this because, in the past, I had admonished him to listen to himself instead of just running on. Now, as he spoke, he began to show some emotion, expressing feelings of deep hurt that no one had called him after he had left the group, most especially myself, the therapist. He acknowledged that he had exploded in the previous session, yet he said that he had expected me to stand by him. Instead I had let him go.

He went on to tell me that I hadn't realized how much trouble he had been having in that previous session, how much difficulty it had cost him to say the things he did. When I added insult to injury by not calling him, he felt quite abandoned.

I took the risk of saying, in front of the group, that I had made a mistake, that I hadn't recognized the things that he had pointed out, and that I should have. I apologized to him, which struck both him and the others in the group. This apology made quite a difference to Samuel, but I had profited as well. I had been given the opportunity to practice soul-honesty.

This confession of honesty and proper humility established a soul-to-soul connection with the patient and the group as a whole. In this manner Truth, which comes from the Divine center, conveys itself, radiates from itself, duplicates itself, invites itself, and leads itself to a higher realm of communication between and within people.

Later in the same group session, I approached another patient suggesting the possibility of his undergoing hypnosis in order to relieve a severe headache. He agreed and I asked the group members to allow themselves to go into hypnosis with him as I chanted the induction. This type of activity increases the group energy and the effectiveness of the hypnosis. As one of the group members went into a deep trance, she "caught" the painful headache that the first patient had been experiencing. In order to relieve her, I induced an even deeper trance, for I knew her to be a worthy inductee. She became very cold, and I gave her something to wrap herself in. She was shaking all over, and complaining of pain in her stomach, a sign of great anxiety as it turned out. Then she began to tremble and to cry and to shout. When I tried to touch her to reassure her she recoiled. "Don't touch me, don't touch me!" she said. At that point she began to whimper, "I want to go home, I want to go home," and tried to rush out of the room with her eyes closed. When the group restrained her, she fell to the floor and began to cry over and over again. When I saw that in the midst of the trance, she no longer perceived me as the therapist whom she trusted and indeed adored, but as a threat, it became clear to me that she was reliving a rape scene. She continued to try to run from the room, to cry and to say that I was going to hurt her.

Despite her demonstrated agony, I let her go through this experience fully. It was a very dramatic episode, but I had an inner surety that she would break through to the other side in spite of her tremendous pain. When the experience and the memory were finally over, she emerged with a clean, freshly scrubbed look on her face. I asked her to look around, for she had felt very ashamed of what she had confessed about being raped. She was comforted and encouraged to see the beaming looks of approval on the faces of each member of the group.

Thus we see the evidence of the universal network that exists among people. Indeed, the group was very sympathetic to her, very caring and very happy for her. She came out of this experience with a peaceful feeling and a beatific glow on her face and personality. This is a wonderful illustration of how the spirit is at work within people, leading the way through the trials of life, giving them the knowledge that the light will be seen after the darkness of the fear has been gone through. The powerful soul-to-soul contact between each of the members of this group clearly shows us the inherent connections between groups of people, the network that is our soul-connectedness.

Our Natural Attraction to One Another

There is a tendency among all people, as they get to know each other, to feel a commonality. I believe that this is a part of the God's universal plan. If we live in a holographic network, and I firmly believe that we do, then we are basically attached to one another. Even though our world works according to a principle of duality--negative opposed to positive, darkness to light--in the end the positive, the light and the love, will prevail.

This natural attraction stands in contrast to our previously held suspicions and distrust and is an invitation to soul-to-soul contact. It is followed by an accentuated love, interest, a liking of people for each other even under the most dangerous circumstances. Among soldiers or civilians in wartime, or among gang members within our inner cities, we see a great loyalty. Even in the Mafia there is a family loyalty, a derivative of love, a bonding of the members with each other. In catastrophes, we witness a mass joining, a collective altruism of group members. In a well-conducted group therapy, it is almost inevitable that the group members will bond with each other.

This desire for connection between people is a "prodrome," a harbinger of things on the march. The Tibetan, in the Alice Bailey books often says, that we are in a stage wherein group consciousness is replacing individual consciousness. What this means is that as individuals we are becoming more and more aware of the fact that our welfare is better served by realizing that we are never alone, that we are part of the group. Following this awareness is a desire to serve the group, even if that means that we must put some of our own desires into the background. Scott Peck has written about this dynamic in his instructions about community building in his book *A Different Drummer*. The popularity of the seminars on community building is a sign of the times, and a very hopeful one.

Impediments to Soul Ascension

Before we can take our place as fulfilled human beings and members of a community, we must go through a process of self-discovery and healing through soul ascension. This is not without its difficulties, however. Even though soul ascension is a process to which we naturally are drawn, there are numerous and ever-present impediments, as can be seen in the case of Angela, a forty-year-old patient who came to me for the relief of her depression. I soon discovered that Angela was terribly afraid of darkness and death. I felt that hypnosis would help her and, indeed, she was a very good hypnotic subject. At one point, however, when I began to speak about entering into the velvet black and quiet bliss, an image that I sometimes use as part of guided imagery, she grew very anxious, and began talking about her fear of death and evil. These feelings were associated with a nightmarish dream that she had had the night before, in which there was a hooded figure that had a white face with a black center. She knew that this figure represented death, and she was greatly frightened.

Angela's experience clearly shows that often when we try to enter into hypnosis, meditation or deep introspection, and complexes of fear and prohibition bar our entry. If we can help our patients to flow past these barriers, however, they can enter into an area that we call deeper, but which might as well be called higher. Within this deeper-higher mind--which is related to the higher bodies, both astral and mental--we have greater perception, greater knowledge and a closer approximation to the soul. We have an entry into an area of intuition called "Knowing-beyond-Knowing." Therefore, it is the job of the spiritual psychotherapist to help the patient to slide past these barriers, and to get in contact with the inner self, closer to the divine self, the soul-vessel.

When a spiritual psychotherapist can accurately interpret a patient's blockages, the consequent freeing of the patient from old fears and fixations allows their physical and astral (emotional) bodies to clear, paving the way for further ascension. This is what I mean when I say, "the inherent buoyancy of the soul."

Many of the impediments to the buoyancy of the soul can be found in the established social relationships, myths, and social surround. For example, in American society, there is much dedication to the pursuit of youth and material beauty, with a consequent overlooking of the inner, more important, and perhaps more beautiful part of the person. Other accepted ideals in our society teach us separateness; for example, "All's fair in love, war, and business." This attitude is re-enforced by the fact that the rich are not only admired in our culture, but also forgiven for all past and present sins. It is commonplace to see businessmen who step on the shoulders of others and symbolically scramble over the corpses of their competitors--even their former friends or spouses--in a frantic climb to the top. Once their high position is achieved, even religious organizations, to which they contribute money, honor them generously. The philosophy that "all's fair in the interest of expediency" is a serious impediment to the rising of the better portion of society.

Another impediment to our spiritual progress is the invitation to the Dark Forces that constantly overarch (in their search for those whom they can influence) as do the Forces of Light. These dark forces can never exert their influences alone; they can only express themselves by being incorporated into some physical vehicle.

Consequently, a human being must first offer an invitation to the Dark Forces. For this reason, these forces are constantly scanning, seeking with their subtle radar, those individuals who are excited by desires for selfish power, for material pleasures, for sadistic revenge. These openings allow human contact through which the Dark Forces can then exercise their power. In turn, such human beings become rooted in their selfish pleasures, and rewarded for them by our society, concluding a kind of Faustian compact. This situation represents an impediment both on the personal and social level to the rising of the soul.

A Gateway to Ascension in Group Therapy

Perry, a thirty-two-year-old who came to me for treatment of depression, illustrates these principles in action. Perry was fully rooted in a rather suspicious, almost paranoid view of the world. A mother who had a struggle-colored view of the world had taught this to him during the course of his development. She dominated him with cruel sarcasm and relentless criticism. Because of this it took some time before he could trust me as someone who would listen without retaliation to his acerbic criticisms. He scoffed at some of my charitable views of the world, announcing that I was naive, Pollyannaish and a weakling. I made no reply in defense of myself, feeling that no defense was necessary. I also knew, however, that my allowing his scoffing would provide him with a new experience, making it possible for him to question his own struggle-colored view of the world.

Perry thought I was absolutely "bonkers" when I spoke about out-of-body experiences or out-of-body realms. Somewhat later, his views moderated when he heard others in group therapy telling of their similar beliefs. As he grew in therapy, he became less afraid of his tender feelings, and their accompanying loneliness. Before the treatment was over, he was able to express his warmth and attachment to me. Whereas this was not exactly an updraft into the realms of the soul, it did provide a gateway. He now has considerable access to his warmer and more tender feelings and to his idealism as well, for he now wants to serve the world through a political career, and by writing books on political science.

Soul-to-Soul Contact in Psychotherapy

Another example of how soul-to-soul contact can release people from the influence of negative forces can be seen in the case of Sean, a fifty-year-old homosexual Irish gentleman who was quite handsome and always took the masculine role in his sexual encounters. When Sean came to me, he was suffering from a major depressive disorder; in fact, he had been in a psychiatric unit several times, once in 1989 and once in 1990.

It was easy for me to see just how repressed and full of unexpressed tension he was. His family background was horrible. His father had married his mother because she was pregnant with Sean and blamed the boy for the marriage from the beginning. Sean's mother was truly a crazy person. She was not only very critical of him but also psychotically dirty. For example, she would leave her Kotex pads around the house, sometimes stuffing them behind wastebaskets and in other places. The entire family was loose and chaotic -- providing him with a miserable beginning. One day, when Sean was eight years old, he came into a room to find his grandmother having intercourse with the parish priest. At that point he was blamed and called a sinner, for having come in! His much older sister became interested in him in a seductive way, and he had to defend himself against her. He repeated similar stories to me time and time again.

Sean came to my office after an eighteen-year relationship with a homosexual partner broke up. Despite his lamentable beginnings and an education that stopped at the ninth grade, Sean was highly literate, sensitive and, in fact, erudite and poetic by disposition. He was also endowed with a goodly store of love-capacity.

Whenever possible, I see my patients in combined group and individual sessions. During group therapy, he revealed that he was very perceptive about people. But despite his many accomplishments, he remained ashamed of both himself and his origins.

One day I was able to gain some important intuitive insights into Sean. Being understood in this manner was a new experience for him, and made an important impression on him. We all like to be understood; even more when the understanding is unsolicited and intuitively perceived. At a certain point I asked him why he wanted to be homosexual, after having asked, "Would you think that I'm a homophobe if I posed that question?" He assured me that he could listen. I went on to say that he really might not be basically a homosexual, that he was a strappingly masculine man who told me poetic things about my wife's being beautiful. He had remarked with considerable appreciation about the love-light in our eyes when we looked at each other. Such remarks were not especially homosexually oriented, I said.

When Sean denied being interested in anything but men, I nevertheless continued, "I remember that you told me how you can't think of a woman from the belt down." He replied, "Well, no I can't because, you know, I get disgusted and I feel like vomiting." I said to him, "Well then you're really cornered, being so entrapped by these ideas." He himself said this led back to his mother and how disgusting she was. What followed was a moment of real communication when I was able to tell him about his positive attributes. Did he remember when I had described his poetic soul and his loving nature? He had reason enough to be proud, rather than ashamed, for having overcome his origins. Suddenly, a beginning tear showed in his eye, giving me the opportunity to acknowledge his feeling of gratitude and happiness at being understood.

At that moment there was great peace in the room. It happened that a younger colleague, whom I was teaching, had been present--with the patient's permission of course. I was now able to say to him, "Can you feel the silence, the peaceful silence, the quiet joy-silence, the feeling of stillness in this room?" Such was the evidence of soul-to-soul contact, the kind of contact and uncommon communication that we make when we are exceptionally at one with each other. At such moments, we each become the other and understand the other. This represents the quiet bliss and joy that denotes a meeting of the souls; the presence of the divine Truth. Both patient and colleague were able to see and to acknowledge. It was an education for all of us.

Unfortunately, Sean eventually disappeared from treatment. I had an episode of severe illness and had to transfer the patient to the care of my colleague. Sean continued for a while, and then vanished. I presume he was carried away by his former defensive style of developing amnesia and disappearing when his emotions became too much to bear. How sad! Yet something considerable had been achieved that Sean will carry with him throughout his journey. Dynamic therapy, especially spiritual psychotherapy, doesn't pretend to produce a "finished product." It strives, rather, to start a growth process that hopefully can continue throughout life; perhaps many lives.

Spiritual Psychotherapy and a Case of Conjoint Therapy: Vera and Dan

Vera, as you remember, was the forty-year-old woman we spoke about in Chapter III who sought treatment because of panic attacks that had begun three years before when someone with a severely gashed face had come to her door. She hadn't liked her psychiatrist and had found her way to me after having learned that we practice a different form of psychotherapy.

Her treatment with us released her from the fetter attachments to her mother, who had always been very critical of her, and from her father who had always been very distant. Such attachments had chained her, preventing her from expressing her natural lovingness and her great soul. A devout Christian, who longed to take part in healing others, Vera became interested in the spiritual realm of our psychotherapy. Soon she was able to release her great stores of love, which she had been unable to experience or even to recognize before. Finally, she was free, albeit in a sublimated way.

As she moved up to this new level, her husband responded with the very attitudes that had frustrated her so in her family--a sort of artificial compliance, an increasing blankness of personality and an exaggerated gentility. Vera grew more and more disappointed until she arrived at the point where she realized that her panic attacks of three years ago, which led her to the hospital, were generated by both her wish to end the marriage and the great fear and anxiety that this realization entailed. After a year of therapy, she had reached the point where she decided that she was almost ready to ask for a separation. The only thing that was standing in her way was her fear of hurting her children. By now Vera had found other outlets for her emotions. She was actively engaged in hospice work and helping people through ecclesiastical adventures within her church.

Because she could finally speak openly to her husband about these matters, he overcame years of resistance and agreed to enter into psychotherapy. He made an appointment with me.

When I met him, I was surprised and impressed to see his flexibility and his ability to respond to my observations with a kind of openness. He responded strongly to the fact that it was my desire for him to become himself, to satisfy himself--that this was the goal of the treatment. I told him, however, that in the interest of satisfying himself, he would first have to discover himself.

In spite of his apparent gentility, we discovered that he had a great deal of aggressive energy; not mean energy -- he was very gentle -- but the kind of aggressive energy that could be sublimated into a dynamic strength. Freud's concept of sublimation becomes important in this connection. Sublimation means refinement, in this case the refinement of the instinct of aggression. Our body energy springs from our raw instincts. In the course of childhood and later development, we learn to become civilized. A part of this civilizing process is being trained to tolerate our raw instincts and turn them to something better, more social, and more useful. The child's initial interest in dirt becomes sublimated into a desire to be clean; childish cruelty into kindness; and the aggression that might remain as meanness becomes refined as energy, tenacity and protectiveness. In this sense, the use of aggressive energy does not mean becoming overtly aggressive, but usefully assertive and courageous.

At one point in his life, Dan told me, he had become so angry at his wife's talking about her love of other things including the "Course in Miracles" that he fairly put his hand through the wall. But he retreated from his anger almost immediately, paying obeisance to his guilt by assuming an exaggerated gentleness. He was unaware of his basic sadness but became conscious of it as we talked. He became conscious of his anger as well.

Dan was unaware of his positive attributes, and I had to point them out to him. He had worked hard to support the family in good style, and always been on hand for his children and his wife, in spite of his crushing schedule. Slowly, he became aware that his overly great gentleness had been determined in childhood during a time when he had been conditioned to take care of an impaired younger brother. Dan had been admonished, over and over again, not to make any waves within his family.

He responded well to his private psychotherapy sessions; in fact he began to express some of his dissatisfactions to his wife, almost for the first time. Finally, I felt that he was ready for the first conjoint session. When the three of us met together, I could see that Vera was really quite disinterested in Dan. She was treating him as if she were a clinical psychotherapist, and he an unfortunate patient. I pointed this out to her. I also indicated to Dan that he was doing her as well as himself a great disservice when he took all of the blame onto himself. This behavior deprived Vera of any opportunity to see what she was contributing to the poor communication between them. With this realization, Dan was finally able to vent some of his criticisms and to express himself in a much more authentic way.

When I showed Vera that she was being clinical rather than acting as a human being, a wife or a patient, she understood. She poured herself out, describing how she had, with so much effort, made herself not care about the marriage. She had been disappointed so many times. This recapitulated the many disappointments at the hands of her father. As she did so, she began to talk about the other side of her feeling, about how she had really loved her husband since she was six years old, how she had tried to take care of him; how she had tried to console him about his family and how she had moved into a big house she hadn't wanted because she felt that it made him happy.

When Dan heard Vera speak honestly about all of these things, he warmed toward her a little. This encouraged her to continue by expressing her great disappointment and anger at having been unappreciated when she gave him a fortieth birthday party. She had worked so hard with his staff and a number of other people to give him a marvelous party and all he had said was that he didn't want it. She had felt so angry that she had wanted to give up on him. That night she slept on the couch.

Surprised at her reaction, Dan confessed, "But I said that because I couldn't stand to have these people love me." She exclaimed, "What?" She was stunned by the fact that he had developed this much access to himself, this much insight; one could fairly see the love-light returning to her eyes. This is not a finished story; it is a beginning story.

Seeing this opening, I invited, fairly prodded, Dan into talking about what he had said to me in private session. He admitted that he sometimes got quite fed up with Vera and that he too thinks about how nice it would be to separate. Then perhaps he would only have to work three days a week instead of working all the time; maybe he wouldn't have to take care of the children while she's out gallivanting around.

This kind of honesty is true "soul-honesty." People respond to real authenticity and integrity. Both Vera and Dan were able to be much more genuine with one another after this; and although they didn't become honey-mooners, there was more contact between them on a sincere level. At one point Dan even said that he thought that they ought to try to make it together. I cautioned him, however, telling him not to have that goal as an aim because it was always best if one were prepared to surrender one-self on both sides to whatever developed in pursuit of the truth. Both of them acknowledged that idea as correct.

Open-mindedly surrendering to whatever truth emerges is central to seeking soul contact. This is love in its most honest sense--love of truth and recognition of the divine essence that we are, in ourselves and in the other.

The concept of "surrender" is of supreme importance, not only to the therapist, but to all of us throughout life. Surrender is like jiu-jitsu where one throws the opposing force by going with it. As often as possible, I teach people to tolerate, to go with their feared feelings. This not only relieves the pressure that tempts us to run away, it also allows us to absorb the feeling, and to make use of it. The surrender of the therapist is necessary too; allowing whatever will develop to occur. This is a noble humility, an open-ness, a receptivity to the greater wisdom that comes through the patient and his/her own intuitive center. It is also the reception of a higher wisdom coming through the therapist's intuition. This recognition process requires a setting aside of the ego and one's private aspirations. It is the only way. If we are to teach the patient to find his/her authenticity, we must own up to our own. It is parallel in essence to the wisdom contained in the following reference from Meister Eckhart:[15]

"Who are those who honor God? Those who have wholly gone out of themselves, and who do not seek for what is theirs in anything, whatever it may be great or little, who are not looking beneath themselves or beside themselves or at themselves, who are not desiring possessions or honors or ease or pleasure or profit or inwardness or holiness or reward or the kingdom of heaven, and who have gone out from all this, from everything that is theirs; these people pay honor to God, and they honor God properly, and they give him what is his." In the exchange between Vera and Dan, there developed a greater openness, leading closer to authenticity. They perceived it, felt it, and it drew them together. It augured a new beginning. This is always so. All of us feel authenticity, both in ourselves and in those with

---

[15]   Meister Eckhart: *The Way of Paradox: Spiritual Life as Taught by Meister Eckhart* (London: Darton, Longman and Todd, 1987).

whom we interact. I was taught that the psychoanalyst is, first and foremost, the representative of reality. I would add, the representative of the Truth.

Additional Examples of the Recognition of Authenticity

Over the years, my practice has been filled with examples of people who have been freed because they were able to acknowledge their truth. One of these examples can be seen in Eileen, a very successful and magnetic woman. Tragically, Eileen also had a paralyzing sense of inferiority about her mind and memory. This was strange because she was intelligent and very beautiful. She had hosted her own television program for a number of years and was highly accomplished. Nevertheless, she felt highly inadequate, and was even more afraid that these emotions would show.

These feelings of inferiority became especially acute when she was asked to remember something. When I asked her to recount something during the course of a workshop I was conducting, she blushed and said that she felt blocked and very, very stupid. When I asked her why, she blasted me, saying that she didn't like my domineering style, which was "so typical of men". I accepted her and what she said, but I also pushed her further using a Gestalt technique. Gestalt is a method in which the therapist encourages the development of the feeling. As I did so, Eileen became increasingly angry--angry enough to hit my arm.

I remained supportive and she was able to come through her transference passion. The meaningful thing was that I had listened to her and heard her as she was. This was a new experience for her, allowing her to express herself more fully than ever, and yet to remain accepted and acceptable. As she became liberated, she was able to become warmly loving toward myself, the very person whom she had derided shortly before as being "so typical." During the Transpersonal Breathwork that followed, she had an ecstatic experience, accompanied by great love that she felt as a release.

This was a true freeing of her personality, releasing it to flow unblocked and to rise to higher levels of love's expression. My full listening without judgement gave her permission to be herself. When this happened, her love-self was able to come forward. Thus, every time a patient is released from an inhibition, there is a movement of the personality upward, in spiritual ascension toward love. This is the natural buoyancy of the soul.

Another patient, Charles, was fixated through guilt to a frigid and restricting girlfriend. During transpersonal breathwork he was able to relive and to realize the demeaning and guilt-making background his family had provided him with during his childhood. As he was delivered from these fixations, he experienced a flood of emotion -- and then an overwhelming capacity to love and be loved. Charles began to look for a larger circle of friends with which to express and fulfill himself. He exclaimed that his life had been changed, and indeed it had. He broke up with his girlfriend and developed spontaneous and genuine relations with other women. He became happy.

Again, there is a lesson to be learned. Discovering one's authentic self is not easy. It requires courage, and a more relentless pursuit of honesty than in almost any other walk of life. But its rewards are very real: relief and freedom to be one's self. This is happiness.

Another example of the natural buoyancy of the soul can be seen in Lillian, a woman of forty-five who had been raped and sexually and incestuously abused. She also went through an experience of emotional release. By being heard, by being allowed to howl with pain, she disengaged herself from the memory, and emerged into a greater lovingness, which clearly beamed, from her face. The "hole" in her chest, which she had formerly called her feeling of emptiness, became filled as my assistant held her and cradled her. What followed was both a greater ability to receive love and a greater ability to give it. Her spiritual ascension manifested as an arising toward love and light.

These momentary experiences of the release of the personality are important, for they provide us with a new outlook on both life and the self. Most important, they provide us with a continual sense of opening in life, an expansion in relation to self and others.

Blocked by her fear of being out of control, Lorraine was caught between the longings for fulfillment of her feminine self and a fear of being rejected in her relations with men. Although these feelings sprang from a deep wellspring in her past, its source remained concealed from her. Lorraine had a deep and abiding love for her father, who was a good man, but inhibited in his own expression. This made for repeated mini-rejections when the little girl tried to approach him. The result was a retreat into an exaggerated independence.

In spite of her autonomy, Lorraine's longings to surrender and be fulfilled remained. She traveled through life using her considerable energy and resourceful intellect to achieve important success in her field, but her relationships with men consisted of affiliations that were not worthy of her. They were not able to complete her, and though they weren't worthy of her, they would inevitably reject her. In this way, Lorraine's defenses against a more complete fulfillment were quite completely developed. Simultaneously a re-enactment of the ancient drama of rejection was taking place. In this way the formative patterns of childhood remain, and exert their influence, until they can be brought to conscious light and reframed. Accordingly her inner glow had been blocked by a fear of surrendering to someone who would be someone worthy and sufficient to fulfill her. Love cannot be received nor can it flow until one is safe enough and ready to fully surrender.

This story has a happy ending, which is illustrative. Lorraine's courage and tenacity expressed themselves in several ways: She sublimated much of her love longings into an intense and rewarding spiritual path. She contributed a great deal in this way. At the same time she undertook to understand herself with determination, and followed several avenues of intense psychological investigation. This led her into opening trial relationships with a different kind of man, one who could give to her, protect her, allow her, and provide the security she needed against being rejected. After a while she met someone who was right for her, and the two have consummated a complete relationship of happiness, fulfillment and service. This is a yin-yang match.

All of the examples above illustrate the natural buoyancy of the soul and the rising of the personality to love and service after its release from the shackles of past conditionings.

These stories and the lives behind them illustrate the fact that, as humanity, we have every reason to be hopeful. Even though our culture is passing though a dark time, if the soul is so ready to rise within us, then this clearly implies that there is a natural goodness in our human fellowship, and that the Light will inevitably pour itself out over the shadows. To honor this truth, however, we must first bring the Soul out of concealment. We must spread the word to all healers, so that new expectations may arise and be fulfilled. In this way society itself will gradually be transformed into a kinder, more cohesive and spiritual force.

Guidelines and Exercises:

1. Let yourself notice when you are with a group that you really like, and with whom you feel completely at ease, how the feelings of togetherness, unity, love naturally rise. This is the buoyancy of the soul, the love portion we carry.

2. Select a situation or a relationship which you fear; invade the fear without danger to your body or future, observe where the fear is coming from (from you and your past conditioning), tolerate it, and see yourself break through to a feeling of relief. This may be true of some emotion you think you can't stand.

3. As you meditate, summon courage to look at your faults - this gives you a chance to practice autheticity, the hallmark of the soul. Practice this in your relationship with people. You may be inclined to rationalize, lie, or make excuses out of anxiety. If you resist this you will be practicing authenticity.

4. If you find yourself with a counselor, or even a counseling friend, make sure not only that you practice authenticity but also that he/she does.

5. Look around in a group of which you are a part. Notice how attracted and affiliated you have become with them and they with you. This is our natural affiliation - the law of attraction, which is a lesson from the soul.

6. Make a list of the resistances you might find in yourself to soul and personality ascension. It might be a fear of change, or a reluctance to make the effort. Resist rationalizing the reason. Invade your fear of change, as you aspire upward to become more loving, less self-preoccupied, more giving in all respects.

7. Practice soul-to-soul contact, appropriately. Select a very close and intimate friend, or your loved one. Exclude everything from your thoughts and preoccupations. Settle into an envelope of peace that will surround you both as you concentrate exclusively and without effort on him/her. Look into the eyes if that is appropriate. You will notice a channel of silent communication, surrounded by peace, in which you can sense subtle emotions. You will be able to understand deeply, without words, and beyond words. Don't be too anxious to talk about this immediately, but later you can, in order to validate it.

8. PRACTICE AUTHENTICITY every day of your life, with others, and most especially with yourself. It is not easy, but extremely rewarding, and will open yourself and others to your soul.

CHAPTER VI:
Alchemy, Sex and
Transcendence

Sublimation And Transcendence -- Sublimation And Transmutation Trans-mutation: Sublimation At The Level Of The Soul -- Transmutation, The Release Of Energy - Alchemical And Psychological -- The Dark Forces At Work Through False Teachers -- The Forces Of Darkness And Light Seen Through Theosophical Literature -- Dark Forces In Action In Our Daily Lives -- Using Past Life Memories -- Creating Harmonious Balance -- Sexual Flow, Harmony, And The Gate To Spiritual Peace -- Working With Sexual Energy To Embrace The Divine -- Honoring The Body And Sexuality.

Sublimation and Transcendence

Sex and transcendence often run parallel to each other, passionately opening up people to their greater fulfillment. We have seen this dynamic in action in the stories of many patients who found permission, through transference, to feel strongly and to allow their love emotions to flower. This achievement is often followed by a "bursting beyond the body" into higher planes, into levels on which we experience more refined feelings, more elevated concepts, a greater aesthetic appreciation, and a more altruistic, expansive and inclusive spiritual love. In short, we find ourselves in God's kingdom.

I was initially trained as a Freudian psychoanalyst. A basic principle of psychoanalysis is to seek and find the inner talents, drives and resources of a human being, and then to liberate the individual from acquired fears and limitations. Once liberated, however, these strivings must be expressed in a way that is consistent with reality. Then both society and conscience can reward the individual for his talents and capacities. This is what Freud meant by sublimation, finding a socially constructive outlet for our instincts, strivings and needs, an outlet that genuinely contributes to the lives of those around us.

"Sublimation" really means refinement. This concept is derived from the idea of the chemical distillation of an element until it is pure: water into distilled water, crude oil into high octane, pig iron into steel, gold ore into gold.

Sublimation is allied to the most basic principles of life. Although

Freud first introduced the concept, his greatest student, Carl Jung, saw the limitations of his definition. Jung, who had studied the Eastern philosophies and journeyed into the higher realms, recognized that Freud's thought was too firmly anchored to the material and the literal. Take sexuality, for example. While sex is not a minor factor in our lives, Freud's view that the mind was run by instincts was too tied to the body, too limited. When Jung gave equal credence to the metaphysical aspects of sexuality, Freud felt that he had become too mystical.

One of Jung's most extensive areas of study lay in alchemy. To understand why he wrote about it so extensively, it is very important to understand what alchemy means in its truer sense. Jung was not interested in it as an activity that transmuted lead into gold, although this is now possible since the smashing of the atom, but as an endeavor that transmuted the baser portions of material human existence into higher human essence. This has always been the transmutation sought by the ancient masters. Jung states:

> "... when I began to understand alchemy, I realized that it represented the historical link with Gnosticism, and that a continuity therefore existed between past and present. Grounded in the natural philosophy of the Middle Ages, alchemy formed the bridge on the one hand into the past, to Gnosticism, and on the other into the future, to the modern psychology of the unconscious.
>
> "This had been inaugurated by Freud, who had introduced along with it the classical Gnostic motifs of sexuality and the wicked paternal authority, the motif of the Gnostic Yahweh and Creator-God reappeared in the Freudian myth of the primal father and the gloomy super-ego deriving from that father. In Freud's myth, he became a daemon who created a world of disappointments, illusions, and suffering. But the materialistic trend which had already come to light in the alchemist's preoccupation with the secrets of matter had the effect of obscuring for Freud that other essential aspect of Gnosticism: the primordial image of the spirit as another, higher god who gave to mankind the krater (mixing vessel), the vessel of spiritual transformation. The krater is a feminine principle which could find no place in Freud's patriarchal world."[1]

In the above statement we see Jung's perception of the krater as the principle of creation. When the spiritual essence from above infills the feminine principle below, the result is the material person. The natural complement to this process is the rising of the material essence to higher and higher levels that approach the spirit and finally the Universal All.

Sexuality as it is popularly experienced has been limited by our cultural myths about this universal human experience. Sexuality is much, much more than a meeting of bodies or a satisfaction of unique pleasures. Both our individual and societal neuroses have distorted the sexual act. The pendulum of community belief has swung from the over-restriction of Queen Victoria's Age to the modern-day overexcited worship of the sensual body - the voluptuous experience. As exaggerated masculine sexual prowess and feminine super-desireablity and glamour have become the cultural myth, what has been lost is the sweet, refined, high-toned harmony of love's union that comes to us more slowly, and in the larger context of personal and spiritual blending.

Just as a log provides the substrate for fire, transmuting the material into heat, a higher form of energy, so too can the material aspect of sexuality, passion, give rise to the higher levels of spiritual experience. The exercise of sexuality for pleasure alone keeps humankind attached to selfish and separatist pursuits. The joining of two in love begins the journey to the higher levels. There is wisdom in the Hippie admonition of the 1960's, "Make love, not war." War and love are incompatible. When the Divine Spirit is poured into the human vessel, it creates the drive for love and attraction. But if love is captured anchored and imprisoned in material expression alone, then we have no chance for the ascension of the human being. He/she remains caught in the physical body.

Sublimation and Transmutation

As many of the stories about transference that I have shared show, the tolerance of love's message, almost always accompanied by powerful sexual stirrings, can lead to a refinement, a sublimation, and a bursting beyond the body into broader and more altruistically serving realms. This process goes far beyond the individual to become a flowering, a mushrooming of light that can shower itself upon the planet and all of its inhabitants.

In the Eastern traditions as well as in Western religions, we are frequently advised to strive for celibacy. Although I believe that the instruction to celibacy has its wisdom, it can also be misapplied. Celibacy should not be imposed to the point where human needs are stifled and dispatched to the underground of the unconscious mind. If forced downward, these needs will persist there, continually making their claim, draining the life energies from a tortured soul or leaking out in destructive actions, such as the sexual abuse of children that is so prevalent today.

When we hear about the inappropriate sexual activities of priests, it gives us cause to wonder whether or not many of these acts are due to prematurely imposed celibacy upon the individuals who have this calling. The time to become celibate arrives only when one has fully experienced his/her desires, has tolerated them, and has allowed them to lose their value through replacement, or expansion into a higher form of satisfaction and creativity. Paula's sexual desire for her therapist naturally waned as she became occupied with higher pursuits--her spiritual reading, activities and service to the community. Vera transmuted the sexual desire she experienced in the transference into her work in the healing profession caring for hospice clients, and her desire to seek ordination as a minister.

Alexandra was also able to transmute her unfulfilled sexual need for Roy into something higher. Due to her high sensitivity, she was able to experience and received visits from Roy on the astral plane. At first the feelings these visits elicited were intensely sexual, reflected in erotic physical sensations and movements. As time went by, however, Alexandra's needs changed, to be replaced with highly satisfying intellectual and emotional exchanges with friends and students, shared interests, and mutual encouragement of her work and Roy's.

Transmutation: Sublimation at the Level of the Soul

In her book *From Intellect to Intuition*,[2] Alice Bailey describes transmutation.

Transmutation is a matter of change, but a change that is upward, the ascension toward, and at the behest of, the soul. It is the spiritual alchemy of the personality, the essence of any system of good psychotherapy, and an integral part of spiritual psychotherapy.

Over and over, the path of ascension is revealed by the teachings of the masters, both ancient and contemporary. The ancient biblical figures of Abraham, Moses, Jesus and the Apostles speak for themselves; but it is important to recognize and acknowledge those modern saints from the East, such as Muktananda, Yogananda, and Sai Baba, who have devoted their lives to the teaching of spiritual truth. Another great modern-day saint was Mother Theresa, who manifested her miracles of healing, and worked tirelessly to change society's attitudes toward the poor and the disenfranchised. At one time, Mother Theresa had no place to put her homeless, so she encouraged them to occupy tenements that were empty, and then fearlessly faced the law on their behalf; faced them down would be a better description, for she prevailed over the authorities. Elizabeth Kubler-Ross, in her turn, has led an unknowing medical establishment to the recognition of the awful loneliness of the dying patient. Almost single-handedly she has established a new specialty that focuses on dealing with the dying.

My colleagues and I witness miracles in our clinic, the Center for Mind/Body Wellness, every day. "Untreatable" pain is relieved when we exorcise the emotional trauma that the patient has been carrying. In one very dramatic case, a young volunteer fireman who was legally blind had his sight restored from 20/400 to 20/40, enabling him to realize a dream of his to attend college. Faith has its miracles, and they reside in the knowledge of the power of prayer and belief, as well as the surrender to a higher power and a higher mind.

The Fruits of the Path of Right Intention and Right Action

If we purify ourselves with good intentions and good acts, we will inevitably ascend, raising our personality and reaching for the light. If we "think good acts, we will act good acts." Such a pathway denotes lifting the baser instincts of desire to the refinement of love and service to others, in fact, to all. This pathway leads us to savor the ineffable and to taste the refined pleasures of the best works of humanity, such as those of Emerson, Whitman, Shakespeare, Beethoven and Mozart. To these we can add the works of the great female creators: Maria Callas, who single-handedly revolutionized the concept of theatrical performance in opera, Martha Graham, who was one of the inventors of modern dance. There are a host of others including the visionary painters Freida Khalo and Georgia O'Keefe; Nadia Boulanger, who not only composed extraordinary music, but instructed an entire generation of American and European twentieth century composers, including Aaron Copeland and Samuel Barber. We can remember, too, Doris Lessing and Edith Wharton, both literary giants of great subtlety, astute social penetration, and enduring human values.

The pathway of right intention and right action leads our attention from the physical, to the higher emotional plane, and even farther to the higher mental plane. All of these ascending planes are described in Theosophy. Happily, as we absorb ourselves in higher efforts, we experience the subtle joys of love on an expanded level: bliss, serenity and peace. Concomitantly, we acquire greater powers of wisdom and intuition. Ultimately, we will achieve the miraculous powers of mind and soul, until we too can perform the miracles of Moses, Jesus and the Eastern adepts. Christ himself foreshadowed the development of these abilities when he said to his apostles, "Greater miracles than this shall you perform in my name."

Even today we witness the miraculous cures of cancer through visualization; the wonder of fire-walking, commonly achieved today in workshops all over the country; and the growing proof of our immortality as many individuals have come forward to share their near-death-experiences.

Trasmutation, The Release of Energy - Alchemical & Psychological Obstacles to the Transmutation of the Soul

When we engage in psychodynamic psychotherapy, the therapy that recognizes the importance of the unconscious mind, we must work from within rather than from without. In this regard, the spiritual psychotherapist is guided by the inherent wisdom of the patient about his/her needs and difficulties. I have found that the best way to release an individual's inner potential is by finding and releasing his/her inherent energies in a self-induced way so that these energies can be free to rise from within. In this way, the personality can lift *itself* authentically to higher levels of spirituality, achievement and service. The energy released automatically expands to be of service to the general good, and rises to meet the Heavenly Creator.

It is well to remember, however, that Dark Forces exist that are always on the alert to obstruct this spreading of the light. They are represented by those who would prey upon people, using them for their own selfish aims. They operate externally by bringing outside pressures to bear upon the person, in contrast to the powers of light that rely upon an individual's inner wisdom to find expression. The Dark Forces produce containment rather than release. They present themselves as "the great authority" and seek to control through intimidation.

The Dark Forces at Work Through False Teachers

James was a young and highly idealistic individual who projected his idealism onto a false guru and became almost hypnotized by him. James was caught at the tender age of eighteen by this sham authority because he was seeking answers for some unusual experiences. In one, he'd been very frightened when he had experienced a powerful flow of energy that shot up his spine and came out of the top of his head. He also began to have visions. In all of the other areas of his life, James was well grounded and quite successful. He was popular, a good student, an excellent musician and a part of a well-known rock group.

When he began tentatively asking several people if they had ever had similar experiences, no one seemed to have any answers. Finally, a friend told him about an East Indian teacher, a guru, in a town that was some distance away. James sought this guru out and was accepted into his ashram and classes immediately.

James was very vulnerable at this point of his life. Because of this, he was captured by the false teachings of this guru, who drew his students in by instilling fear in them. James was taught that this "guru" was his only authority, and was intimidated into obeying all of his directives about meditation and spiritual practice on threat of ruining his entire chakra system. In this way, he was progressively robbed of his confidence in himself--when he could not fulfill the impossible expectations put upon him by this false teacher, he was made to feel that his failure was a sign of his continuing spiritual deficiency.

In despair, James took to alcohol and drugs. He ventured into the most hazardous of neighborhoods disdainful of the danger, for he had grown hopeless. All of these activities drained vital life energy from his internal self. His subservience to the false guru enabled his teacher to pull energy from him until he was virtually enslaved to his teacher's whims.

When James finally came to me for psychotherapy, his personal development had been arrested. It took us a considerable amount of time to wash out the psychological implants placed within him by his false teacher. For example, James had been taught that unless he meditated only in the way that the "guru" had instructed, with his eyes open, that his nervous system and chakras would be permanently harmed. Of course, no one can meditate like this, and his inevitable failure was followed by the despair and self-hatred that lead to his desperate adventures with drugs and alcohol.

When he entered therapy with me, I had to rely on my knowledge of the Eastern philosophies and instructions in order to win his confidence. I had to go slowly, for the young man still felt that he was in mortal (even worse, spiritual) danger if he disobeyed his former teachings. Over a period of time, however, and after several relapses into addiction on the part of the patient, I won his confidence enough to have him consider reviewing his experiences. One of the most telling blows delivered against his belief in his former mentor was the observation that this guru was so full of arrogance and self-congratulation. James finally came to understand that these characteristics stood in stark contrast to a person's level of evolution into spirituality.

Today, James is still in treatment with me, but has been restored to his very good family, and is working with his father in the family business. He attends his recovery from addiction with dedicated tenacity, and with equal intensity, his pursuit of his personal and spiritual development. The meeting with the false guru had corrupted this young man's initial spiritual emergence--turning him temporarily into a slave, and then into a force of self-destruction--but, fortunately, this story had a happy ending.

James' story is revealing of the fact that spiritual emergence is often misunderstood in our society, with tragic consequences. When people admit that they are having a spiritual emergence--an experience that might be accompanied by unusual and dramatic energy flows within the body, profound religious feelings of unity with the world, states of bliss, and even visions--these experiences are almost always misunderstood by psychiatrists. These individuals are often placed in an institution for "treatment," or forced to take anti-psychotic medications that smother the spiritual event. Needless to say, after such treatment an individual no longer seeks out these spiritual experiences, for they seem too dangerous.

James' spiritual emergence began when he had a transcendent experience of bliss, accompanied by a sense of light and energy emerging from chakra at the top of his head. Mystified and frightened, he went in search of answers and found, instead, the false guru. Not only did this "guru" arrest his spiritual development, but he put a distinct wrinkle into James' personality development during the important time of late adolescence. James had already become a celebrated musician, and was honored for his talent and his family background. All of this could have ended permanently with his suicidal forays into dangerous parts of the city in search of drugs.

The Forces of Darkness and Light Seen Through Theosophical Literature

The ensnaring of an individual through the agency of a false guru is one example of how the Dark Forces work upon humanity. We can also see examples of the dance between the forces of light and the forces of darkness in Theosophical literature. It is always important to acknowledge the presence of darkness, both in the personality of someone whom we meet and in the overarching forces that employ that person. Why is this important? The spiritually advanced are often naive and therefore easy prey for those who would take advantage of their innocence. It has been said that all that is needed for the triumph of evil is for good men to say and do nothing.

Alice Bailey and her Tibetan master talk about this dynamic in *A Treatise on Cosmic Fire*: ".... in the transmutation process the magician or alchemist works with the deva essence through the control of the lesser builders in cooperation with the greater Devas."

Therein she speaks of transmutation, and the different kinds of transmutation in the hands of the Brothers of Light and those of Darkness.[3]

In this quotation, the Deva essence represents the inner essence and power inherent within individuals and material substance. The magician represents the highly advanced being with extraordinary powers gained through study and ascendance.

Bailey goes on to speak of the distinction between transmutation in the hands of the Forces of Light as opposed to the Forces of Darkness. It is important to understand that when Bailey speaks here of electrical energy, she is referring to the fact that the Ancient Masters considered cosmic energy to be an electrical force--and so it may very well be. In fact, our modern experience of electricity is probably the material counterpart of a higher form of energy.

Bailey clearly points out the differences between how the Brothers of Light work and how the Forces of Darkness work. The Light strives to bring forth the inner rays, the inner forces, while the Dark seeks to constrict and shape material form to its own purpose. This becomes quite understandable when we remember that the essence of spiritual psychotherapy is to recognize the individual's soul potential and to release it from the "sheaths" of inhibition that surround it. These inhibitions represent the acquired restrictions that were placed upon the soul during childhood development.

On the other hand, the Forces of Darkness can always be recognized by their need to constrict and shape us according to their own patterns and uses. We often see this technique at work in the opportunistic and self-seeking entrepreneur who uses people to fulfill his or her own selfish purposes, rather than releasing the person to flower into his or her own talents and instincts.

The Dark Forces in Action

A highly successful financier, who was also a skilled and psychopathic opportunist, lured people into handing over their personal savings and their lives to him by promising them power, profit, and spiritual advancement. Working delicately and playing on these people's idealistic desires to help humanity, he promised to help them found a health center that would serve the community with advanced techniques in psychological care, using many of the discoveries of alternative medicine and humanistic and spiritual psychology.

Before long, this small group had become entirely dependent upon this man for financial support and the fulfillment of their ideals for the health center. Unfortunately, the center never developed as is should have, because its operation and profits were undermined by the greed for more and more money on the part of the entrepreneur. His selfish schemes were not unmasked until it was too late, because he was protected from public scrutiny and discovery by the honest facade presented by the idealistic staff. In the end, many who followed him were not only disappointed, but also disillusioned and deeply hurt, both personally and financially. Ultimately, the financier went to jail for his schemes, but nothing could make up for the time and opportunities lost in the lives of those who had believed in him.

In *The Key to Theosophy,* Madame Blavatsky[4] tells us of the wonders of our inner divinity, and how this becomes more and more manifest as we depart from pre-occupation with the physical body and the lower emotions.

"We assert that the divine spark in man being one and identical in its essence with the Universal Spirit, our 'spiritual Self' is practically omniscient, but that it cannot manifest its knowledge owing to the impediments of matter. Now the more these impediments are removed, in other words, the more the physical body is paralyzed, as to its own independent activity and consciousness, as in deep sleep or deep trance, or, again, in illness, the more fully can the inner Self manifest on this plane. This is our explanation of those truly wonderful phenomena of a higher order, in which undeniable intelligence and knowledge are exhibited."

This too fits in with the fact that the outer sheaths (the physical body, the lower emotions, the lower mind) surround the spiritual essence of the person, the divine spark, the Universal Spirit. The more the individual pursues the lower elements of self-importance, self-fulfilling power, selfish acquisition of property and selfish addiction to lustful states, the more these sheaths hypertrophy and enclose the spirit.

On the other hand, if the inner fire, the call of the soul, the lure of psychotherapy are allowed to invite the inner essence to express itself authentically, then these addictions to personal power and sensate experience are resolved in favor of the rising of love for service, humanity and nature in general.

It is interesting to note that the inhibiting "sheaths" are related to the physical body and the intellect: When allowed to "run the show," so to speak, the intellect is capable of all sorts of rationalization and self-deception. When put to sleep or into a deep trance, however, the intellect allows the inner essence of great knowledge to arise. This is consistent with the fact that the cortex of the brain is an inhibitory apparatus. When its activity is suspended, greater intuitive knowledge is allowed to enter into consciousness. It is also true that the inhibitory function of the cortex is a necessary function in life, otherwise we would constantly be flooded with useless information. We need only look at the example of the idiot savant to see how overwhelming this would be. Although of limited mental capacity, the savant has access to a very narrow band of unlimited information that allows him or her to recite the weather report on any given day for the past hundred years, or to tell you what date the first Tuesday in November fell on for the last thousand years, automatically making adjustments for the switch to the Gregorian calendar. Whereas this is indeed an extraordinary mental feat, it is of no use whatsoever in the real world, because it is completely unconnected to any other type of practical knowledge or insight.

Psychological Alchemy and the Philosopher's Stone

In her book *A Treatise on Cosmic Fire* Alice speaks of "Alchemy."[5]

The scientific understanding of alchemy has clearly been distorted from a higher meaning to a literal one. This viewpoint is consonant with our modern materialistic way of looking at things. Plato and other high teachers of the Greek era understood alchemy differently, as the symbolic process that brought about the trading of the dross of personality for the refined and precious advance toward the soul. This transmutation of personality has been known, through the centuries, as initiation.

In *The Holographic Universe*[6] Michael Talbot describes the alchemical process in a way that helps us to make sense of the transformations that occur both in the subtle and visible realms. He suggests that the "retreat into the implicate essence, which is the seat of the holographic pattern" is the real source of creativity. Remember the holographic plate that was made up of squiggles that could only take form in the explicate realm when light was shown through the plate. When we are able to retreat into this implicate essence, the very real things that we bring forth into the light of day form the basis for transmutation and alchemy. That is why the highly evolved Indian Guru Sai Baba is able to materialize dust and jewels from thin air. He has gained access to the implicate essence to such a degree that he is able to create not only transformations of emotions, insights, and personality, but also material objects. While this ability may seem astonishing to us, it is well to remember that Moses and Jesus were also able to accomplish such miracles. Madame Blavatsky could perform miracles as well, but she was largely disinterested in them. She used them only to demonstrate that these achievements came from a better understanding of the laws of nature, which was a natural consequence of study and personal ascension.

Nowadays respected researchers and scientists at major universities are investigating the seeming miracles of psychokinesis, remote viewing, and accurate medical diagnosis by those who are psychically sensitive. What unrevealed miracles lie ahead for us to discover, and in fact grow into.

I believe that our ability to access the implicate order is something that we are doing all the time. One example of this process can be seen in how the causal body stores up positive experiences and then reincarnates, creating another body. Thus it exercises its influence on the lower realms, according to the need of the individual soul for further evolution on the material plane and finally on the higher planes. In so doing the psychological needs of the soul are transmitted to the physical plane through accessing the implicate order.

This is a good time to review the process of our downward journey from God and the Light. We descend from the highest planes, and traverse through levels of descending vibration and power till we arrive at the level of the soul, the causal body. Having stored learned experience from previous incarnations, the soul then creates a body to both continue the journey of knowledge, and to eventually return to God. The soul creates the physical to the physical.

This process of the soul gathering energies to itself continues throughout the incarnation. For this reason, I believe that the psychology we bear and create has its effects upon the body. Occupation carves its influences upon our personalities and our bodies so that cops look like cops, and psychiatrists look like psychiatrists. People who live together long enough even begin to resemble each other. We are never separated from the influence of the subtle bodies that created us, and continue to create us. We are the manifestations of our psychology, both past and present.

This signature that our souls place upon our physical manifestation is one of the reasons that I believe in past-lives. Freud showed that a neurotic symptom or present-day behavior was determined and maintained by repressed memories. I have applied the same rule to believing in my patient's' memories of past life experiences. If these events arise spontaneously as memories and if they are relevant because they explain some of the mysteries of the patients' present-day difficulties, then there is a scientific reason to think they are valid. Furthermore, it has been my experience that the exposure and resolution of these past life memories and neuroses creates a greater sense of freedom in the patient's life.

Using Past-life Memories in Therapy

Donna was a forty-year-old woman who had come to me for the treatment of anxiety and depression. She was full of frustrated sexual energy and a wild desire to dance. Under hypnosis, Donna remembered a past life in which a similar desire to move about and to dance had been crushed by an individual who, currently reincarnated as her mother, was now trying to control her behavior in this lifetime. Only when Donna's need to dance and her repressed sexuality were released by psychotherapy was she able to experience the fulfillment of these two very powerful qualities of her soul. Her body reflected her need. She was built with power and strength from the navel down, so that one could actually see the material expression of her sexuality, and her desire to dance, which only later in life found a way to express itself.

Tapping into the Implicate Order Through Visualization, Meditation, and Hypnosis

Hypnosis is not the only way that we can tap into the implicate order, informing and transforming our experience of reality. We can also use visualization and meditation to heal the body. In so doing we are tapping into an implicate primordial essence that allows us to recreate the body in a better form. Advanced cancers and other illness can be healed using these techniques.

As I've worked with Olympic figure skaters over the years, I have seen that asking them, while under hypnosis, to visualize a perfect performance dramatically improves the skating of even the most super-athletic and gifted.

In terms of the soul-body-mind transaction, this represents the alchemical process, psychologically mastered, and psychologically produced. We see this process more often than we might think in our daily lives. For example, because the mind creates the body anew, people who live together in love and devotion begin to resemble one another.

Sexuality

Because the mind creates the body, it is important that we not constrain the sexual instinct too early. By this I mean that we should not make people feel so guilty about their natural sexual feelings that they push them into the unconscious or into the back of the mind. It is as natural to have sexual feelings (at all ages) as it is to pump blood or to breathe air. In fact, sexuality is a natural part of the metabolism of the body, manufactured in the body's very cells. Our sexual nature is, at the same time, an expression of the descent of divine energy into our cells. This does not mean that one should become libertine. Indeed, any drive must be disciplined before it can be really enjoyed.

The expression of any basic human drive in a way that serves only the individual carries both the seeds of its own destruction and the destruction of others. The rampant sexuality of the past few decades has led to the destruction of many human relationships. The structured family loyalty that helped to form the heroic character that created the American democracy has been undermined. Purely self-serving sexuality has also destroyed the human body, the human spirit, and the human heart by stifling our natural and creative needs.

Creative needs may be expressed in many ways: procreation, art, surgery, building a business enterprise. If one is addicted to the pleasure of the loins or the taste buds, - so much pre-occupation will rob energy from the creative source. I believe that this is also expressed in our fascination with the youthful body, or the oh-so-macho theme of the movies. This is a substitute for what could otherwise develop as a higher form of art. The addiction to the pleasure of the loins degrades what would otherwise sublimate as higher forms of music, altruistic service, and poetry.

Creating Harmonious Balance

We seek the best in life by striving for a harmonious balance, avoiding the path of too much expression on the one hand and too much restriction on the other. At the Center for Mind/ Body Wellness, we strive to teach this sense of balance, flow and access to all parts of the personality: the needs and drives, the moral precepts, the desire to please spouse and family. We also teach balance in terms of leading the good life: a dedication to meaningful work that raises self-esteem balanced with a dedication to satisfy one's personal needs. In advocating this approach, we follow the philosophy of the ancient Greeks who instructed that the best path to follow was the path of moderation. This philosophy is also consistent with ancient Chinese wisdom. Chinese medicine advocates balance in all things--in the body, in life and in conjunction with nature. This is the secret to balancing the energies of Yin and Yang, which can be thought of as the masculine and feminine components within ourselves, and the masculine and feminine aspects of Nature's world.

How does one find balance? One of my teachers was a direct disciple of Freud. Some say he was a genius in his own right, and often his genius would express itself in pithy statements of truth. One day, in speaking of raising children, he said, "Too much discipline damages the instincts, too little damages the ego." By this he meant that too strict an upbringing damaged the free flow of desire and drive, and that too liberal an upbringing damaged the controlling part of the personality. I have often observed that the most miserable people are those who have been indulged too much in life. They can't find satisfaction in anything, for the more a desire is indulged without limitation or discipline, the more demanding and unfulfillable it becomes.

My teacher's aphorism applies to more than just raising children. It applies to our present culture and how we live life. To achieve balance we must recognize our needs and talents, and experience them--this is a matter of finding and following one's truth--but we must also do this in a context of limitation and discipline, finding pleasure and recreation, but also finding reward in constructive work that contributes to the life around us. To paraphrase my teacher: too much pleasure and indulgence brings jaded instincts; too little brings exhaustion and burnout.

Sexual Flow, Harmony, and the Gate to Spiritual Peace

Wilhelm Reich, a student of Freud, advocated many principles about human sexuality and human energy flow that are only now coming into recognition. When I was a young psychoanalytic student, I had been told that Reich was a brilliant man who in his early days had made impor- tant contributions to psychoanalysis, but then became "psychotic". A closer study of Reich's discoveries, however, indicated that he was far from mentally disturbed. He was actually an individual who was too far ahead of his time, swimming upstream against many popularly held views, such as looking at a patient to discover his/her emotional postures, and then working on them for release of emotions. He discovered that people hold themselves in, in body as well as emotion, and that the release of one leads to the release of the other. This has brought about the science of bioenergetics, which discovers that the mind is in the muscles as well as within the cortex. His biography, *A Fury on Earth*,[7] showed his fierce and penetrating inquiry into the nature of humanity and the nature of Nature itself. This resulted in discoveries such as the discovery of the "orgone," a packet of energy which exists in the atmosphere, and influences our general well- being or lack of it. In his own time, this discovery was thought to be a part of Reich's psychotic thinking, but now we can understand it as part of the universal energy which is known as prana by the Hindus, Chi by the Chi- nese, or electricity by the Theosophists.

He discovered the vortex-rotation of energy expressed in cloud for- mation. This counter-rotation is now visible as we study the geometry of the clouds as seen by satellite. He went further to discover how the orgones, which are related to this cloud energy could be attracted to water. Applying his theory, he was able to influence weather, to become a "rainmaker." This work is being carried on, with some success, by Dr. Richard Blasband and others in the Institute of Orgonomy.

Reich's basic thesis was that a free flow of energy was the sine qua non of a healthy life. He advocated full sexual expression in order to achieve this. But he was concerned with larger issues, not libertine freedom. His larger issue was that of relieving the individual, and indeed society, of the false blocks which prevented a free flow of personality, sexual expression, giving.

I don't agree that sexual release is the essential ingredient of health; but I do believe that an untrammeled energy flow is necessary for our health, harmony, active interest in life and essential happiness, and that sexual fulfillment, in union with love, is the highest expression of love's alliance in this material world. In this way, sexual energy can be a preamble to a yet higher movement of energy toward the higher bodies and a more elevated spiritual reach.

Eva Pierrokos, a student of Reichean Psychology and highly psychic in her own right, said:

"In reality there is essentially no difference between the ultimate, spiritual state of bliss and the human potential for it. Only the degree of intensity varies. Although no human being is capable of the depth of experience which is possible for unstructured highly developed consciousness, pleasure remains pleasure. Spiritual pleasure is not bodiless. Even unstructured consciousness is not formless; it creates the subtle bodies, which consist of streaming energy in purest form. This energy form is without obstruction. It is pleasure itself. The gross matter of the human body represents an obstruction that can be overcome only when the total personality attains harmony with the energy streamings of cosmic origin."[8]

Working with Sexual Energy to Embrace the Divine

A parallel philosophy has been recorded in a beautiful little book entitled *The Jew in the Lotus* by Rodger Kamenetz, which describes the dialogues between the Dalai Lama and six Jewish rabbis including the Hasidic rabbi, Zalman Shachter. The Dalai Lama originally invited these individuals to his headquarters in Dharamsala India, with the purpose of learning how the Jews had managed to maintain both identity and religion throughout the trials of their Diaspora. This subject was of great interest to him, for the Tibetans were enduring their own involuntary dispersion. Much of the exchange that took place during that visit was between him and Rabbi Schachter, an individual in whom the Dalai Lama took great delight because of the many similarities that he discovered between the teachings of Tibetan Buddhism and Hasidic Judaism. Describing these similarities, the author writes:

"As the Dalai Lama told us, the goal is clarity. The noise coming out of the sense organs has to be quieted, including the powerful sexual impulses. In the puritanical religions, this is done through suppression, denial, and hatred of the body. As D. H. Lawrence memorably, defined it religion is bad sex. The daring of Buddhist tantra is to work with the energy, rather than suppressing, denying, or opposing it...

"The whole issue of what to do with sexual energy, or how to accommodate it in religious contexts, goes to the core of life today. The highly moralistic and rigid approaches of some religious denominations to sexuality have led to schizophrenia and denial. In his discussions Zalman Schachter had touched on the Hasidic approach of the Baal Shem Tov and his doctrine of `strange thoughts' - namely, that even thoughts of lust come to the mind begging to be raised up. This is probably something Jimmy Swaggart never thought of. And reflecting on the Dalai Lama's explanation that the whole purpose of tantric meditation was to `actualize concentration,' I thought again of how distracting our culture's obsession with sexuality is, and how dealing effectively with such energy is crucial in having a spiritual life. (This was also true in the time of the Baal Shem Tov when in order to continue their studies, the best students had to put off marriage.) So I delighted to discover that in both kabbalah and tantra there are attempts to recognize the whole human being and all of our impulses, lovely and unlovely, body and soul."

He continues:

"We did not discuss in Dharamsala what might be called Jewish tantra. But, in an utterly different context - the marriage bed - Jewish mysticism also teaches certain techniques for raising sexual energy to celestial realms. The very first written description of Jewish meditation is found in a marriage manual, *The Holy Letter,* attributed to the kabalist Joseph Gikatilla.

"As described in Tabi Aryeh Kaplan's *Jewish Meditation,* the partners meditate throughout the sexual act, becoming `aware of the spark of the Divine in the pleasure itself and elevating it to its source.' According to a contemporary Hasidic description by Yitzhak Buxbaum in *Jewish Spiritual Practices,* the Zohar teaches that when man and woman in sex are both directed to the Divine presence (Shekinah), the Divine Presence rests on their bed ... [It is taught that] a man should make his house a Temple and his bedroom a Holy of Holies.'

"In Jewish mystical thought, then, there is a sacralization of the erotic and an eroticization of the sacred. But this mixture of the erotic and the holy, though very salient in kabbalah, is highly suppressed in mainstream Judaism." [9]

Being instructed by the wisdom of Pierrokos' beautiful passage, and the guidance offered to us at Dharamsala, we can understand that the journey for spiritual ascension is also a journey in sexual or pleasure ascension. This journey, however, must be one in which there is a meeting of the divine energy, the spiritual energy, God's love-energy, with the physical pleasures of the body. In this union love is never selfish. Instead, it becomes progressively less materially sensate and more and more other-conscious and of service to others in place of being used in service to the self.

This journey begins, however, with friendliness toward one's body and an acknowledgement of one's sensate needs and pleasures. It continues as a refinement as one elevates the personality into an effort to reach upward and join hands, Michelangelo-style, with the Divine Source.

There is a holiness to love's union, and an ambience that fills the room when a sexual marriage has reached its fulfillment. I remember a fifty-five-year-old woman, who had been forced into abstinence for many years by her husband's impotence. Resigning herself to this necessity, she had been living a life that was only partly fulfilled. After her husband died, and a suitable period of mourning had passed, she allowed herself to date and eventually remarried, this time to a man who was very much in love with her. Together they filled the marriage bed with passionate and loving communion. When anyone came into this woman's presence, they immediately sensed the aura that she carried, a spreading light that portrayed her fulfillment and the expanding energy of love's soulful message.

Honoring the Body and Sexuality

It seems to me that, in our culture, the sexual drive has been altogether slandered and misunderstood. If we are honest with ourselves, we must admit that sexuality is, after all, evidence of a number of things that are to be valued spiritually. First of all, Judaism and Christianity both speak of the body as the temple of the Holy Spirit; and, indeed, it is. This would imply that body is to be honored, not tortured--that it should be given its due in a holy, love-infilled, spiritual manner.

It is also true that the denial of the body and the sexual self keeps us anchored to the material. There is a vast difference between letting a desire drop away because its time has come, and forcing an instinct to be gone. The latter choice leads to a battlefield rather than to a gradual process of ascension. Too often people assume that, having subdued their enemy, "sex," that their enemy is gone; but, in truth, an unresolved instinct will go to live in the unconscious where it will pressure our conscious mind for expression until it has found an outlet. This is the foundation of the tortures of neuroses, and the denial of our self-expression and self-fulfillment. This is the source of many an unhappiness in misfit marriages.

Recognizing that the sexual drive is a part of our physical self, we should also recognize that it is the basic element from which the heat of love arises. It is to be enjoyed, but within limits, for any instinct must be limited in order to be enjoyed. It is to become refined by love's joining so that it can carry the two partners with it into the higher reaches of love's embrace, and beyond that, into surrounding spheres and planes of spiritual ascension. Sexual magnetism is an expression of a basic law, the law of attraction. This is the law that brings negative and positive together in balance. Its energy begets group-cohesion. It is related to the law of gravity and to the laws that keep our planets and the solar system in ordered and regulated proximity as gravity is balanced with the centrifugal forces of repulsion.

It is important to know that the Dark Forces can easily employ sex. Its spiritual essence can be distorted if it is poured into the deformed vessel of a neurotic, sadistic or selfish human being but this is not the essence of the law nor of the sexual drive itself. In other cases, the human vessel may become too easily expansive, leading to the dullness of sexual gluttony. This leads to an addiction that knows no limit in pursuing satisfaction. The craven individual (or society) will be pushed through a restless indulgence to seek one outlet after another after another. Such people are to be pitied, for only discipline and commitment to something higher can allow sex, hunger, possessiveness or the acquisition of power to be satisfied.

The Holy Marriage with Spirit

What about those who, for one reason or another, have no partner in life? Where is the love path to their ascension? I believe that, for these individuals, the course is mapped in several ways. One route might be masturbation; but while there is no physical harm in this outlet, there is an inherent emptiness about it, a lack of completion for mind and soul, a longing-remainder that is felt in the heart.

On the other hand, some who practice celibacy, such as the followers of some of the religions of the East and some Western priests and nuns, can reach soul-completion without a partner. While I believe that celibacy before its natural time can be harmful, it can also become part of a natural flow leading to a different kind of partnership. I believe that the nuns married to Jesus can be in a soul relationship with him, and that Mother Theresa is married to her followers in spiritual union. Anna Freud, the founder of child psychoanalysis, never married, but found spiritual love and satisfaction in the children she treated. When one restrains physical expression for a higher purpose, one can transcend the bonds of the body and allow one's sexual energies to flow into a higher realm of creativity. I wish to reiterate my belief that sexual energy is better disengaged when its time has come, when the body is satisfied enough to allow a flow upward into soul-creative realms. When, authentically, does this happen? When the body as well as the mind gives approval--when the body is no longer tortured to do so.

Sexuality ultimately can become refined into an ineffable bliss that soars into the upper strata, carrying with it the soul and spirit. For this to happen, however, one must break the bounds of the body. Satisfying sex for sex's sake only keeps the individual rooted, anchored to the material self. If the sexual instinct is allowed to be felt, and alloyed with the love that it carries; if it is properly restrained, while at the same time allowed satisfaction for its flow, then the time will come when the cravings of the body will be replaced by a movement beyond the body into an ascent to higher realms of bliss. This is the ultimate aim of ascension--to move from the material human to the soulful. The important principle is this: the balance lies between satisfying the needs of the body on the one hand, while on the other restricting these needs sufficiently to give shape and direction to the energy of Divine Essence. Once this has been accomplished, one's aim can be a balance and flow through the physical form to the higher bodies, and then on to the soul.

Alexandra illustrated this balance so well. At first, she expected to have a sexual relationship with Roy. When this didn't happen, however, she conquered her hurt pride and continued the relationship on to another level. Developing their soul connection through their correspondence and the times they spent together, she and Roy eventually began meeting in astral visits. These visits led to a sexual consummation that was so fine and loving; that it surpassed anything that Alexandra had experienced in marriage. In the higher realms colors are more beautiful, music is more exquisite, sex is more joyful, love is more complete.

Any energy must be limited before it can become useful, even enjoyable. And so it is with the law of attraction in general and the energy of sex. Much as the cocoon gives way to release the butterfly within, the day will come when the urgent sexual needs of the human being will drop off, giving way to a more beautiful creation. Then life's energy, the sexual energy, will soar into higher realms.

Guidelines and Exercises:

1. Examine yourself in reference to your sexual feelings and sexual life. Is there too much preoccupation with shame or fear? Is this an inappropriate inheritance from your childhood? Is it interfering with your freedom to give yourself? On the other hand, are you too driven by pre-occupation with unsatisfied sexual feelings? Remember, the union of sex and love is a great and creative harmony, leading to balance and sublimation to spiritual peace and togetherness.

2. Do you find that you have no partner, or do not wish for one? Practice raising your mind and sexual feelings to the level of creativity, to sublime areas of art, music, altruistic service, love of children - whatever is most satisfying to you.

3. Become aware of your naivete in regard to the presence of darkness within yourself and other people. Become aware as if witnessing it, and then do whatever you can to remain aware, to change your own personality upwards, and to become less naive about the darkness around you. In doing this you will not only protect yourself, but will teach, for we teach what we are.

4. Sensitize yourself to the presence of past life influences on your life NOW. Respect deja vu experiences, feelings of familiarity or repulsion with someone, that might not have a logical basis. Let these feelings help you manage your life and relationships.

5. Strive to create balance in your life. Acknowledge the darkness, such as temper, and raise it, sublimate it into tenacity, energy, courage. Alloy it with love so that it can become milder and more useful. Alloy your loving characteristics with the strength of the aggressive instinct, so that you can become protective, active with your partner, etc.

6. Cultivate a rich sexual-love life union. The greatest harmony in life is achieved when lovers unite in body and soul, though this can become refined over the years into a harmony that is on a yet more refined level. Even thoughts of lust beg to be raised up.

7. Remember that there is also sex in the astral realm. Thus there is a union of marriage with spirit, possible for those who have achieved the sublimation of bodily sex into a union with Spirit.

8. Honor the body - it is the temple wherein resides the soul. As such, do not torture it or profane it with too much denial, or too much indulgence.

9. Work with someone (whether spouse, deep friend, lover or

otherwise soul mate) who is compatible, who recognizes you, who affirms you, who can inspect you and see your hidden talents.

    10. Participate in an Enlightenment group.

CHAPTER VII:

The Flowering of the Tree of Life:
The Releasing of our Innate Capacities through Transference

Spiritual Psychology Seeks To Release The Individual To Full Potential Including The Release Of The Soul -- The Use Of Transference To Release Capacities -- Freud And Transference -- Full Flowering Through Transference -- "Short Courses" For Release Of Potential, Opportunities And Cautions.

Spiritual psychotherapy has the power to release the "life energy" of the patient, and to bring to a full flowering, the person's soul and self-potential. This bespeaks the difference between this therapeutic approach and the classical one. Spiritual psychotherapy allows for a fuller expression of the transference experience, and a recognition that transference is an expression of the patient's own latent capacities for love, service and creativity. In such a setting, the feelings that arise during transference are treated as more than a memory--as passions that belongs to the past--but as expressions of the patient's life-energy. These vital, powerful qualities express the strengths that have always been lying in wait in the patient, but under repression. By acknowledging the patient's love (or hate, when it occurs) the spiritual psychotherapist validates each person's vital capacity.

Too often in traditional practice, the transference energies are feared, and too quickly translated into neurosis. The fear that arises, however, in the presence of such devotion or anger from the patient may well be the therapist's own fear of the intensity of his or her love, anger, excitement or fear of life itself. To truly understand and facilitate the transference, the spiritual therapist must learn to build a tolerance for passion and, in the course of this tolerance, allow and acknowledge the fullness of the patient's living force. This greater freedom of expression is to be respected, and so is the nascent fear that the therapist may harbor.

Freud and the Transference

If we look at the history of psychoanalysis, we can see that psychiatrists often feared the power of the transference. Freud's mentor, Joseph Breuer, fled from the transference of his patient, Anna O. when she fell in love with him and invoked the jealousy of Breuer's wife. He turned the case over to Freud who was able to view the transference from a greater distance and to see it as an expression of the pent-up love longings of the patient rather than as something that he had created.

In spite of his courage in taking over the case of Anna O., and his genius in recognizing her love feelings for what they were, Freud's attitude toward transference had its limitations. Although he understood its dynamics, Freud was still a Victorian moralist who instinctively kept his distance from his patients. This attitude is not to be criticized; it was a part of the times. Unfortunately, however, his example is still followed by the present generation of analysts. Psychoanalysis in its most pristine purity still constrains the patient to the couch, and allows the analyst to remain hidden behind the so-called blank screen.

In contrast, I have learned that the patient always scrutinizes, always inwardly knows the therapist for what he or she really is. While it is true that patients do project their feelings and ideas onto the therapist, these projections are almost always grafted onto the reality of the therapist's actual personality. To relegate the patient's genuine love only to the realm of transference is to denigrate his or her innate power and love capacity. The same is true of aggressive feelings. These too may be inhibited by a too hasty interpretation instead of recognizing the reality of what the therapist may have done to invoke this hostility in the patient. Whether the transference feelings are positive or negative, the principle remains the same.

The Full Flowering of the Individual Through Transference

We can see these dynamics of transference at work in both Paula--the woman with environmental allergies and muscle spasms, who was raised so elegantly that she lived almost without feelings--and Vera, the individual who developed panic episodes when she witnessed the boy whose face was torn off. The allowance of their passionate love transference onto their therapists, and the acknowledgement that each therapist possessed real qualities, to which the patient was responsive, permitted a fuller flowering of the love capacities of both of these women. Of course, this did not legitimize any acting-out on the part of either therapist or patient, nor would it have excused any ethical transgressions. Instead, transference acknowledged in this honest way, within healthy boundaries, nurtured the fuller flowering of love by creating a series of steps toward its realization. First there was a feeling of near-intolerance of the emotion;

then each woman developed a tolerance of the love feelings; and, finally, there came an expansion beyond the body and the limitation of their previous orientations, into a higher realm. From this new plane both Paula and Vera could view themselves more realistically and, released from the passion of the transference, enter an infinitely larger and higher place. Within this high realm there is a serene and quiet joy, a bliss, an expanding love of humankind, an appreciation of aesthetic things and an altruistic embracing of our planet and all its creations.

Naturally any therapist must be careful to avoid becoming the victim of his/her own narcissism. One must avoid believing that the love feelings of the patient belong exclusively to him or her. They are to be recognized for what they are: outflowings from within after the restrictions of both training and repression are loosened. In this connection, I once more recall Muktananda's wise response when I was mystified by my love for him. He told me that this love was my own love capacity. Not only love longings are to be tolerated to the point of breakthrough, but other strong emotions as well. Tolerance is always followed by breakthrough into higher realms. Listen to what Paula wrote to me:

"I praise you, I praise you, I praise you and thank you for your continual persistence and adherence to practicing the knowledge contained within your psychiatric principles intertwined with the intuitive Spiritual Wisdom of your inner self. I left your office yesterday, not shattered completely as I was last week, but feeling somewhat rejected, separated, lonely and hurt. To me the opposite of that, the duality of those feelings, was depression, accompanied by a certain closed-down 'posture' that my body, my personality assumed. Last week I could not attend the Science of Mind class and the spiritual love contained within it ... I somehow had to go along with feelings that were shattered to the fullest. This week, my feelings of rejection felt `old' -- the same old redundant `story.' I was tired of them. I was tired of what I thought I 'had' to feel -- either desolate or depressed. My feelings of isolation are so old that I cannot remember when they did not exist. They may actually date back to other lives, other incarnations. Dealing with them may also be the reason that my soul came to earth this time -- to learn about love via the limitations of the physical body.

"You mentioned that my feelings of a clinging love dated back to the age of one to one-and-one-half years--to another baby-clinging relationship--to a baby who did not want to be separated from its mother. At age one my sister was born. During a transpersonal breathwork workshop,

I discovered that I had wanted to kill this new baby. At that moment, the feelings of my one-year-old inner baby were brought to the surface, to a real awareness. I was horrified that I had wanted to kill, but at the birth of my sister, I no longer had the undivided love of my mother. I felt separate and rejected--desolate. I assumed a defensive `posture.' I did not realize that there were options. There seemed to be no alternatives. But finally the teachings of A Course in Miracles have begun to sink in: I do have a choice. I can choose to feel any way that I wish. I can choose `love' or I can choose fear.

"Your wisdom imparts to me that you want me to be free of the clinging, dependent side of the love I have for you. You want me to find love in other places, other people. It dawned on me that you wanted me to be that freestanding, well-nourished, tree, whose roots and branches intertwined with others in the forest of those who connect with love.

"When you told me the story of Muktananda, I applied `That love is your love' to my own situation. The `L' becomes capitalized -- the Love of God. Using you as a vehicle has helped me to deepen, expand and transcend until I experienced Divine Love. Knowing that love is within me is what produces the freestanding tree, not the finding of love outside of myself. I cannot seek love in others, but I can associate with others in the spirit of love.

"The trees in the forest on this earthly plane are visually separate, but the trees in the heavenly forest are not. In essence, I feel no separation from you. I feel that there is only one tree, one soul, one God. Two souls have become one--all are part of the Divine Life, the Divine Soul, transcending to being at One with God."

I can find no greater wisdom in any of the ancient wisdoms or philosophies than in what is expressed here by Paula. In spite of this, I believe that the beauty and talent shown by her words is not unique to this patient; rather, these things have been liberated from her--given access by her openness to the higher mind within her and the higher mind that surrounds us all. This is the more gratifying when we realize that she was a woman who had walked through life for fifty-eight years as an automaton, shut off from reality and from her feelings.

Both Vera and Paula have risen above the goals of "love and work" described by Freud. Both women have become capable of fulfilling their responsibilities to themselves, their families and their fellow human beings, and fulfilling them well. Their work has expanded beyond ordinary work, and their love has expanded beyond the ability to love only a marriage partner. At the same time, not one jot of feeling has been taken away from their spouses. With the help of their treatment, their loyalty and tenderness toward their husbands has been enlarged, just as their feelings for all humankind have been.

The down-to-earth descriptions of their experiences testify to the fact that these two women have bridged the gap between this earthly plane and the high spiritual realm. Their experience, understanding and activities remain practical rather than symbolical or archetypal. The proof of this can be seen in how both women have dedicated their lives to service to their fellow beings in the most devoted of ways.

The Quick, Short Route

Many "fast-help" psychological groups are forming nowadays, and these seem to be highly successful in attracting clients. Although my experiences have taught me that these groups are capable of doing much good--challenging and opening people as they push them through their constricting anxieties--I still have some reservations about the ultimate depth of the "quick-fix" approach. In one sense the presence on the scene of such groups is welcome, a measure of the changes our society is undergoing toward recognizing the all-importance of the mind and of psychology. In this sense, these self-help groups represent a kind of rising of the mind in society. But their lack of a deeper approach strongly limits what they can accomplish and bring forth in their participants in the way of growth.

I attended a seminar once called "Educational Enlightenment," which was followed by another, yet more advanced course. Both of these seminars greatly helped me to reach some hidden feelings that I had been carrying around inside of me, and I deeply admired the workshop leader who had helped me. Later, however, when I took a third course, I discovered, to my great disappointment, that all of the leaders seemed alike, as if created by the same cookie cutter.

This discovery was confirmed when I invited my much-admired teacher to dinner. I said to her, "I know that you are happy, very happy, with what you are doing. Yet there might be something unsatisfied. If you could have one wish, what would you wish for?" She said, "I would wish that the President of the United States would do the course." I followed with, "If you had yet another wish?" She replied, "I would wish that everybody in the United States would do the program." When I continued, "And yet a third wish?" her reply was, "That everybody in the world would take the course."

While this may sound like dedication and altruism (for the course is quite proud of its spiritual and altruistic orientation) it ultimately impressed me as an indication of the inadvertent narrow-mindedness that this program had fostered in my most admired and talented friend. Although her idealism was indeed expressed through the seminar, I also learned of the limitations that associating her entire energy with the "program" imposed. From my point of view, her training had caused her to become "one of them," without a full knowledge of herself, for she seemed to have been poured from a mold rather than enabled to emerge from within. Observing others in the Educational Enlightenment Program and similar fast-help groups has reinforced my opinion. It is as if the teachers apply a trademark brand to personal development, as if "one-size-fits-all." This is different from individualizing and customizing one's inner progress toward self-knowledge through a deeper wisdom that leads to authenticity and soul-honesty, inside and out. It is all the more dangerous when this lack of a deeper understanding extends to the teacher. If he or she lacks the tools for a deeper understanding of the self, surely that will lead to a failure to understand others. This deeper understanding of the self is necessary for the enlargement and growth of the personality, and for soul ascension. A limitation of this kind within the teacher is all the more to be mourned for we teach what we are.

This cookie-cutter constriction defines the lack of sufficient goal, a lack of deep understanding and a lack of depth-release. I believe that this soul-release is only achievable when combined with a profound understanding of another human being and a liberating deliverance. Within everyone there is a driving force to become authentic. When this authenticity is achieved, there is always a rising to a more divine self.

Both Paula and Vera have certainly risen to undreamed of heights of fulfillment in both their personal lives and their work. Paula has gone on to express herself more and more artistically, in the field of spiritual inquiry, and in volunteering her efforts to support spiritually oriented groups. She is an elegant lady, well spoken and increasingly coming into her leadership. Her former environmental allergy has given way to a spiritual and intuitive sensitivity. She had always had an exquisite awareness of touch--she could quickly recognize the difference between one type of leather and another--and a sensitivity to art and to the aesthetics of a fine table. This type of discriminating awareness has now been released to rise to more elevated realms--of the soul, the astral body, and the spiritual heaven of God's love. This release is easily recognized in her writings.

As for Vera, she continues to authentically fulfill herself as an exemplary wife and mother. Through therapy, her husband has become freer, but his is not yet fully realized, although he continues to grow and change. Vera has gone on to become a hospice worker, helping the dying to achieve an acceptance of their deaths as well as a vision of higher realms. Although she is more religiously devout than ever, she has also become more independent-minded as far as religion is concerned. Since the Catholic church does not allow women to become priests, she is now training for ordination in another religious denomination.

In summary, we can see that such joyous and quiet bliss-experiences expand into realms beyond the physical body, and that they are much like the experiences of ecstatic mystics, saints, and other holy people. Such experiences are ready and available to all of us.

The highly poetic writings of these two patients indicate the release of their capacities, as well as their contact with the more elevated levels of mind that become receptive to transmissions from On-High. May we help others to find such realization.

Guidelines and Exercises:

1. Train yourself to be on the lookout for overstated loves and hates. Use them to know yourself better, by knowing they indicate past experiences, but also needs, such as love needs. Then release yourself appropriately so that you grow, and so do those with whom you transact.

2. Find the "short course" institutions, such as Landmark Education, Silva Mind Control, and others, and use them. But be aware, that they have limitations. Get what you can, but keep your independence.

CHAPTER VIII:

Witnessing

Three Important Principles In Insight -- The Witness, The Self-Observing Self, The Out-Of Body Self, The Soul-Infused Self -- Attention, The "Vivifying" Element -- Detachment -- Surrender -- The Soul Is Too Big For The Body -- Employing Tolerance -- Case History Showing Rewards Of Surrender -- Meditation, Hypnosis As Related To The Witness -- Hypnosis And The Feeling Of Falling As Related To Surrender -- Falling In Meditation And Lucid Dreaming -- Some Authorities Speak About The Witness.

There are three important principles at work in insight-producing dynamic psychotherapy: tolerance, detachment, and surrender. Spiritual ascension and the growth and expansion of the personality are the natural results when these rules are followed. An individual's progress along this path can be seen by the shedding of selfish aims, and the increasing love for others accompanied by joy in service.

Detachment, Tolerance, Surrender and the Witness

Detachment, tolerance, and surrender are all related and continuous processes along the road to becoming a fully realized human being. To understand this journey, however, we must take each of these qualities and closely examine them.

The Witness

The Witness is the self that observes, the out-of-body self, the soul infused by the Holy Spirit, the divine quality that distinguishes us from the animals. To make contact with the Witness, we must detach from our fears, anxieties and daily distractions, surrender to our higher Self by entering a state of mind akin to meditation, and then go with the flow of whatever comes to us in this state.

In meditation the mind is stilled. Only when one is removed from the preoccupation with bodily and material distractions, can the Witness appear. When I meditate, I often find myself initially occupied with physical and material concerns. I may be preoccupied with the latest session with a patient, a lecture that I will be giving that night or little physical aches and pains that seem to hem me in. As the meditation deepens these kinds of fixations are softened, and I am released to enter into quietude. Once I reach this point, however, I may again have feelings that disturb me. These feelings must be tolerated rather than combated; and, when one learns to do this successfully, they claim us less and less. Quietude and mind-still follows--a pleasant emptiness that is almost blissful. In this receptive state, one experiences an openness to wisdom from higher sources, and inspirations come in easily. This state of mind must not be sought actively or commanded, however; that would be coming at meditation from the ego and would be counterproductive. Inspiration arrives in its own time, and we are guided by the injunction to remain open, with no expectations. The revelations that follow can be thrilling, but they can also be veiled, surrounded by a curtain of doubt. When knowledge does come to us, however, it is critical that we resist thoughts such as, "This isn't significant," or "This has been said before." I find that it is important to make a record of the messages we receive in the meditative state as soon as possible; otherwise they may go the way of the dream, into forgetfulness.

Here is a meditation that taught me that the spiritual path is paved with surrender. By surrender I mean "going with the flow" of divine guidance, events and obligations in a sedate, detached, yet joyous manner:

In my meditation, I was thinking about some new opportunities that were presenting themselves in my practice and the fact that undertaking them would not give me much time to read and study, and get on with my spiritual path. Thinking of these things, I felt anxious, but realized just as quickly that I was in a controlling mood, and that my anxiety was based on my trying to control things. I saw that the best path for me to take was the one that would allow me to surrender, to go with the flow. If I did that, that would mean choosing to go with the new opportunities, but in a different mood. If my plans matured, I might make money, but I would also be disseminating knowledge of what it meant to live as a better human being, both within and without. I would be able to teach others valuable tools for spiritual growth, such as how to break into infinity, enter mind-still, and travel on other planes. I would have the opportunity to share with others how to live fully in the moment in joyous surrender. This insight from my meditation followed me for the rest of the day, and when I thought about it, I tried to control my life less and allow more.

During another meditation I learned something valuable about how to approach meditation. I came to know that "I wanted," and that this disturbed the peace of my meditation. I "wanted" a better meditation. I wanted to get to the place of blank-mind. I wanted to get to the high planes of knowing-beyond-knowing. But then I realized that wanting these things was the same as controlling the meditation--and I let these feelings go. It is hard to let go; yet this is the essence of a good meditation. In finally understanding this I became peaceful. Throughout the day, I remembered what I'd learned, and when I felt anxious or too excited, I remembered to let go. It was not easy, but each time I succeeded, I built psychological muscle. I am in training to surrender to life.

Attention

I believe that our attention to things is what maintains their "aliveness." This is true not only of the various components of the personality but of the bodies that surround our material self. When we remove our energy of attention from something, its mental representations dissolve from our consciousness. This is what happens in meditation. As meditation progresses, our physical body disappears along with the emotional turmoil that exists in the emotional body. The demands of the physical body--hunger, itching, noisy distractions, emotional heat--all become less inviting and, therefore, less powerful. The final result is that we are in a state of quietude and receptivity to a higher wisdom that comes from the higher planes and is transmitted through the soul.

Detachment

Detachment describes the removal of our attention, not forcefully, but gradually, gently and naturally. It is not indifference, but a standing apart, as if one is a viewer from a higher place looking down upon a scene. In this way, one can experience self-observation and a distant, more objective view of people and events. Detachment is not a state of "not caring," but rather a lack of involvement with feelings that lead to assessment, a kind of objectivity. When we are in a detached state, we are not swept under or carried away by feelings, losing a necessary sense of proportion. This was the state I experienced on the first day of medical school when I had to remove myself (mentally) from the room in order to be able to make the first cut in the cadaver. It is also the state of "witnessing," a point of view that we want to encourage in our patients when we ask them to "analyze" themselves.

Detachment is related to tolerance because by accepting what we fear, we detach from it -- progressively. At the same time, the more we learn to detach from things, the more we can tolerate. Detachment gives us that sensation of being above a situation and looking down on it, the same kind of awareness that characterizes out-of-body experience. It indicates that the angel within the self has arisen, allowing the entry of a greater wisdom into our lives, and putting us in touch with the soul as we leave our body's environment.

Surrender

Detachment and tolerance require a concomitant attitude of surrender. This can be described as an attitude of "not-expecting," a readiness to accept whatever comes along, be it emotional pain, excitement or anxiety. When surrender, tolerance and detachment lead us to this readiness, a new wisdom descends, opening us to the Witness, and through the Witness to the Whole.

The Soul is Too Big for the Body

Because this dimension of the soul is so overwhelming, our body/mind has erected defenses against the experience. In daily life, distractions creep in whose main purpose is to keep us from connecting with our soul. Normally, we avoid any kind of stimulation that would increase our feelings. We also use physical activity as both a distraction and an attempt to discharge energies that might be leading us soulward.

Employing Tolerance

In contrast to Society's usual advice for dealing with overstimulation--essentially, by avoiding it--at the Center for Mind/Body Wellness we teach our patients to face their fears and to abide them. When this happens, the pressure of these fears actually becomes less, and the expected explosion does not occur. Consequently, the power of the fear dissipates.

Once we have broken into the quiet of the higher mind, we find ourselves in a superconscious realm, denoted by a feeling of quiet joy, bliss and peace. Entering into this realm, one comes into increasingly higher states of mind, eventually approaching a place of "knowing beyond knowing."

I have had many "knowing beyond knowing" experiences while meditating. During one such meditation, I experienced a loss of feeling in my body and a progressive movement upward of the energy toward my crown chakra. By the end of the meditation, I had a wonderful near-psychedelic feeling in my head accompanied by a realization. I now understood that the Devachan (heavenly plane) was an area of bliss on which all one's dreams come true; but I simultaneously knew that these were "dreams about a dream" because life on this planet, in its limited sense, was a dream. Embedded within this psychedelic feeling was a realization that beyond the Devachan there is a further realm of knowing even beyond dreaming. The dream, or what is called by the Eastern masters the world of illusion, represents the limitation of our intellect. The knowing beyond knowing we experience during meditation senses something more, and in this sensing there is a different and better type of perception, one that can move beyond our present limitation. And why should this not be so? Through meditation, we often transcend our subtle intellectual arrogance.

Another insight into deeper knowledge came to me as a reflection while I was reading. For me, really informative and gripping reading has always been a kind of meditative experience. The passage in question was one by Aurobindo in which he speaks of the "Gnostic Soul"--the soul that knows, explores and identifies with a higher mind than the one that is familiar to us clothed in our intellect. He then went on to describe a yet higher realm, a higher soul known as the bliss-soul. He describes this in his book *Synthesis of Yoga*:

"In its infinite consciousness, the gnostic soul creates a sort of voluntary limitation for its own wisdom-purposes; it has even its particular luminous aura of being in which it moves, although beyond that it enters into all things, and identifies itself with all being and all existences. In the Ananda all is reversed, the center disappears. In the bliss nature there is no center, nor a voluntary or imposed circumference, but all is, all are one equal being, one identical spirit. The bliss soul feels itself everywhere; it has no mansion, it is _aniketa,_ or has the All for its mansion, or, if it likes, it has all things for its many mansions open to each other for ever. All other selves are entirely its own selves, in action as well as in essence. The joy of contact in diverse oneness becomes altogether the joy of absolute identity in innumerable oneness.... In this absolute truth of its being the eternal soul of Ananda lives, here deformed by contrary phenomena, there brought back and transfigured into their reality."[10]

Undoubtedly Aurobindo can teach us these things because he has visited and lingered in these realms. We can understand, however, that the journey upward is for all of us. It begins with our material selves, longings and fixations. We then travel upward in our material bodies, including our brain, until we exist in the realm of higher thoughts, devotions and feelings, the land of aestheticism and altruism. In this manner we occupy the higher astral body that surrounds us, and the higher mental body that surrounds the astral. From here we move onward in our journey to realms of quietude in which we sense that there is more to know, that we do know more than we think we do. This is the realm that I call "knowing beyond knowing" and that Aurobindo calls the Gnostic Soul. And yet there is something even beyond that, as he has so clearly indicated, for insofar as we know, and know that we know, we are in fact limiting this expansive feeling of being ecstatically joined with the All. When we can surrender that final limitation, we participate in the ecstasy of joining.

This journey to the upper realm is not achieved all at once. It is really a matter of stepping upward and then stepping back, and stepping upward yet again higher and then back, developing the ability to sustain the higher for longer and longer periods of time. As we do so, we get flashes of yet higher realms.

Sam, a twenty-six-year-old physician who was so emotionally reserved that he couldn't get close to his fiancé, let alone his therapist, illustrates this process. One day during therapy, however, his resistance melted away and he experienced an emotional high. He felt a sense of deep closeness to me and a oneness with everything around him. Reveling in this state of Ananda-bliss, he began to laugh ecstatically, enjoying the moment. This experience did not last for long, and did not occur again for a while, but this was his first delicious taste of connection with the realm of the bliss-soul--an experience that left him hungry for more.

I have seen this breakthrough into Ananda in a number of people. It may last only briefly, but it creates a map, a vision, of the territory that can be inhabited more and more in the future as the work of ascension is done. Some people describe it as the light that burns over everything. They tell me of becoming one with the leaves, as they join with the wind, the sun, and the All. I have also heard similar descriptions of bliss in my patients who have returned from a near-death experience. All speak of the indescribable bliss that accompanies such realization. And then it all disappears.

This is the absolute truth of "the eternal soul of Ananda." When we must return to ordinary life and ordinary material representation, this experience is always deformed by the "contrary phenomena" that we must face and the resistances that enclose the bliss-soul.

Vera and Dan: The Rewards of Surrender

When Vera and Dan attended conjoint therapy sessions in my office to try and save their marriage, the most important lesson they both learned was how to surrender. Early in the sessions, Dan had suggested that they try again to make their marriage work. I objected, saying that such a solution was premature -- it would be better to surrender to whatever truth would emerge. At that time they courageously agreed, open-mindedly resigning themselves to whatever came out as truth as their communications became absolutely honest.

As Vera and Dan followed this principle of surrender to the truth, they experienced an inevitable contact with their own soul-essence, as well as with the essence of each other. This is love in a better sense--the love of truth and of the divine essence that is found both in ourselves and in the other.

Meditation, Hypnosis as Related to the Witness

As the highest portion of the personality, the Witness hovers over the scene observing, guiding and critiquing. It absorbs into itself our endeavors and experiences as we course through each lifetime on our road of ascendance. In everyday life, it is the self-observing faculty.

Meditation, hypnosis, and true prayer are all portions of the same whole. They ally themselves to higher consciousness, helping to free us from the fixations and constrictions of the material-physical brain, helping us to enter higher realms. We actually experience types of light hypnosis and meditation all through the day during times when we are completely and happily absorbed in activities such as reading or staring into space and thinking, or so focused on a loved one that all else is excluded from our mind. These types of experiences happen frequently during our lives. If we can acknowledge this, then we can enter more consciously and frequently into these higher places.

A great deal has been taught about meditation throughout the centuries. Meditation is certainly the road to ever-deepening self-discovery. I believe that meditation becomes simpler to achieve and more available to us if we link it with life as we live it every day, and with a better understanding of both mind and personality.

Meditation means going inward and achieving a state of "mind-still." When we surrender to mind-still, we stop trying so hard, learning to expect the unexpected and suspend our doubts. Meditation is helped by letting the self flow past resistance and distraction. It is deepened and increased when we resist doubt. The products of meditation are often receptions from On-High, and they can be kept conscious by removing uncertainty. Doubt will often say, "This wonderful insight you have received is only your imagination," but we must not succumb to this belief. It is important for us to see doubt for what it is, an attempt to repress newly arrived information. In this way we lift the veil of repression that tries to hinder growth and change in our lives. It is not surprising that our minds use doubt to block out our new insights, because true growth and change are often difficult. It often means giving up old comfortable patterns and journeying into new potentials and possibilities that challenge our entire being.

Alice Bailey in her book *From Intellect to Intuition*[11] speaks of the reception of inspired messages from on high, through the intuition which is opened by meditation.

Hypnosis and Falling as Related to Surrender

Wilhelm Reich once said that the sensation of fear is often accompanied by a feeling of falling. This could be described as a kind of helpless feeling, but it is also a kind of surrender. We experience surrender when we fall in love--or fall for a lie. The sensation of falling is often felt in meditation, as we allow ourselves to surrender. We become a part of the flow, turning ourselves over to a higher order of things, becoming receptive. This is a way of letting go of the ego.

The process of surrender can be seen in the work of my colleague Rena, a therapist with a lot of healing power. Rena was treating a patient who had a distressing physical problem. On one occasion while they were talking together, she allowed herself a moment of silent meditation in which to form an envelope containing the two of them and excluding everything else. While this was not specifically a "falling" on her part, the inner experience was the same. Rena allowed herself to enter into a new realm, as if she were falling into the depths of herself and of him. The envelope was formed within those inner depths, creating an exchange of energy and a tube of connection between the two of them. This sort of surrender to our essential oneness happen quite often in psychotherapy.

Rena was also psychically gifted in interpreting her patients' art. When she examined their drawings, she would sometimes get frightened and not be able to see anything. Upon surrendering, she would get an intuitive flash about what was being expressed, always on target and always highly insightful. The frightened feeling was due to her ego and its fear that she would not be able to accomplish her task. Once she surrendered her ego, opening to higher realms, she would receive her message in the form of the intuitive flash. This happens to all of us as we surrender to a higher power.

When I conduct a hypnosis session, I always allow myself to go into an altered state. I experience this first as a descent into myself, and then as a mutual falling and surrender. Hypnosis is very much facilitated when the hypnotist allows himself/herself to yield to a relaxed, almost helpless state of mind. In this way a corridor of open receptiveness forms between the therapist and the patient accompanied by an inflow of energy, through which extraordinary powers of the mind are called up.

Falling in Meditation and Lucid Dreaming

Lucid dreaming is a state in which a person becomes aware that he/she is dreaming, and can even take conscious control of the dream, directing its outcome or asking it to take the dreamer somewhere.

The state of surrender and the quietude that accompanies meditation is very much akin to lucid dreaming. In this state pictures and thoughts arise, and at the same time the meditator has a self-reflective realization of what is happening.

One day, while in a state of deep meditation, I saw myself comfortably lounging in the corner of the couch. In a moment I realized that this was a dream state, and that I was actually sitting in my meditation chair. In reality, I was hovering between the two states of consciousness, functioning with a "Janus-eye"--facing in two directions at once. This state is akin to lucid dreaming and defines the entry into the "second gate of attention" as described by Castaneda in *The Art of Dreaming*. This attitude of mind is achieved after one has trained oneself to remain alert in the dream state. I knew that I could use such a condition to understand myself and my dreams better. I also knew that if I could achieve such a state of mind in waking life, I would have more access to my intuitive and higher-knowing center.

Here is an example of the heightened knowing that occurs in lucid dreaming:

In a dream, I was in a small lobby titled the "Information Center of Scandia." The doorman appeared and wanted to wave me out. I said, "No, I belonged in that information center." I then knew the interpretation of the dream, that the gate was the gate through which most of humanity is ushered out. But I wanted to stay and be informed, as I always want to be informed in Krishna Consciousness, Spiritual Consciousness.

In another meditative episode I heard a voice directing me. This voice came not from my high self, but from something higher still, beyond even intuition somehow, a link to a guiding agency On-High. I had received both guidance from above and receptivity from within. For example, in a meditation, I was bothered by physical discomfort, a pain in my groin. Then I heard a voice say, "Suffering is present only on the physical plane. In higher realms there is no body, and no pain or suffering, only peace and quietude." Then I knew that if I would quiet myself, I would rise out of my body and out of my pain. I did!

The higher mind and higher self, along with the openness I had achieved during meditation, provided me with the opportunity to receive, and thus formed the channel. Eastern masters, including Aurobindo, Ramakrishna and Krishnamurti teach that "knowing" and "knowledge" denotes a very high state of consciousness. This is not to be confused with the emanations of the brain, but is something religious, spiritual and beyond humanity as we know it. They teach that each level of knowing and consciousness opens to yet another level. The achievement of each of these planes is an "initiation" of sorts. This is why they say that God is not limited to our ideas of perfection, but supersedes them. He/She is ever creative and creating; and we, in our union with God, in our essential Divinity, are also ever creative and ever creating. This is what causes the expanding nature of our "knowing," imaginative originality, lovingness and spirituality. When I sensed this knowing beyond intuition, I was permitted to peer into higher realms that will surely lead to even higher ones.

Lucid dreaming occurs when one stays in the meditative state of mind, characterized by a relaxed consciousness, while still in the dream. In lucid dreaming, we are not only allowed to go into other planes, such as the astral, but we are also able to emerge, to witness and to guide. In this way, <u>a bridge is formed between the material and the logical planes of mind, on the one hand, and the astral plane on the other.</u>

In *The Bhagavad-Gita*, Krishna admonishes Arjuna not to decide his time of death, but rather to surrender completely to Krishna consciousness. Then his arrival into Krishna-Loka (the highest heaven) will be assured. How similar this is to our setting our ego and its goals aside and surrendering to a Higher Wisdom.

The Hierarchy of Needs and Its Relationship to the Accessibility of the Soul

In his famous description of the "hierarchy of needs," Maslow showed how a need, when fulfilled, allows the personality to rise to the next higher level, beginning with the needs of survival and ending with loftier needs of creativity and spirituality. In my own experiences with patients, I have found that there is also a hierarchy of needs that must be met in our ascension toward the soul. It is never wise to force ascension, as in forcing celibacy before we are ready for it, or forcing faith in intuition. We must rather <u>allow</u> our needs to be fulfilled, level by level. As this happens, we can naturally expect an elevation of the personality. Needless to say, the needs in question must be fulfilled not in a selfish context, but in the context of our living in society within our own moral precepts. The ascension of the soul is also enabled when an individual has released the constricting bonds of anxiety, fear and guilt.

Maslow's theory was articulated from another point of view by Anna Freud who spoke of the smorgasbord of needs and solutions that must be offered during the psychotherapy of children. She discovered that no matter what interpretations are given for the child's problems, the child would take from the treatment what he or she needs at the time. The same is certainly true of adults. Anna Freud also spoke of lines of development, natural sequences that can be impeded by anxiety or deprivation. Again, this is parallel to what Maslow has said: a need fulfilled allows for development onward, for when anxiety or deprivation are removed, progress and ascension of the personality follow.

Elizabeth Kubler-Ross' description of the process of dying is another example of how developmental needs are fulfilled. She pointed out that there is a hierarchy of stages through which the patient traverses before reaching the final and desirable stage of acceptance. She spoke of death not as a dead-end of despair, but as the final stage of growth. Such growth indicates that there is a continued ascension after death.

Clearly, there is a natural buoyancy of the soul that carries the personality upward with it as it rises. This process occurs quite automatically when we open ourselves in surrender, experience release from the bonds of anxiety or constriction, or find fulfillment of an important deprivation in our lives or our development.

Some Authorities Speak about the Witness

The idea of the Witness is not unique to either the meditation experience or to the kind of spiritual psychotherapy that I practice. We read about the witness in many great myths, in the writings of many philosophers and in the holy books of many religions around the world. In *The Bhagavad-Gita As It Is* by Swami Prabhupada, we read:

"And present in the body along with the individual soul is the Supersoul, a plenary representation of Lord Krishna. The Supersoul...is situated in the heart.... The Supersoul, the Supreme Personality of the Godhead, seated beside the individual soul, is the witness of the individual soul's activities and is the source of the soul's various types of consciousness. The Supersoul gives the individual soul an opportunity to act freely and witnesses his activities."[12]

On the other side of the world, in nineteenth century New England, we find Ralph Waldo Emerson saying something very similar:

"We distinguish the announcements of the soul, its manifestations of its own nature, by the term Revelation. These are always attended by the emotion of the sublime. For this communication is an influx of the Divine mind into our mind. It is an ebb of the individual rivulet before the flowing surges of the sea of life. Every distinct apprehension of this central commandment agitates men with awe and delight. A thrill passes through all men at the reception of new truth, or at the performance of a great action, which comes out of the heart of nature."

Note that Emerson speaks of the same intuitive thrill and emotions of "agitation" that attend the soul's perception of truth that I remarked on earlier.

Swami Muktananda says in his *Siddha Meditations:*
"The Self is the witness of waking, dreaming and deep sleep. It is as a witness that He enjoys these states, without undergoing any change. He is indeed Shiva, the supreme Lord. In the waking state He functions in the gross body and experiences gross objects with the five organs of action, the five forms of prana and the fourfold psychic instrument. In dreams He experiences the subtle objects of that state. And in deep sleep, He experiences joyful and dreamless oblivion. That Self is none other than Parashiva. Parashiva is the real experiencer of all the states. It is a delusion to believe that you are the enjoyer."

These authorities define and describe the witness as the higher Self and make clear its closeness to the soul. This understanding is also consistent with my experience, both in my private meditations and in my encounters with patients. The loss of self--self-consciousness and self-concern--is rewarded by the ability to soar to the higher level that is the seat of the Witness.

And so, meditation, hypnosis and the witness are intimately related. Meditation, and its ally, prayer, opens the way to contact the soul. Hypnosis assists in removing interest from the lower bodies, followed by a release to ascension. In these endeavors, the witness hovers over the scene, watching, waiting and guiding. The witness is the part of our soul that draws, watches, and invites entry into itself.

Guidelines and Exercises:

1. Familiarize yourself with the seat of your self-observing self. Notice that it is not inside the skull. Is it above your head and slightly behind? Is it above and in front? Where is it in relation to you? Notice how you can see both yourself and the person you are talking to.

2. Observe attention as the vivifying force. Notice something out of peripheral vision, and then look straight at it. Notice how it becomes vivid. Notice that the same thing is true as you observe your thoughts and feelings.

3. Practice detachment. When you are in the midst of a heavy feeling or a slight argument with someone, pretend you are someone else, perhaps a spirit hovering overhead and watching, notice then the feeling of detachment. Practice this for it is a real benefit in life, self-observation, control of emotions, relationships with people.

4. Practice surrender. Perhaps when you are meditating, you will feel restless, or hungry. Tolerate it, surrender to it, let it fill your body. You will notice a breakthrough into calm after a while. As a result, you will have built psychological muscle, and achieve entry to the realm of the soul, the peaceful realm.

5. Observe yourself as you are "falling" asleep. Keep yourself in the semi-sleep state for a while. That is the entry point for good meditation and reception of inspired messages. It is a way of gaining access to lucid dreaming as well.

CHAPTER IX:
The Creative Power of the Soul

The Soul Has Wider Perceptions -- Seeing The Astral Presences -- Feeling At One With Someone -- The Soul Creates The Body During Our Lifetime, And In Re-Incarnation, Proofs -- A Case Of Re-Incarnation Which Created Her Body -- The Soul Receives Knowledge From Above And Transmits It -- Becoming Aware Of Dark Influences In The Astral Realm Of The Subtle Planes -- "Hagging," Instances Of Hagging, Instances Of Visits By A Dark Force -- Opening To The Divine.

Remembering that the soul resides in the fourth ascended body surrounding the physical self, we can remember too that the soul, known also as the causal body, is the receptive vehicle for divine energy in its transmission to the lower bodies (mental, astral and physical). In the course of fulfilling its mission on earth, the soul will acquire experience through the physical life of the human being; it will store positive experiences while discarding negative ones. It will seek a new life, a new incarnation, by gathering unto itself the bodies needed to manifest. It is important to recognize that surrounding the physical body is an etheric net that acts as a template for the laying down of the physical-material self. This etheric net closely surrounds the physical body and is perceived as a part of the auric glow by sensitive people. It is also the agency that contains, in its Electro-magnetic energy, the acupuncture network (the meridians).

As we all know, physically, the cells of the body are being constantly replaced. It is also true that the physical manifestations of the person change in an ongoing fashion over the course of a lifetime. There is very good reason to believe that mental influences, combined with the creative power of the soul, continually relate to and create the body as an ever-changing manifestation.

No doubt the lines, the scars and maps of our experiences are engraved on the face, the posture, and the body itself. A person's occupation is imprinted upon his/her face and behavior. For example, academics look like academics. Typically, their hands are fine and unscarred and they might have a slight stoop and less than 20/20 vision from doing so much sitting and reading. There is a social personality, too, to which they conform. It is wise and expected that the academic will be "proud to be poor," thus showing disdain for the affairs of the materialistic world. Gardeners and landscapers, on the other hand, also look alike. They often have darkly tanned or sun-damaged skin, rough or scarred hands, a more developed musculature because of the lifting and digging that they do, and clearer eyesight because they do not have to peer at the printed page or the computer screen for several hours a day. They, too, are part of a social climate, and their bearing, posture and carriage speak of it.

Presidents seem to become more presidential in bearing after assuming the office with its many responsibilities, new perceptions and challenging experiences. Harry Truman changed remarkably after assuming the presidency, seeming to become tougher and more direct, though undoubtedly his steel was there from the beginning. There was a change in President Clinton's attitude and bearing after his election. He seemed to transform from a brash young man into a more mature individual. His hair even mysteriously changed from dark brown to silvery grey, although that might have been through the agency of a hairdresser given the directive of making this youngest of all elected presidents look older, and therefore more "distinguished" and trustworthy.

There are laws that influence the body, laws related to the powers of the mind, that extend far beyond the boundaries of modern science and we see manifestations of these laws in such activities as fire-walking, viewing at a distance and the healing of serious diseases through visualization. David Bohm spoke about this responsiveness of material reality to the higher mind, calling it the implicate order. According to Bohm's definition, this order is the seat of potential that, under the proper circumstances, can be made to manifest as the explicate order -- that which can be seen and expressed in the material world. The implicate order has no particular allegiance to any one definition of reality, but holds within itself everything that is possible. Sai-Baba and Madame Blavatsky could make precious gems appear out of the air, simply because they understood that the "laws" of reality, as understood by any particular society, were a construct of the mass mind. Even the laws of physics are a manifestation of the explicate order. People once believed that Newtonian physics explained all there was to know about the laws of science. Since then, we have seen two major revolutions in physics, through Einstein and the quantum physicists, which have superseded Newton's unalterable rules. Someday, we may very well break another rule and travel faster than the speed of light. Non-locality, the ability of two particles separated by space to have instant access to the same information. may very well be pointing us in the right direction. The possibility that fire does not burn exists within the implicate order, and can be demonstrated by the actions of tens of thousands of men and women who attend the rapidly spreading fire-walking workshops across the United States. These workshops demonstrate that the "laws" that influence the body are directly related to the powers of the mind, that extend beyond the boundaries of modern science.

More proof of the existence of the higher mind and body and their ability to transcend time and space can be seen in Michael Talbot's book, *The Holographic Universe,* in which he discusses the work of Professor Ian Stevenson, a psychiatrist at Eastern Virginia University who has conducted exhaustive studies of reincarnation. Stevenson's work with thousands of individuals has led him to dramatic evidence of the power of the unconscious mind to influence our current life circumstances:

"He has found that a person's previous incarnation can apparently affect the very shape and structure of their current physical body. He has discovered, for example, that Burmese children who remember previous lives as British or American Air Force pilots shot down over Burma during World War II all have fairer hair and complexions than their siblings.

"He has also found instances in that distinctive facial features, foot deformities, and other characteristics have carried over from one life to the next. Most numerous among these are physical injuries carrying over as scars or birthmarks. In one case, a boy who remembered being murdered in his former life by having his throat slit still had a long reddish mark resembling a scar across his neck. In another, a boy who remembered committing suicide by shooting himself in the head in his past incarnation still had two scarlike birthmarks that lined up perfectly along the bullet's trajectory, one where the bullet had entered and one where it had exited. And in another, a boy had a birthmark resembling a surgical scar complete with a line of red marks resembling stitch wounds, in the exact location where his previous personality had had surgery.

"In fact, Stevenson has gathered hundreds of such cases and is currently compiling a four-volume study of the phenomenon. In some of the cases he has even been able to obtain hospital and\or autopsy reports of the deceased personality and show that such injuries not only occurred, but also were in the exact location of the present birthmark or deformity. He feels that such marks not only provide some of the strongest evidence in favor of reincarnation, but also suggest the existence of some kind of intermediate nonphysical body that functions as a carrier of these attributes between one life and the next. He states, `It seems to me that the imprint of wounds on the previous personality must be carried between lives on some kind of an extended body that in turn acts as a template for the production on a new physical body of birthmarks and deformities that correspond to the wounds on the body of the previous personality.' ...

"As unorthodox as many of Stevenson's conclusions are, his reputation as a careful and thorough investigator has gained him respect in some unlikely quarters. His findings have been published in such distinguished scientific periodicals as the *American Journal of Psychiatry, the Journal of Nervous and Mental Disease,* and the *International Journal of Comparative Sociology.* And in a review of one of his works the prestigious *Journal of the American Medical Association* stated that he has `painstakingly and unemotionally collected a detailed series of cases in that the evidence for reincarnation is difficult to understand on any other grounds . . . He has placed on record a large amount of data that cannot be ignored.'"[13]

Rupert Sheldrake, a British biologist, also subscribes to the idea of a higher mind or energy field that encloses consciousness outside of the realm of time and space. He calls this concept "morphic resonance." This theory states that a product--be it material, behavioral or mental--once formed, creates its own morphogenic field of resonances, waves of influences, that remain forever. As these fields are repeatedly formed, they create a kind of piling up, a coalescence, of former resonances and more recent ones-and as these accumulate they create a stability of the newly formed product or behavior.

Using his theory of morphic resonance, Sheldrake is able to explain the factors that give form to a body. The chromosomes can hardly explain these factors or genes alone, since the latter (being ubiquitous in the cells of the body) do not explain the differences of configuration of the various organs of the body. The theory is also used to explain why there are such things as dominant and recessive genes. Dominant traits are results of longer established and therefore more accumulated experience and waves of resonance; the recessive, lesser-established resonances.

It is interesting to note that these waves of morphic-resonance-influence are consistent with Eastern philosophy, which describes the causal body as creating a new body for itself at the time of the new incarnation.

It is always satisfying to see more than one line of investigation converging on an explanation and when a number of lines converge, there is a growing sense of conviction that this is the area of truth.

A Case of Reincarnation: Morphic Resonance, The Implicate Order and The Shaping of the Body

Janet, a forty-year-old woman, met a man for whom she couldn't have cared less in terms of his physical appearance. Yet at a certain point, when Samuel touched her, she felt a strange sexual and love excitement--much to her surprise. Even though, looking at him, she knew that he wasn't at all what she wanted in a man, she felt a strong connection that kept on growing. When she finally allowed him to kiss her, she was swept away. Samuel confessed, in turn, that he had wanted her for a very long time.

It seemed to me that this mysterious attraction bespoke a meeting of more than physical bodies. It is likely that there was also a meeting of souls that preceded their physical connection. For example, long before they had ever formally met, Janet had a dream in which she had been taken care of and kissed by a man who looked much like Samuel. She was puzzled by this dream because, even though at the time they were working together in the same office, she felt rather cold toward him. Apparently, the astral person was alive and working within the dream, working beyond physical recognition.

When Janet came into therapy with me, I discovered that her physical body, which had been laid down by an etheric net influenced by past life experiences and present life desires, was operating in a state of repression. Under hypnosis, Janet remembered a past life when she had been a free spirit dancing wildly in the fields. At that time, she had experienced a passionate and highly sexual love affair with a teacher. This teacher was the man Samuel to whom she was powerfully attracted in this life. When the past-life affair had been discovered, she had been locked in a room from which she could not escape. She remembered finally becoming immobile, with only her mind and eyes free to wander about. As Janet relived the experience in my office, she lay quite still, telling me very fearfully that she was paralyzed and could only move her eyes.

In her present life, Janet had been raised by a severe and highly critical mother who lost no opportunity to blame her for anything that went wrong. If the mother spilled a glass it was because Janet had made her nervous. Janet was frequently and publicly admonished and humiliated, and was constantly reminded that if she gave into any of her passions, she would wind up pregnant and disgraced. Having been so educated, she held in her passion. Like many other women in a similar situation, she had chosen a husband who repeated the repressions of her past. He was sexually cold, and constantly critical.

In spite of all these constraints, Janet was very attractive and emanated an aura of sexuality. Physically, she was endowed with generous proportions from the navel down. Her thick legs seemed urged to move about and dance. This was a passion that she learned to satisfy later by going to dance clubs where she could express herself for hours on end.

It was almost as if, in this life, Janet's soul-person had been constricted. Her physical body, instead of being the agent of her passion and self-expression, had become more like a casket as her mother's disapproval weighed down on her. Yet her body also found expression for itself through her generous proportions and the urgent movement in her legs.

When her new relationship with Samuel developed, she began to change physical style. Melting the influences that had formerly formed her thick shell, her inner persona was allowed to break out and find expression. In essence, this is what happens in successful psychotherapy: the healing process takes on a spiritual cast when we begin to think of it as the soul trying to find release, to ascend into its love-self.

I believe that love is very much linked to sexuality, that is, after all, the burning source of love. And so it seems that love opportunities in life, and in psychotherapy, release the person in just that way, by melting the internal resistances and external influences that create the body.

The Creative Power of the Soul

Janet's story describes the creative power of the soul as it relates to the shaping of the physical vehicle. There is much to be said about the creative power of the soul when it is receiving information, inspiration and creative knowledge from above. The soul is a satellite dish that faces in two directions, turning one face toward the higher and divine forces, while with the other it witnesses, creates and interacts with the lower bodies. This process can be seen when one goes into deep meditation, hypnosis or even reflection. In these states the inhibitory powers of the cerebral cortex are diminished; and as they are diminished the intuitive powers are released.

In *The Key to Theosophy* Madame Blavatsky speaks of the desire of the inner self to be released and its realization of this state when the body is paralyzed in sleep. She speaks also of the power of the inner self to see and interact with the astral presences of both the living and the dear departed.[14]

Many people may find the idea of interacting with the astral presences of the dead far-fetched, a product of the imagination. But, I ask, "What is imagination?"

The unabridged *Oxford English Dictionary* defines imagination as follows: "the action of imagining, or forming a mental concept of what is not actually present to the senses; the result of this process, a mental image or idea (often with implication that the conception does not correspond to the reality of things ...)." But what is the reality of things, and what senses are employed? Surely not the ordinary five senses alone, or we would not believe in X-ray images. "Yet," someone might argue, "we can see X-ray images." But again, we can also see with Kirlian photography the images that sensitives can see with the naked eye.

There are so many things that we shut out with minds that are less than open, minds that have been forced to close by the fear of challenging the accepted belief. I have had my struggles with new beliefs. Here is an account of one such struggle, which ended in a new and inspiring insight.

The Water Deva:

I had long lamented the fact that I could never see "Devas," nature spirits. Once, at a spiritual retreat, I had heard someone speak of seeing a massive nature spirit hovering overhead. I wondered why I couldn't. Someone else spoke of the nature spirit that ruled the mineral kingdom; I wondered again why I was lacking. But then I learned that we see such things, not with the retina, but with the eye of the thought realm; not straight on but in the periphery of vision. Now I was freed.

This was my experience:

I was swimming, and I felt the water. I had a thought which became a perception: I knew I was feeling an expression of the water spirit. I could feel the water around me as liquid, mobile, graceful, adaptable, fluid. I remembered that at another time, when I would be tired, or when the water would seem thick, I would feel a different expression, an expression that created resistance. I understood that the water itself was a presentation of a higher something, something which in its own way was a delegate from God's realms. I knew that I was seeing out of the corner of my mind; I was seeing water expressing itself as the manifestation of the water spirit. In this realization, I was able to swim the more easily, in "flow" with the water and the water spirit.

This awareness meant a lot to me. It meant that if we allow ourselves to enter into the current of things, we become "in communication"; we become messengers. But more than that, since we are sufficiently developed in our consciousness, we can also seize the idea; putting it in writing we communicate it to others. We become scribes, servants and messengers from the On High.

In God's dominion, we are messengers; we are scribes.

Aldous Huxley once said, "If the doors of perception were cleansed, we would see the world as it truly is, infinite." Open perception, greater perception!

Becoming aware of astral presences is one of those greater perceptions.

Contact with astral presences is a more common phenomenon that one might think. I have already described the experiences of several of my patients who sensed an astral "presence" close to them in bed at night. In this case, the experience was pleasant and reassuring. Sometimes, however, the experience can be disturbing. Professor David J. Hufford of the Hershey Medical Center and the University of Pennsylvania, has written a book entitled, *The Terror That Comes in the Night* that describes the research he has done concerning folk tales that describe what is commonly called the "Old Hag" experience:

"The experience of being hagged...may be summarized as follows: (l) Awakening (or an experience immediately preceding sleep); (2) hearing and/or seeing something come into the room and approach the bed; (3) being pressed on the chest or strangled; (4) inability to move or cry out until either being brought out of the state by someone else or breaking through the feeling of paralysis on one's own."[15]

One of Hufford's informants described his experience in this way: "You are dreaming and you feel as if someone is holding you down. You can do nothing, only cry out. People believe that you will die if you are not awakened." Hufford described the experience of another subject as follows: "Every night when he went to bed, it was as if someone was pressing across his chest - it was as if he was being strangled."[16]

Perhaps Professor Hufford would not claim that these were astral presences, but he does describe something that his subjects have found palpable. Furthermore, when he examined one hundred college students, he found that a full twenty-three percent of them had had at least partial hag experiences. Surely, this phenomenon is thought provoking, although it describes the dark side of the mind.

When my friend Joy Parker read this section of the manuscript, she made some valuable comments about this. She suspects that the phenomenon of hagging has something to do with being profoundly disturbed about issues in one's life that one is in denial about--as if the thing one is trying to avoid actually takes on physical form. She bases this suggestion not only upon her reading of folklore and literature in which hagging is described, but also upon the many stories she has heard throughout the years from friends, acquaintances and relatives.

I think there is a truth to the idea that hagging might be the unconscious mind's way of bringing something that we are in denial about to consciousness, but this idea needs to be elaborated. I believe that the agents in the Supersensible Realms, both the agents of Light and those of Darkness, can operate in the physical sphere only by invitation. Since we all have within us elements of both the Light and the Dark, we are vulnerable to attack when we hide our dark feelings and dark fears from ourselves. In sensitive people, these feelings can manifest as the astral presence. Similarly, the Agents of the Light arrive only when called in by the aspirations of the holy portion of ourselves. Neurotic fears that are based on repressed feelings make one susceptible to these presences. We certainly feel them in nightmares.

One of the most interesting of the stories that Ms. Parker shared with me concerns the sister of a psychologist friend who was trying to deny to herself that her "perfect" marriage was not all that she wanted. Although she had everything that society recognized as important--money, a house that was a showcase, and social position--she was afraid to admit to herself that she wasn't happy. This woman was hagged almost every night by a white dog (they had no pets). It waited until her husband was asleep, and then came into the bedroom, its toenails clacking on the hardwood floor, jumped up onto the mattress, and then placed itself across her legs. The woman lay awake in terror, unable to get the dog to move off her. One morning, when she was standing in her dressing room putting on her makeup, she heard the heavy footsteps of a man walking loudly across her bedroom. When she looked out, there was no one there. At that moment, she vowed with all her heart to leave her marriage. The footsteps went away, and she was never hagged again.

In another incident, a relative of Ms. Parker's was going through a difficult emotional time. As she reached a crisis of anxiety, an astral presence came into her bedroom, sat on her chest, and tried to kill her. After fighting it off with frantic pleas to God for help, this woman was able to awaken her husband who said, "Mary, there was something evil in this room." The dog was also aware of the astral presence, and was cowering on the carpet, whining in fear. Mary had been aware that when the presence had left their bedroom, it had gone out into the hallway and stood in front of the doors of her children's rooms, but had been unable to enter them. When her husband went out into the hall, he could sense where the presence had walked. It was very real.

Ms. Parker also told me about an incident described in Maxine Hong Kingston's book, *The Woman Warrior*. While living in China, attending medical school and agonizing over whether or not to follow her husband to America, Kingston's mother was hagged one night by a presence that came into her room, sat on her chest and tried to kill her. In China, hagging is a commonly acknowledged experience, and the astral presences are called "sitting ghosts" because they often sit on the chest of their victims.

One of my own clients endured a series of severe hagging events that almost choked her to death. A very sensitive and perceptive individual, she ascribed these incidents to Dark Forces. At the time, she was denying all of the abundant anger and hostility that she felt toward the husband who abused her, and whom she subsequently left.

I believe that these terrors are the projection of unconscious products within the people who experience them, but I also believe that these projections also join with "shades" who are all too willing to come in. There is wisdom to surrounding one's self with white light at these times, including the light of introspection that reveals the dark corners of our mind.

After looking at the widespread folklore, religious writings, and modern accounts of encounters with astral presences, both angelic and dark, it is hard to justify the claim that dismisses them all as just fantasy and imagination. Those who know that they have felt the touch of the divine are those who have fallen silent enough to catch these subtle perceptions. Paula, firmly in touch with her abundant capacity to love, has these kinds of experiences all the time. Alexandra, a high sensitive who meditates regularly, invites high experiences of loving contact with her guide and inspirations that become the basis for poetic productions in her writing. I have experienced many messages myself, as well as a widening vision of God's plan for us, in my own meditations. This almost always happens when I have been able to surmount the initial period of restlessness, and enter the quietude of the subtle realms.

There are wonderful love experiences with the dear departed on the other side, and some of my patients have not only experienced them, but been healed by them. Madame Blavatsky has said that one of the ways that we can recognize the presence of these loving souls is by the feeling of a passing soft breeze.

Listen to the beautiful words of Sri Aurobindo:
"FIRST RESPONSES OF THE DIVINE. They come rather as a touch, a pressure; one must be in a condition to recognize and accept, or it is a voice of assurance, sometimes a very `still small voice,' a momentary Image or Presence, a whisper of Guidance sometimes, there are many forms it may take. Then it withdraws and the preparation of the nature goes on till it is possible for the touch to come again, to last longer, to change into something more pressing and near and intimate. The Divine in the beginning does not impose himself - he asks for recognition, for acceptance. That is one reason why the mind must fall silent, not put tests, not make claims; there must be

room for the true intuition that recognizes at once the true touch and accepts it."[17]

The perception of astral presences is neither fantasy nor imagination, but the experience of those who have fallen silent enough to catch the subtle perception. When the experience of so many bears witness to these claims, who can confidently say that those things that do not fit the parameters of present day perception cannot exist. There may be a greater wisdom about such things in indigenous cultures. The West African Dagara tribe has no word for "imagination" because they believe that anything that can be thought of is possible. Also, the Cherokee religion has much to say about the Dream Lodge in the Medicine Wheel as an actual place of reality.

So I say, "Perhaps there is no such thing as imagination, - only perception on planes that we may not yet have visited." Perhaps our dreams arc not imaginary, but instead perceptions--simply on another plane.

Guidelines and Exercises

1. In your dreams, you will notice the wide number of perceptions. Obviously you are not perceiving with the retina, or hearing with the eardrum. These are the perceptions captured by the perceptive apparatus of the astral realm, closer to the soul.

2. Become alert to the feeling of "presences." They are easily seen in dreams, but in waking life are felt as "feelings" or "sensings" of something. Trust these feelings. The more you do, the more you will have access to them.

3. Observe groups of people: policemen, lawyers, doctors, teachers, carpenters. Notice how they assume similar attitudes and behaviors. In a sense they begin to look like each other. Observe people who have lived together a long time. Sometimes they begin to resemble each other. Thus the soul creates the body.

4. Watch your nightmares to become alert to dark presences. Suspend doubt for a little while, and you will become more familiar with their reality, so that you may deal well with them. Depression is often heightened by the invasion by a dark force entity.

CHAPTER X:
Conflict Resolution In Spiritual Psychotherapy

Meetings In The Subtle Realm, The Astral Plane, Can Be Healing In Terms Of The Dear-Departed: Two Case Histories -- How To Gain Access To The Subtle Realms -- The Power Of The Subtle Realm (The Realm Of The Soul) To Perform Miracles On The Body -- What Is "Imagination?" -- Perhaps Imagination Is A Higher Form Of Perception.

Conflict resolution in spiritual psychotherapy is comparable to conflict resolution in classical psychodynamic psychotherapy, but with one important addition: in the former, further advancement of the personality is available after resolution. When the spiritual psychotherapist recognizes the fact that the material body is only a part of the person--that we live also in the higher bodies, and that the expansion of the mind includes the ability to contact those who have passed over--then we have the potential to expand the tools of therapy, benefiting our patients and humanity at large.

In line with this, I would like to share some case histories that illustrate how spiritual psychotherapy takes classical psychodynamic methods one step further. In the first history, a patient was actually able to make contact with her departed husband, resolving a grieving process that was so intense that it had begun to affect her physically.

A skeptic could easily say at this point, "But this only happened in her imagination." To this I would respond, "Imagination or no, the resolution took place when the woman allowed this possibility into her belief system, whereas before it had not." Again, we must ask ourselves the all-important question, "What is imagination?" Is it not possible that the imagination is merely perception in a realm beyond our present five-sense sensory perception?

Resolving Grief in the Realm of the Soul
Emma was sixty-four-year-old woman who had been referred to me because of chronic pain. The purpose of her visit was to get psychiatric approval for an electrical implant to be inserted at the base of her spine in a desperate attempt to control that pain. It was my job to assess her psy-

chological readiness for this procedure.

Emma was a woman completely unschooled in psychological matters. She was accompanied on her visit by a son who must have been around forty-five years old, who was a farmer. As I later learned, he was totally skeptical about the referral and wondered what she was doing here after all; what she needed was an electrical implant. By the end of the session, however, Emma was able to change his attitude completely.

Emma was an obese woman with a missing right forearm and hand, which, she quickly explained, was a birth defect. She was jolly and congenial, and spoke rapidly and continually, which, as I learned, was a strategy for keeping her mind occupied so that she would not be sad. During the course of our interview, I discovered that sixteen months ago she had lost her husband, whom she described as her best friend and companion. When she told me this, she displayed just a moment of sadness, but quickly suppressed it. When I suggested that she might be keeping herself busy to avoid her feelings of missing him, she confessed that this was true and that she was very sorry that she had never had the chance to say goodbye to him properly. When I asked her if she would like to say good-bye to him now, she eagerly agreed.

I put Emma into a relaxed state and asked her to follow my instructions. When I began a hypnotic chant, she went into trance very quickly. I then asked her to meet her husband on a soul level and to say to him all the things that she had wanted to say. I also gave her a pillow and told her to let herself hug him. She immediately embraced the pillow, full of love and with a kind of sad happiness, telling me that she does this at home when she thinks of her husband.

The experience of communicating with her husband was very real for her and very fulfilling. To hasten the healthy progress of her grief, I suggested that she continue to put herself into this state of hypnosis morning and evening in order to continue her experiences with him on a soul level. When Emma came out of her trance, she had a beatific smile on her face and a glow to her personality. When I called her son in, she was so insistent about the value and pleasure of her experience with me that she made him change his mind about bringing her back.

Emma returned one more time. It was easy to observe that the hypnosis had a great effect on her. She was easily induced into trance again, and waited patiently until her beloved husband, Alonzo, appeared. At the time, she told me that her breathing had also been better all week. The pain diminished, she said, when she went into the relaxation. At such times, she found herself in a beautiful and peaceful realm where she could invoke her husband's blessings and appeal for his help. She invoked his blessings upon me as well. She told me that she had never in her life achieved this much peace and that it was a transcendent experience for her. I encouraged her to continue to practice this soul connection with her husband.

It seemed to me that she had entered another realm, a realm of beatitude, peace and quiet joy, a realm of meetings with her spiritual partner, a realm of love.

Repair of Childhood Wounds in the Realm of the Soul

Freda was a forty-two-year-old beautician who had been severely injured in an automobile accident. As a result she had developed pain in her neck and a disc disorder that led to lower-back pain and weakness in her upper extremities. She was referred to me by a psychologist who had seen her without success for a considerable time for treatment of depression. He had hoped that I would treat Freda with antidepressant medication, which I was happy to do. The medicine did help her in some respects, giving her a general lifting of her mood, increased energy and a better sleep pattern, but her pain and depression continued, even though it was clear that she was receiving increasing benefits from her psychotherapy sessions with me.

As Freda's pain continued, her family doctor referred her to a neurosurgeon who had operated on her previously, removing two discs from her neck. Seeing that the operation had done nothing to relieve her pain, he decided that it was caused not by the accident, but by arthritis. Subsequently, he referred her to someone who gave her cortisone injections.

Meanwhile, I had been using hypnosis on Freda and found her to be a good subject. On one particular day, I decided to have her go very, very deeply into trance and to get in touch with the origin of a feeling she had described. She had told me that she felt as if she were now a stranger in her body. At my invitation, Freda went all the ways back to the beginning of this feeling, and began to speak about several significant things. So far we were in conventional psychotherapy. She rued the fact that now her physical incapacity made her feel as if she were struggling through the day when before she had always been so active and independent, able to clean the house and carry on all of her duties as a beautician. The pain kept her from being what she was; therefore, she felt like a stranger in her own body.

As she continued, she discovered that she had never felt loved enough by her mother. Her mother was a true stoic who hadn't even cried at her husband's funeral, or during the entire time her own mother was dying of cancer. Freda had always wanted to be strong like her mother so that her mother would approve of her and love her. Sadly, she realized, her mother had never really loved her. She then told me that her fifteen-year-old brother Kenny had raped her when she was only nine and how it had hurt her all over, much like the pain from the accident was hurting her now. Her mother clearly loved her brother Kenny more than she did Freda and, for that reason, wasn't there to protect her. Freda couldn't go to her father because she knew that he loved her so much that he would have killed her brother and surely have wound up in jail.

In hypnosis I suggested that Freda see herself united with a blue-white light that was her all-knowing and all-healing God-self. Then I asked this all-knowing Self how the information that Freda had shared with me related to her pains from the accident. She said these pains reminded her of her experiences with Kenny, experiences that she had been forced to keep secret all of her life. Since Freda was a particularly unsophisticated individual, I was startled to hear her say that keeping the secret had caused her pain. She continued, saying that in order to heal herself she must now go to her brother, whom she has seen little in recent years, and straighten things out with him. This seemed to me to be a knowing far beyond the patient's level of sophistication, a kind of Soul-knowing.

As we continued, Freda kept coming back to the feeling that her mother didn't love her, especially because she was being weak and crying so. Even though her mother had died some years before, I suggested that she try to contact her on a soul level. Freda did so--fully. Her mother thereupon reassured her (within the hypnotic state) that she did love her, and that she was sorry about what Kenny had done to her. I further suggested to Freda that her mother was wiser now that she was in another realm.

During this communication, her mother also told Freda that she had perhaps loved her less because she resented her daughter's close relationship with her father. Whenever her father and mother had an argument, her father would pick up Freda and take his little girl over to his sister's house. The father almost always spent more time with Freda than with his wife. This was quite a confession on the mother's part. When I suggested to Freda that she must have understood this situation unconsciously at age nine or ten, as well as the fact that her mother was jealous of her, she agreed. I suggested that perhaps she couldn't know these things consciously at that time because she looked upon herself as only a little girl; however, her God-self knew, even as it knew about these things now. Freda experienced a great healing during the course of this hypnotic encounter with her mother.

Freda also went on to cry about how much she had missed her father after he died; he was her best friend. I suggested that she might want to contact her father as well. When she did, I asked her what he looked like. She replied, "He is full of life; he is light--sort of transparent." The light was so bright, in fact, that she couldn't see his face. When I asked what kind of a light it was and if it hurt, she said that it didn't, but that it was very bright, beautiful and happy-making, very healing. Her father told her that he would be there to help her as he had always said he would.

Even though the results of these sessions were similar to those achieved in conventional psychotherapy in that the patient healed painful memories associated with her parents, the dynamics of spiritual psychotherapy provided a qualitative difference. Both the patient and I believe that she was actually in contact with the astral presences of her departed loved ones, by calling upon her own higher Self and releasing knowledge that she otherwise would not have in her conscious mind, given her level of sophistication. Having access to this type of perception, and knowing that the presences contacted are not simply memories, allows the patient a view of a larger dimension. This understanding adds a kind of palpability, a "realness," to the exchange between the patient and the parents; therefore it has greater healing potential. I anticipate that it will not be long before Freda will be pain-free enough to terminate her cortisone injections.

Although traditional psychiatry and psychology might raise objections to the idea of astral presences, attributing them to fantasy, my work with my patients over the last forty years has convinced me that there is much more out there than meets the eye.

Dogs surely have greater auditory and olfactory perception than we do. Who knows what else they may perceive? I have no doubt that sensitives can discern much more than I can, and frankly I envy them. Even at that, we see more now that Kirlian photography has arrived, photographs of auras that are invisible to the naked eye of most of us. These photographs confirm the perceptions of energetic or "psychic" healers who accomplish their results by actually being able to "see" and physically manipulate the body's energy systems. Barbara Ann Brennan, the internationally known author of the book *Hands of Light: A Guide to Healing Through the Human Energy Field,* has written extensively about this process.

In order to gain access to subtle perceptions, one must suspend judgement momentarily, and settle into a calm, quiet and receptive state. There are so many new experiences available if one will only do that, demonstrations in the subtle realms that cannot be explained by present-day science with its limited parameters. For example, the body must be able to surround itself by a protective envelope of energy never described by science if one can walk on hot coals heated to 1200 degrees without burning either one's feet or one's clothing.

There is another possible explanation for this phenomenon that my friend Joy Parker has pointed out to me, and one with which I too agree. In their writings, both Joseph Chilton Pearce and Michael Talbot remind us that objective reality is a consensus opinion. We believe that fire will burn us because we have been taught that it does so. In *The Crack in the Cosmic Egg,* Pearce described how, as a college student, he became convinced one evening in the student canteen that he could put a lighted cigarette to his hand without being hurt. He did so successfully all night long. He also helped his wife to go into remission from cancer for over a year when the doctors had given her very little time to live. Based on this line of thinking, a group of people can all walk over a bed of hot coals because they all agree that it is possible to do so. Reality always responds to our thoughts because, essentially, it is created by thought.

Joy has told me a humorous story about this. She related how she and a friend of hers, a network chiropractor named Silvana, were talking about how they were always trying to "help" and to "save" their mothers, and how hard it was for them to remember that this was not their job. Silvana told Joy that she had literally dragged her mother to a fire-walking demonstration one weekend to "prove" to her mother that she should take her daughter's spiritual path seriously. While Silvana sat raptly listening to the afternoon's speaker, her mother sat next to her yawning and fidgeting. She finally said, "I can't stand this. I'm bored to death, and I'm going back to the hotel to take a nap." Half an hour before the fire walking was to begin, Silvana raced back to the hotel, dragged her mother out of bed, and made her come back to the workshop. "Now you are going to see people walk on a bed of hot coals at 1200 degrees without being burned!" Silvana said smugly. Her mother said, "Oh, is that what all this is about?" stood up, and walked over the coals herself to the complete shock of both the people who were watching the demonstration and those who had been psychologically preparing for the walk all weekend. At that moment Sylvana decided that she had better stop judging her mother and trying to lead her to her own brand of spiritual "truth."

Where do such observations lead us? They lead to a speculation that the things that our culture calls "imaginary" may very well not be imaginary at all, but merely perceptions on another plane, much like the things we see, touch, and interact with while in the dream state. In dreams, our minds and perceptual apparatus are very active, but in another realm. Therefore, if we do have the ability to imagine certain possibilities and to make them real while dreaming, to peer into other domains, perceive other realities and enlarge our vision, then perhaps there is no such thing as imagination, but only reality on another plane This may be, in fact, a new reality that we are contacting. If we can palpate pressure in the "empty" space between our palms, why would it be unbelievable that we could feel the presence of someone beloved to us (or even those dark energies that walk the earth) as we become more sensitive to subtle perception?

Conflict is supposedly the bane of our neurotic existence. This is what Freud discovered. Conflict resolution is the healing factor. But conflict resolution in the spiritual realm leads us higher. Resolution now turns adversity into advantage. Spiritual resolution, which invokes the soul, creates something beyond solution -- an invitation to ascension into God's Domain.

Guidelines and Exercises:

1. Sensitize yourself to the subtle planes by reading again the beautiful injunction by Sri Aurobindo, and then practice it. You will be surprised, as you become more and more aware of the subtle sensations and messages that have been suppressed by doubt and cultural conditioning;

> "FIRST RESPONSES OF THE DIVINE. They come rather as a touch, a pressure; one must be in a condition to recognize and accept, or it is a voice of assurance, sometimes a very `still small voice,' a momentary Image or Presence, a whisper of Guidance sometimes, there are many forms it may take. Then it withdraws and the preparation of the nature goes on till it is possible for the touch to come again, to last longer, to change into something more pressing and near and intimate. The Divine in the beginning does not impose himself - he asks for recognition, for acceptance. That is one reason why the mind must fall silent, not put tests, not make claims; there must be room for the true intuition that recognizes at once the true touch and accepts it."[18]

2. Give free range to your imagination, and record the ideas that seem valuable to you. Value yourself and your creativity. There will be a time when you will manifest your imagined creations. It may not be through a magical act, but it is the beginning of realization of the creative capacity of the imagination, which then can become more and more useful. There are highly advanced human beings in the East who can actually materialize a product of the mind.

CHAPTER XI:

Accessibility to Higher States of Consciousness
Ascension Versus Impedimenta

Accessibility To Higher States -- Ascension Vs. Impediments -- The Hierarchy Of Planes -- The Hierarchy Of Fixations -- Too Strong A Fixation To The Material Prevents Ascension, Case Illustration -- Case History, Not All Soul Releases Are Recognized As Such -- The Power Of Money To Limit Ascension -- A Case Illustrating Transcendence From The Material Level All The Way To The High Plane Of Love -- Miracles Are All Around Us, They Need Only To Be Recognized, Case Histories.

In his hierarchy of needs, Maslow stated that one's basic survival needs had to be met before an individual could turn his or her attention to matters of the spirit. I have seen this idea at work in my own practice as well. Once I have been able to aid a patient in releasing individual fixations, I can always see the natural buoyancy of the personality as it begins to come into play. As the personality rises, the soul is released as well.

When I speak of impedimenta, I am referring to those fixations, those "chains" that bind the personality to archaic levels of belief and behavior. Before I became a spiritual psychotherapist, I thought that these fixations were exclusively ontogenetic, that is, arising only through the experiences one has in this lifetime. Since I have learned of the immortality of the essential person and of the soul's journey through a series of lives, I can also speak of phylogenetic (racial) fixations.

In my years of practice, I have seen this process, the rising of the soul to higher states of consciousness, over and over again. I would like to share some of these stories with the reader, demonstrating the irresistible freeing of the self once the anchors of fixations and impediments from both this life and those previous lives are released.

The Hierarchy of Accessibility
It is unfortunate that, in our society, the prevailing opinion is that we are only our physical selves; that we end our journey and our consciousness when we leave this earthly coil. Majority opinion scoffs at ideas of immortality, of past lives, and even at our inherent divinity. I would like to

share again with you the somewhat difficult path which led me to a conviction of our immortality. It was related in terms of my own wish to be immortal, and the growing evidence in my practice and readings that led me to it.

The only divinity that gains much official acceptance these days is the kind that is practiced in the most custom-bound and ritualistic of ways in the churches, mosques and synagogues. The fixation our society has on the idea that organized religion is the only path to truth creates one of the strongest obstructions to the ascension of the personality. Too often this belief literally impedes entry into higher levels of group love, altruism and self-realization. The fixation of society to separatist rules such as "the ends justify the means" impairs the ascension of both the individual and society.

A Series Of Case Histories Illustrating Ascending States of Realization

Rachel's Story

Rachel is now seventy years old and I have known her for twenty-five years. Long ago, she came to me as a patient in the midst of a depression accompanied by a number of phobias, and she remained for a considerable time in a thoroughgoing, classical psychoanalysis. The important ingredient of her "cure" was the transference belief that I was the reincarnation, so to speak, of her mother, whom she had lost at a very early age. Rachel had achieved abundant insight into the fact that this was transference, but continued to extol me as if the relationship were real.

I remained a friend with her after her treatment was over, and maintained sporadic contact with her throughout the years. It was a minor triumph that she was able to have her husband visit me, despite his initial belief that psychiatrists were an unnecessary extravagance. In spite of this, he and I became friends as well as patient and doctor, and I was able to give him considerable support throughout his terminal illness.

During this final illness, I tried to comfort them by telling them about my faith in the immortality of the soul, which, I explained, was also the essential person--but they would have none of it. They had lived like two peas in a pod, and were not about to change their basic beliefs now. The loss of her husband should have been well-nigh disastrous for Rachel, all the more so since she had, not long before, watched her son grimly succumb to a wasting muscular disorder, anterior lateral sclerosis. Nevertheless, my words about the spiritual realm, which were designed to comfort her, fell noiselessly on her ears. In spite of this, she did receive comfort and support from her visits to me. It was the transference that comforted, and not any resolution through knowledge of higher realms.

In the realm of human relations, even in the relationship between a psychotherapist and patient, we must often be content with incompleteness. That is part of the human condition. Furthermore, everyone has the right to be what he or she decides, and this most certainly cautions any therapist, counselor or friend to avoid imposing his or her values on the patient. Rachel had severe self-imposed restrictions when it came to the spiritual realm, and had the right to not believe me when I told her that her soul was immortal. But she did have the comfort of feeling safe in my care, much as a child knows that her mother will make everything "all right."

When the Defenses Are Strong, and the Release is Minimal

Born of German stock, Herman is a sixty-five-year-old of definite tastes and opinions. A successful financier, he thinks strictly in categories, and his opinions, likes and dislikes are rigidly defined. He is too embarrassed to express or even realize his more tender feelings, and will act disgruntled and slightly aggressive if exposed to these emotions. In this respect he is not unlike the American hero, John Wayne. He is a good man who practices his charity in the most conventional ways but, nevertheless, gives with a full heart. He is deeply involved in the Boy Scouts of America and has taken important administrative posts in that organization, contributing his financial knowledge as well as his personal wealth. Herman's interests are family, money, wine, gourmet dining and sports. According to German tradition, his family life is strictly ordered and he is unquestionably the head of his household.

So far we have seen the portrait of a good man, a family man, and a man of charity. However he is clearly limited in his openness to emotions of love, let alone to any kind of knowledge that is beyond the conventional.

Herman's adjustment has recently been challenged by his wife and adult son. Both are in treatment and are loosening their ties to their former ways of looking at things. As they do so, they are becoming interested in spiritual affairs. Herman remains closed to this. He does not interfere with their beliefs, and remains the benign despot. Without acknowledging any changes in himself, however, he is inevitably changing in response to his wife and son's new openness.

I have invited Herman to my office several times as an adjunct to his wife's and son's treatment. Each time he has come, he has been terribly uncomfortable in spite of my best efforts to put him at ease. I believe this is because he thinks I'm going to make him talk about himself. He is basically very shy.

This man is a good person and a good member of society. He shows a degree of flexibility (witness his response to the changes in his wife and son), but remains fixed in his conventional beliefs, firmly attached to the teachings of his early upbringing. His mind is closed to any possible exploration of realms beyond the conventional. In this, he represents much or perhaps most, our society.

Herman finds his security by staying within the strict confines of his upbringing, and experiences change as threatening. Deep down, he fears that the changes he has seen in his wife and son mean a change in their attitude toward him. While he shows adaptability in allowing these transforming experiences in his family, he does not allow them to seep very far into his interior to release the softer, more soulful parts of himself.

Not All Soul Releases Are Recognized As Such

Richard is an eighty-year-old financier who, much like Herman, is a very upright individual whose integrity can be seen in all his endeavors. His reputation in business is impeccable. Devoutly religious, he is a pillar of strength in the Jewish community and has presided over several synagogues in his lifetime, continuing to do so even at his advanced age. Richard has also occupied important positions on the national Jewish scene. He attends synagogue religiously and prays in private daily. While his practice of religion is certainly sincere, it is limited to the beliefs that he has been taught since childhood. To my knowledge, he feels no need to explore spiritual areas that extend beyond his present belief. His rabbi, however, with whom he has a close friendship, has developed an interest in *A Course in Miracles*, bespeaking this rabbi's remarkable open-mindedness. This has created the beginning of a broader perspective in the mind and heart of this eighty-year-old "youngster."

Not all religious practices are spiritual, as is demonstrated by those who will attend Temple and then commit an advanced sin in business. Worse than this, more than one priest in Bosnia-Herzogovina has given religious sanction to warlords in return for financial support of his church. By contrast, strong spiritual forces within himself move Richard. I believe that these forces are both advanced and limited at the same time. One does not have to go outside of the traditional church or temple to find a deeper spiritual context. Perhaps there could be an even greater opening for Richard if he were to undertake an exploration of his Jewish beliefs in a more expanded sense. The Kabbala is based upon Jewish mysticism, and combines the basic tenets of traditional Judaism with the extended approach that Kabbalistic teachings bring. This implies an open-ness to ecumenicism, which, I believe, is closer to the soul, advocating universality, rather than separatism.

The Power of Money -- To Limit Us!

Solomon was a thirty-two-year-old physician who had been phenomenally successful in building a huge patient base in the first few years of his practice and had managed to put aside a large amount of money in those years. In spite of his success and financial security, he was exhausted at the end of the day and found himself coming home late at night feeling so depleted that all he had the energy for was passively watching TV. He spent what little free time he had in superficial and material pursuits.

Solomon is representative of someone who has a fixation on material values, the power and pride of money. Ironically, impoverishment of spiritual and emotional values eventually follows such a fixation.

Solomon had been raised in a family that had similar values. Because of this, he invariably took my interpretations of the problems he presented to me as a call to action instead of reflection. In his life, action and material orientation took the place of introspection and the altruistic motivation that should have been the principle behind his practice of medicine.

In spite of all of these things, I could clearly see that he had not only the power but the desire to rise to higher spiritual levels.

Solomon was now separated from his wife because he had remained too attached to his family of origin, and they had rejected her. In spite of this, he longed to be rejoined with her. In the course of his treatment, he began to treat her more kindly, evoking her love for him in return.

My aim in treating Solomon was simply to release him to be what he inherently was. I anticipated that as he was freed from childhood fixations he would rise in his orientation to higher levels, serving the higher needs of both himself and others. I expected that he would become more giving in showing his love for his wife, which he wanted to learn how to do, and, finally, to the extended family of his practice and to his community.

Solomon made progress along these lines. He opposed his brother, his wife's archenemy, and had her move back with him. He took short vacations with her, re-establishing a closeness, which had been interrupted. In so doing, he began to substitute family life for his overextended and overly pressured medical practice. All of these changes occurred under the auspices of his therapy, and the lure of a better and more love-filled life. After a while, however, the lure of becoming richer proved too much for him. Without giving notice he informed me that, although he was grateful for what we had achieved together, he was stopping his treatment.

Everyone has the right to decide at every moment of their lives where he or she wants to put their energy or interest. At the time when Solomon left therapy, he had already gained some release from his attachment to his family of origin. Perhaps, as his need for power and money is further satisfied he will be able to move on even further -- and perhaps not.

Slow and Steady -- A Challenging, but Full Release

Will Rogers once said, "I never met a man I didn't like." I have often admired this tolerant, even-handed philosophy, but thought that it was practically impossible to achieve, especially in my case. But I have learned through my practice that once I understood someone, I could also say that I genuinely liked him or her. Potentially, I think this is true of all of us.

Morris is one of the patients who have taught me this. In the beginning, the two of us didn't even like each other. He thought I was too idealistic, a "Pollyanna." I thought he was somewhat repulsive in his habits. Both of us were finally able to move beyond those feelings.

Morris was thirty-one when he arrived at my office. He came under pressure, for he had been admonished by his supervisor that he must do something about his performance at work. He was depressed without really realizing it, since he was in such poor contact with his feelings. Bored with his work, he was a terrible procrastinator. I diagnosed Morris as an obsessive-compulsive neurotic, which meant that he was someone who kept a very tight lid on his emotions. Instead of feeling things, he thought things, racing his mind in order to crowd out feelings. In spite of the fact that he was practically ordered to treatment with me, he became very attached to it, and made considerable sacrifices to continue our work together.

There was also something challenging about Morris, especially in light of the fact that he gave the feeling of being somehow dirty and lacking in his personal care. In spite of being meticulously clean in his general habits at home, he would pick his ears in the session, and at other times put his stockinged feet right in front of my face. All of this was enacted completely unconsciously.

We worked together for a long time on getting him to recognize his feelings. For the most part, he was quite afraid of himself and of his quick and ready-to-emerge sense of shame. He always expected to be criticized, having grown up under the auspices of a 4'10" Tarzan-mother who would intimidate his father and humiliate Morris both privately and publicly. His father was Morris' only source of emotional support, but he was passive and no match for the mother.

When the treatment was well underway, Morris confessed, with great difficulty, that he was a thirty-one-year-old virgin. A little later he shared his favorite and most private sexual fantasy with me. He would find himself nestled in the arms of a highly muscular Amazon woman. He would be very tender to her, caretaking her and servicing her while softly stroking her muscles. He would masturbate prolifically to these day-dreams, trying to discharge his tension, but he never could find sufficient release.

Freud has described this kind of behavior as an anal-sadistic fixation -- a fixation of the personality to a level appropriate to a two-year old child who is strongly invested in controlling his bowels, himself and others. In the context of this fixation, Morris also had a strong, albeit unconscious, interest in cruelty, as can be seen in his physical behavior toward me and his fantasy of being at the mercy of the Amazon. For the most part, however, he was a good citizen. His fixation and struggle-orientation were well earned at the hands of his domineering and cruel mother.

After Morris had been in treatment a sufficient length of time, he began to see the possibility of a new outlook on life. The key to this insight was his gradual understanding of his own propensity to see life as a struggle.

One Year of Treatment: The Transference is Fully Established

After Morris had been in group and individual treatment for almost a year, I noticed that in the transference, he was agreeing with any number of things I would say, and then passively waiting for me to "analyze" him. One day he was telling me that his supervisor, who had a special interest in him, had given him hell, telling him that he was fed up with him and that he had made all kinds of allowances for him; one more time and he was out. Morris felt very badly for having let his supervisor down.

I told him that I didn't think he really felt so bad. He had said these things many times before, yet continued the same pattern of behavior at work. Then I had a flash of insight that led me to say: "Are you aware of the fact that you are having a high sexual experience, both in here and with your boss?" Morris' face flushed. Since this encounter happened during a group therapy session, I asked him for permission to share with the group his sexual fantasy about being overcome, dominated and pleasured by the muscular Amazon. Now the overpowering woman had become his boss, albeit a man. This was accompanied by other pleasures, I said, such as being treated specially by his boss, in the midst of all of his punishments at work. I indicated that Morris was doing the same thing in group therapy. Instead of exercising his own judgement about what was going on, he had shut down, looking to me for all answers, waiting for me (symbolically speaking) to muscularly take care of him, to enfold him and overpower him.

The Spiritual Dimensions:

In spite of his weaknesses, Morris was an independent thinker and he acknowledged fully and powerfully that this interpretation of his behavior was true. Meanwhile, the rest of the group listened in silence and appreciation. They seemed to acknowledge, and even participate in the "goodness" of Morris' release from such a pattern--to share the joy of his treatment/ liberation. Furthermore, Morris himself had now become liberated from the unconscious pleasure he took from setting up struggles in order to get special attention and inner satisfaction. As Morris gave up this pattern, I watched him become more group oriented and more giving. As his personality ascended, he quite naturally found more room for giving.

The group session was ended with a prayer from the Arcane School of Theosophy:

"I am a point of light within a greater Light.

I am a strand of loving energy within the stream of Love divine.

I am a point of sacrificial Fire, focused within the fiery Will of God.

And thus I stand.

"I am a way by which men may achieve.
I am a source of strength enabling them to stand.
I am a beam of light shining upon their way.
And thus I stand.

"And standing thus, revolve
And tread this way the ways of men and know the ways of God.
And thus I stand."

Ending with this prayer, I pointed out that it contained admonitions of the soul, the high self, the high personality toward which we strive, and which we can achieve by trying to make ourselves better people.

Struggle is Transcended - Soul-Warmth and Love Emerge

Morris' struggles were not quite over, but in the end they were transcended, giving way to a new warmth and expression of his innate loving capacity.

One day, during a group session, he was fairly bristling at whatever I would say to anyone, immediately taking it up for debate. Indeed, he was a very sharp and skillful antagonist. I tried to point out, as I had done many times before, that he was no longer seeing the world through struggled-colored glasses, but my suggestion didn't quite take. Finally, I pointed out that he was being very hostile to me and that his anger seemed to be leaking out all over.

When I saw that Morris did not quite believe me, I turned to the other members of the group for their observations, and they agreed that he was struggling. One patient told him that not only was he arguing with everything, but that he was acting very much like her ex-husband to whom she used to be attracted. This attraction ended, she explained, because he put her down all the time. She warned Morris that if he continued to be so critical, he would remain lonely in life because women wouldn't want to have this kind of a relationship.

The following day Morris arrived very much subdued. I learned that, for the first time in years, his stomach had been so upset that he had thrown up--nor was he able to sleep that night. This revealed just how capable of being hurt he was. I regretted at this point that I didn't yet have that kind of soul-to-soul contact that would allow me to be empathically joined with him. Gradually, however, as the session continued, I could feel the empathy growing between us, helping me to realize that what Morris needed was to be assured of his positive side as well as his negative side. Once the group and myself had done this, I saw the color return to his face and I knew all the more how hurt he had been. I also became aware of my own countertransference feelings of hostility toward him, and it dawned on me that I was not being the well-trained psychoanalyst that I should have been.

I also began to understand that Morris was very heavily engaged in transference to me. This included not only his expectation that I would criticize him, as his mother had done so liberally during his upbringing, but also his fear of being rejected if he allowed himself to feel love toward me. I said to him, "You know, if you were so hurt by me that you vomited and couldn't sleep all night, then you must really think a lot of me." He began to confess, if only a little, that he did admire me. I then said, "You must also be afraid of that feeling somehow or other. Maybe that's why you're bristling like a porcupine, trying to push me away because you are so afraid of your love/admiration for me." This interpretation began to open the door, and Morris was able to speak, for the first time, of his fear that if he ever did let himself to express his feelings for me, then he would become vulnerable.

By acknowledging this vulnerability and helping Morris to under-stand that he was really safe with me, I was able to take the next step. In doing so, I pushed much more quickly than I usually do. I said, "You know, perhaps what you're afraid of too is that you might even be having sexual fantasies about me, a man." I felt that he would understand what I meant by this, for I had explained transference to him many times before, telling him that it is a therapeutic truism that the most important thoughts, feelings and conflicts that a person has will always center around the therapist after a period of time. When I suggested that he might be afraid because he was having sexual feelings toward me, this led to an openness in Morris, allowing him to say that he had found himself looking at men with muscles from time to time and that perhaps he was afraid of his feelings for me. I reminded him that his father was the nourishing one in his family and that perhaps all of his hurt and hostility toward me was based upon his wish--and the fear of his wish--to be very close to me, as if I was a father.

At this, Morris really began to open up. At the end of the session, this man who had always been so distant that I had never been able to hug him at the end of a session, but only shake his hand formally, actually bent toward me and asked for a hug. He held me for a long time and hugged me so hard that he almost sobbed with repressed joy. This was true communion, evidence of soul-to-soul contact leading to a bettering of understanding and the emergence of the joy that was buried underneath all his fear and love.

Full Release

As time went on, Morris began to open himself more and more to myself and to others. One day, during a private session, he began by telling me how much he had looked forward to his appointment today because he didn't like to go for long without seeing me. On this day I noted how much softer he was. I noticed, however, that it was still extremely difficult for Morris to say all of this, in spite of the security of the therapeutic situation. His voice, while he was telling me this, came out in an intellectual and colorless way, due to his shame and his fear of being vulnerable. I suggested that, like many men in American culture, in his unconscious mind he might have such feelings tied up with wanting to get physically close to me, homosexually close. He accepted the interpretation without much anxiety and perhaps with only little realization. He went on, however, to tell me how afraid he was of his warmth and intimacy with people. He admitted that he was still preoccupied with his picture of his mother and still expected others to be as sharp and critical of him as she was. In fact, he was tempted to act the same way as his mother did when he was with people. He went on to say that as I had guided him through the years, he had dropped that way of behaving, allowing his softer side to come out, but he also confessed that he still felt unworthy of being loved.

I suggested that perhaps, now that he had received a new insight and was fully aware of feeling unworthy that he could neutralize this feeling by acknowledging the many, many good things about himself. At this point a feeling of great peace pervaded the room. Previously, Morris had always felt restless, on edge and never quiet except when he was lying in bed reading, but now he felt a great sense of peace as he thought of my relationship with him and of spreading his idealistic works.

In Morris, we have an example of spiritual psychotherapy, but a therapy without talking in spiritual terms. His ancient adaptation and old ideal of being like his mother, his expectation that the world would criticize him as his mother had; all of this was given up. In essence, he let go of a fixation to the lower mind and the lower astral self, along with the equivalent physical body-orientation, for these things are, after all, exercised in behavior and in speech. Having given this up, Morris rose to a higher level of idealism and lovingness. For the first time he could express caring, not only for me, but also for those in his therapy group and for humanity as a whole.

By the time we reached his final session, Morris' soulful lovingness had been so fully released that this man, whose feelings had been encased in a struggle-oriented, sado-masochistic outlook on life, actually threw his arms around me and sobbed a loving good-bye.

A few days later, I received a carefully selected greeting card, on which he wrote:

"To the world's best psychiatrist. From the world's most grateful patient. Thank you for sharing my initial five-year journey of self-discovery and exploration. I will use your insights (and mine as well) for the rest of my life. My work and therapy with you equal my greatest and most meaningful experience in life! The journey will continue, but now the rest of it is up to me."

His current goal is to elevate society through teaching and by achieving a significant governmental position.

In Morris' progress we see the gradual unfolding of a personality, and the growth of his warmth and happiness. This unfolding spontaneously occurred as he was released from his former adjustments and constraints and led to a higher level of personality and orientation, one that is closer to the soul.

What is the hallmark of closeness to the soul? Love-wisdom. And what is wisdom? The Tibetan teaches us, in the Alice Bailey books, that wisdom is "knowledge, gained by experience, and exercised through love."

The Universality of Spiritual Striving

It has always deeply impressed me to witness, over and over again, the easy openness that people, even the most unlikely ones, have for these discussions of spirituality. Once they are given permission to be open about these matters, revelations of hidden spiritual experiences always enter the scene. People in our society have a great deal of fear about taking a stand on anything spiritual. In spite of this, more and more individuals are admitting that they believe in the higher mind and the soul. Here are two examples:

First Example

Marie was a thirty-five year old nurse, who had been raised in a physically abusive and alcoholic household. Because of this, she had learned to make her way through life by becoming "hard." She expected abuse and was constantly prepared for it. In time, however, she quickly saw that she was unnecessarily distancing herself from her husband, and blinding herself to his obvious devotion. When she finally understood this, however, she softened.

In the midst of a discussion in group therapy one day about the possibility of the immortality of the essential person, she told us a story about a six-year old boy who had died of cancer a short time before the group met. She spoke of how he had seen Jesus twenty-four hours before his death. He had not been talking, only waving at people as they came into his room. Suddenly, he opened his eyes brightly and said, "Mommy, look. Look at the beautiful lights. Aren't they beautiful and gorgeous?" His mother said, "Where, what lights?" A little later he said, "Look Mommy. It's Jesus. I knew there was a Jesus. He's smiling at me." With that, he put his arms straight out in the air, as if to go with him. His mother then said to him, "Go, Jake, go with Jesus." Then he said, taking his arms back, "Jesus told me it's not time yet." Twenty-four hours later he died.

In truth, I was astounded to hear these revelations from a woman who seemed so hardened, and who was operating in the academic environment of the hospital in which she worked. But I have often been taken by surprise, gratifyingly so, in this respect.

Second Example

Mark was a thirty-year-old man, fiercely intelligent, but full of obsessions, depression and self-doubt. His obsessions were so severe that one could hardly get him out of the room at the end of a session, because he would obsessively ruminate about the path he should take, asking questions and requesting reassurance. Over time, however, these neurotic handicaps lessened and he was able to more easily continue his search for the self.

One day in hypnosis he had a major breakthrough that totally transformed his vision of himself. He was surrounded and filled with what he described as the blue-white light that was his soul self. When he saw who he truly was, he realized that this was all he desired for his life: to remain in contact with his divine self, his loving self, the productive self that created poetry and authorship. In the previous three months, in line with his progress in treatment, he had made more friends than in all his previous life. He began to realize that the former restrictions that he placed upon himself--that he was too big and clumsy, that he had not achieved enough in the way of credentials, that he was dumb--were all opinions born of his upbringing and, therefore, no longer appropriate. The essential thing, he decided, was to be himself by caring for people and producing beauty through his writing. He would, however, complete law school in order to achieve the necessary credentials to give him enough power and influence to spread the message of spiritual love.

Mark is a living demonstration that the realization and releasing of a high spiritual goal, and the knowledge that one can contact the divine self, leads to higher achievement and greater authenticity.

Spiritual psychotherapy enables any individual willing to look deeply into his or her essential self to achieve this greater authenticity of being. Paula, the woman who suffered from severe allergies and muscular spasms, was able to free herself from the emotional straightjacket she had lived in for fifty-eight years and discover her authentic self. Following the release of her emotions, she experienced an irresistible surfacing of a love capacity that extended first to me, as a transference object, and then broadly to her family--and then to the world at large. Beyond this, she had ecstatic, blissful visions and feelings of union with God, the All and nature. She had an irresistible drive to investigate spiritual literature and teachings, devoting herself to hospice activities and to the establishment of a spiritual community.

Vera, the woman who found herself in a psychiatric hospital after manifesting panic episodes, is another example of how the self ascends after being released from impediments. Conventional psychiatry had looked only at her surface manifestations and did not see the real inner person. When that person was discovered, validated and released, a true servant of God emerged - the servant who had been waiting. Vera went on to become quite a power in her hospice activity, and is now pursuing her credentials as a minister in a church.

These two women are both highly developed, both on the ladder of ascension and both available for yet more advancement toward the soul. It was only necessary to uncork the bottle that had imprisoned the genie.

Everyone has a spiritual center, a latency, and inner divine self wanting to be revealed; but there are also layers surrounding it and preventing its emergence. Some people, though good and admirable individuals, remain attached to their material beliefs, their spiritual armoring, and travel upward only so far. Sadly, consensual belief in our society makes it all too easy to cling to this "material-above-all" orientation. On

208-

the other hand, throughout our culture there is a progressive yielding of these armorings as more and more people turn their attention to matters of the spirit. The more we hear of these spiritual adventures in personal stories, in the media and in books such as *The Care of the Soul, The Celestine Prophecy,* and *The Seat of the Soul,* the more they are becoming acceptable.

In this chapter we have seen the armorings and sheaths of defense that inhibit access to the more authentic part of ourselves, the soul. We have also seen the ever-readiness of the soul to be found and to be expressed, as the acquired sheaths of defense, both individual and cultural, are released. Individuals always have varying degrees of access to the soul according to their willingness and courage to face themselves. If the readiness is there, however, what follows is the wonderful release of authenticity. Sharing this experience, through both words and the message of experience elevates both the individual and society.

Exercises and Guidelines:

1. Know your fixations: Study your language, dreams and mental preoccupations; that which preoccupies you is your fixation. Then raise your mind, aspirations and actions, day by day, to thoughts and acts of senseless kindness.

2. Know the planes: material-body; lower emotion; higher emotion; lower mental; higher mental; intuition (soul); higher planes beyond the soul, from On-High.

3. Practice suspending doubt. Take your intuitions and meditation messages seriously. Again, value imagination and see how you can apply it.

4. Know your immortality. Practice the knowledge of it. Reread why I have come to believe in immortality.

CHAPTER XII:

The Dark Forces

Balancing The Dark And The Light, Both Within And Beyond The Personality -- Ideas, Altruism And Naivete Make Easy Targets For Darkness -- A Case Of Idealistic Strivings That Was Used By The Dark Forces -- Neurosis, The Achilles Heel, Inlet For Darkness, How To Deal With It -- Seekers Of The Dark Forces -- Neurosis And Seeking Glamour Opens The Way -- The Ascent Into The Light (The Forward Movement Of The Personality) -- Case Histories: One Who Was Too Fearful To Face The Dark; One Who Saw The Light.

The moment the Void bestirred Itself, duality was created: light and dark, positive and negative, male and female, good and evil. The Princes of Light vied with the Princes of Darkness, each seeking their representative energies in the lower physical realm--spirituality, love, altruistic endeavors in the part of the one; neurotic, selfish, sadistic strivings on the part of the other.

The overarching forces sought to form a channel, each with its own. The Brothers of Light sought those who were appealing to them through their ascendancy into the higher mind, higher emotions and higher striving to serve others. The Brothers of Darkness sought others in the lower realms of the mind, where the coarser emotions and material strivings are focussed. Each of these powers endeavored to form a completion of the channel (with the human on earth who would be receptive to them) in the course of fulfilling or obstructing the Divine Plan.

While spiritual psychology acknowledges love as the overriding influence in the universe, it also admits to the reality of the destructive forces that we call evil--the Powers of Darkness. While we can recognize that these negative powers have their evolutionary purpose and contribute in the long run to the advancement of the whole, in the short run they can play havoc in the life of the individual and retard that person's spiritual progress. All of these forces must be understood and properly employed if their useful purposes are to be fulfilled. It is the task of the awakened spiritual therapist to delve deeply into the mind of both the individual and society, and to bring forth the secret strivings of evil. In such endeavors, courage is the byword for both the patient and the therapist. Finding the strength to face the most feared feelings and tragedies in the patient's life is an absolute necessity, but this endeavor can also be supported by a firm confidence that Light will prevail, that the Light will dispel the Dark.

For human beings to grow and develop spiritually, the Forces of Light and the Forces of Shadow must be in balance with one another in each person's life. This balance, once properly achieved, will enable us to use adversity as a toughening agent, seeing it as a warning that we must awaken and learn, rather than allowing it to be a destructive force in our lives.

It is incumbent upon the spiritual therapist to recognize the Shadow Forces as pitfalls that face spiritual seekers.

Many of the dangers that spiritual seekers face arise out of naiveté, denial and through ignorance of the trickery of the world. By looking at some case histories, we will examine how these forces work, often under the cover of good deeds and good intentions.

Psychological Training Is No Insurance Against the Dark Forces

Manfred was a man much given to idealism. In spite of being a specialist in the mental health field and having a profound understanding of the human psyche, he was completely naive about the way things worked in the world at large. This naiveté was inspired by his upbringing. His parents were themselves good people, but they had been too indulgent and overprotective of their son. In this way, he grew up filled with an overweening idealism that poorly prepared him for the darker aspects of society, especially for the more shady machinations of the business community.

Eventually, Manfred's naivete led him into the hands of a psychopathic businessman named Ron who was a willing servant of the Dark Forces. Contrary to common belief, the psychopath is not insensitive. He or she has an exquisitely developed intuitive apparatus, resonating to the needs and vulnerabilities of each and every intended victim. Unlike those of us who use our sensitivity to respect the feelings and boundaries of others, the psychopath uses his/hers for selfish manipulation, sensing the field like a hunting carnivore.

In this way Manfred's advanced training, credentials and idealistic plans provided fertile ground for the businessman, who was looking for opportunity. This self-styled "entrepreneur" seemed to warm immediately to the doctor's desire to build a research center, even offering to finance it. This research center, Ron said, would be a model facility that would spread education and welfare. Underneath, however, the motives of the two men were polar opposites: the businessman was moved by the opportunity for a huge illegitimate profit, and the doctor was moved by a dream.

A plan went into operation to build a psychiatric hospital, and assign a part of the profits to fund a research center -- a wonderful design! Idealism was served, but so was gullibility. As project delays arose again and again, Ron explained each of these in turn to Manfred, who continued to believe in him and to remain tenaciously loyal to the project. While the financier was feeding the psychiatrist's belief system, he was simultaneously undermining it with other operations that were far from ideal: cheap, expedient, and even at times on the edge of the law. The psychiatrist's sterling reputation, coupled with innocence and naiveté, served the businessman well. The final result was that the research center was never born. Years of life, effort and reputation were consumed and those who had been caught up in the idealistic excitement generated by the project were disappointed and hurt.

In this situation, the Dark Forces prevailed. They were able to keep Manfred in a destructive partnership with the psychopathic businessman for a long time, drawing on both Manfred's idealism and his desire for financial security.

Idealism and Altruism Often Make People Easy Targets

Another example of how evil feeds on naive idealism and good intentions can be seen in the relationship that developed between a businessman named Fred and a spiritually committed professional couple named Eugene and Jacqueline. Fred, who had formerly worked in advertising, had become a dabbler in the healing arts, in spite of the fact that he had no proper training or professional credentials. He also had great charisma and a large fund of knowledge concerning the extraordinary powers of the mind and of parapsychology.

When he met Eugene and Jacqueline, he was able to convince them to dedicate themselves and their financial resources to the project of creating a special birth center on a faraway island. According to Fred, this center would lead to the development of highly advanced human beings, and the three founders of the project would become spiritual leaders in a better world. The couple soon became persuaded. They sold their possessions, abandoned both practice and roots, and ventured forth. Over a period of time their financial base was misappropriated. The wife had become pregnant and was told that she was carrying a spiritual leader of mankind. She lost the baby through careless medical attention on the island. The dentist was not only deprived of his possessions but of his self-esteem as well. He was harangued and constantly held up to ridicule in the island group. Eventually the couple left, starting over with nothing but their spiritual beliefs and inner guidance. They are now operating a healing clinic in the United States, more enlightened about not giving their trust too lightly, but still optimistic about their commitment to creating a better world.

Here we see how Darkness targets its agent, how it plays upon ideals, naiveté and the ignorance of evil. In line with this, the Tibetan states that when the student is of sufficient importance to attract notice, the attack may come from those who deal purely with matter (meaning physical matter in human beings) to the hindrance of spiritual growth.

Stories such as the ones I told above are not uncommon. Those who are altruistic and spiritual must be alert and educated about the darkness in the world. Surely, there are many idealists who are especially practical and seasoned and we sorely need this combination but there are just as many who consistently project their own goodness onto others, at times indiscriminately. Evil opportunists are always on the lookout for such types and know well how to manipulate them.

The careless desire to project the image of goodness onto everyone does not make the world a better place. It supports blindness. It endows the Dark Brother with a mantle of light that, lamentably, discretion can not penetrate. Worse yet, it provides him with a false glow, within which the psychopath can operate concealed. We owe it to ourselves and to others to be aware of the darkness in the world, and to be knowledgeable about the self. At the same time, we must balance caution with wise optimism. I am not calling for cynicism, but a sense of realism, for one's own sake and for the sake of others.

Idealistic Strivings Used By the Brothers of Shadow

James, the young, talented, spiritually seeking individual we met earlier, is an excellent example of how the powers of good are often co-opted and corrupted by the powers of darkness. When he sought answers from the guru in the far-off city, he was taken in with open arms and housed in their small boarding home where he was taught about many useful and genuine things, such as Kundalini, the Nadis and the energy forces that circulate throughout the etheric body. Unfortunately, he was instructed in an atmosphere that mandated that he "listen only to the guru." His mind was filled with danger and the fear that if he did not do things exactly as the guru said, all would be lost. Since the goals that were given to him were impossible to fulfill, he soon developed profound feelings of failure and despair and his guru was quick to remind him that all his failures were due to his not following instructions properly.

Thus, the circle was closed. The power of the guru became more and more entrenched and James sank into deeper and deeper inferiority and dependence. Finding himself gloomy and hopeless, James became involved in a cycle of drinking and drug intoxication. After each destructive bout with alcohol or drugs, he would return to the "guru," only to be told that he must try harder. In this small cult-like setting, James was captured and caught in progressive dependency and despair, especially since all of the false instructions he was given for soul ascendancy were allegedly offered only for his personal development.

The badge of the false guru is often exhibited in the form of arrogance, a short temper, the selfish exercise of power and an overt conceit. James' guru had all these traits in abundance. In spite of his miserable experiences, however, James was reluctant to leave this "school" lest he be lost forever.

Over time, his drug addiction became severe, and, on many occasions, he wandered through dangerous city streets seeking drugs and putting his life at risk. James not only understood the risk but, at times, was actually hoping to end his life in this way.

Fortunately for him, I was able to speak a language that was not unlike that of the guru. I was familiar with Eastern religion, and was therefore able to participate in James' experience. I intuited immediately that I had to move slowly in discrediting his former teacher, or James would not believe me. His affiliation to this belief system and mentor were so deeply entrenched that he could only detach in small stages. It was necessary for me to both participate in James' belief system and to understand his spiritual striving in the context of the teachings to which he was still adhering--and I did so. Gradually, however, I was able to point out the clay feet upon which his false god stood. Little by little, I was able to help James to see the difference between the self-extolling conceit of the spiritual egoist, and the easy self-effacement of the truly humble spiritual seeker. I did not expect James to graduate into a vacuum either. Week by week, I helped him to replace his former belief system with the teachings of *A Course in Miracles* offered in our clinic, along with the many living examples of individuals who were in service to others, rather than in service to themselves.

Under this gentle guidance, James' fears of meditation were alleviated. When his false guru had told him that he must never close his eyes in meditation, unless he wished to court disastrous consequences, he had effectively bottled up the incredible energy that was trying to move through James' body. Once James began to trust me, and was willing to close his eyes, this energetic bottleneck was alleviated so that he could fully participate in his "streamings," the vibrations that he quite often felt, and in the glories of his music-making that had always carried him into higher planes in the past. Gradually, James lost his former affiliations and fears, and was able to emerge more fully into his true, spiritual Self.

James is a perfect example of how the Brothers of the Shadow use humanity's idealistic strivings to find their way into an individual's inner world. From there, unless stopped, they are able to let their dark essence expand to destroy the seeker, keeping him or her from the journey up into the light -- the release of the true self.

Those Who Seek The Darkness

While there are many whose naivete make them the unconscious prey of the powers of darkness, there are also those who consciously seek out evil in the form of the many sadistic and satanic cults that are widespread in our culture. I have not had much experience with the victims of such cults, but some of my colleagues have. Their stories about the ritual sacrifice of babies, sadistic tortures and sexual sadomasochistic indulgences are not exaggerated. Furthermore the slavery of the one who is incorporated into the cult is complete, and his or her life becomes dedicated to the cultist activities.

I have had two patients who were each raised by devil worshippers. As such, these girls were witnesses to cruel and horrific practices, which they were also forced to participate in. In these instances, the incorporated emotional trauma was enormous, causing the patient to slip away into another personality. In this way, multiple personalities were formed in each of these individuals. The experiencing of a repeated emotional horror that is too much to bear is the common mechanism for the development of multiple personality disorder. In such cases, it is as if the former personality with its accompanying experiences never existed.

It was not easy to detoxify these women from their experiences. It was as if the Prince of Darkness himself had insinuated his power into the bodies of these innocent young women to such a degree that it seemed at times as if they were possessed by a shadowy force that was autonomous from themselves. Indeed, in order to release them from their patterns of continual fear, helplessness and anxiety, it was necessary to provide a constant holding environment of security, availability and relaxation-safety. Hypnosis and meditation helped greatly in teaching them to visualize inner pictures of safety.

But there are also those who, for their own reasons, seek out the Darkness, such as Delilah, a sixteen-year-old girl who was much favored by her father in a very sinister sense. Although they had not engaged in overt incest, there were most certainly overtones of emotional incest in their relationship. The bond between the two of them excluded the girl's mother almost completely. Together the father and daughter would share experiences, scoffing at the mother and pouring themselves into the perfumed essences of material and sensual abundance: food, expensive clothing and even sexual teasing.

At the age of sixteen, Delilah was in so much trouble that her father was finally forced to ask that she be boarded with a foster family. She arrived in a home that was well integrated, whose children--close to her own age--were well disciplined, quite happy and indeed filled with good intentions and a good orientation toward the world. Instead of benefiting from these healthier influences, however, she soon became bored with them. In her room she lit candles, made a shrine to the devil and practiced to be a witch.

Her foster family took such a notion lightly, as the expression of a young and undeveloped mind. Unknown to them, however, Delilah's cruelty was very well developed indeed. She worked tirelessly to discredit the foster parents who had taken her into their home with a desire to improve her life, hoping to help her to overcome her psychopathic and sexually profligate activities. In the end she succeeded in defaming them in the eyes of her father, and she was taken away. The once close friendship between the foster couple and the father was broken forever. Mysteriously, shortly thereafter, the couple began to experience significant setbacks in their lives.

Certainly this is an example of an individual who desired to meet the forces of darkness and to incorporate their ways into herself. She was clearly well met and well used.

Neurosis Opens The Door for The Dark Forces

Another opening for the forces of darkness lies in the neurotic aspects, strivings and handicaps of the personality, which are often manifested by fear and feelings of inferiority. Such feelings inhibit the natural light and love within an individual, and must be resolved in order for the personality to advance to levels of love and true spirituality. Personal greed and the promise of fame, wealth and sexual pleasure can also lead people into selfish and self-aggrandizing pursuits. The Forces of Darkness commonly often use this route, as we can see in those whose personalities changed for the worst after they become successful or famous. Other avenues for the Dark Forces are available through the employment of neurotic preoccupation with feelings of depression or sadism. Feelings of being an abused exception in life (and therefore entitled to compensation) often opens the door for the Faustian contract, as can the overdeveloped and selfish pursuit of sex.

The Tibetan (in *Letters on Occult Meditation*[20]) inveighs against giving into the lower emotions, including discouragement, emotions which he equates with "glamour":

"Glamour may be either on the emotional or mental levels but it is usually on the former. One form employed is to cast over the disciple the shadows of the thought of weakness or discouragement or criticism to which he may at intervals give way....they (thoughts of discouragement, my addition) loom in undue proportion and the unwary disciple, not realizing that he is but seeing the ... outlines of his own momentary and passing thoughts, gives way to discouragement, aye even to despair, and becomes of little use to the Great Ones."

The Tibetan goes on to speak of the descent of a blackness of despair in which the disciple considers that all past effort has been futile and nothing remains but to die. This state of mind certainly sounds like what we call "major depression." Anyone in the grip of this kind of emotional illness certainly becomes useless and their energy as a servant of the light is lost. The Tibetan goes on to admonish that one should not despair, but remember the inner divinity which will surely shine through as victory and optimism.[21]

It most certainly is true that the darkness of despair, especially as experienced in a major depression, paralyzes the efforts of the seeker of the light to foster his or her own spiritual and personal development. Neurosis can also inhibit an individual's ascent into the light.

An example of the individual who is inhibited in his upward progress by his neurosis can be seen in David, a professional man who was in the prime of his life. David was endowed with a creative intelligence, energy and a strong will to do good. Unfortunately, he suffered from a strong feeling of inferiority that led him to be a lieutenant rather than a captain, a follower rather than a leader. This inability to rise to his true level was born of his desire to be close to his father. His father was a man who, in spite of his good character and integrity, was unable to relate emotionally to his son. He would come home from work and hide his face behind a newspaper.

Throughout his life David hoped to find someone whom he could serve and by whom he could be recognized. This pattern caused him to make himself subservient to people who were, so to speak, lesser than he. They did not have the same talent or drive, or the same will to do good. Accordingly, his feeling of subservience and need to be recognized caused him to unrealistically value himself less than he should. This pervading sense of inferiority inhibited David from carrying out his own plans and his own creative productivity. It prevented him from using his altruistic energies to their fullest until much later in life when they were recognized, uncovered and offered many affirmations by valued colleagues and his successes in life.

As David's life illustrates, the Agents of Darkness who oppose the ascent of the individual into personal and spiritual development often use the vulnerable points of the disciples of the light to hinder them.

The Ascent To The Light

What is the ascent into light? It is the constant movement forward of the personality, the striving to raise the mind and emotions to levels of love, high thinking and high striving so that wider circles of humanity can be served and raised up by the work of the human Agent of Light.

All of this describes the aims of spiritual psychotherapy. These goals are also articulated by the Tibetan, who instructs: "In terms of the opposite of the ascent to the Light, that adherence to material pursuits will not only shut out the Light, but also open the individual to the temptation of the darker side of himself/herself."[22]

The experiences that I have described regarding the manipulations of the two psychopathic businessmen are clearly being described in this passage. These experiences denoted the absolute absence of empathic feelings in these men for the individuals they so heartlessly exploited, and many were hurt in the course of their actions. Prominent businessmen who operate in corrupt ways often literally enslave working people and the aged, by incorporating their savings into their personal coffers.

The most extreme example of the mercilessness of the Dark Forces is shown in the life of Adolph Hitler. It is said that Hitler studied the parapsychological powers of the mind, and there can be no doubt that he was an agent of the overarching Forces of Darkness. He appealed to the sadistic, selfish power-motivated cravings of an entire nation. These corrupt drives increased as a nation abandoned its early warning signals and its pain of conscience in its belief that the reign of the Third Reich would create a nation that would last a thousand years.

It is well to remember Elizabeth Kubler-Ross' caution that there is a Hitler in each of us. Only by recognizing this can we expose him to the light so that he will lose his power. It is important to be on guard always against these tendencies within ourselves, so that we do not become prey to them, either through innocence or through selfish desire. These sorts of vulnerabilities lead to the invitations of a Dark Brotherhood.

Bailey writes about this in her book *Letters on Occult Meditation,*[23] wherein she indicates the lure of those who masquerade as agents of light and charity. She also advises the reader to remain firm in purity of character, in body, and emotion.

These warnings remind us that in order to elevate the mind and the emotions to higher striving, we must continually nourish and stimulate the personality, mind and soul to this level. Eliminating fear is something that we work on a great deal in our clinic, advocating that the individual faces the fear, tolerates it, and finally allows the light to be shed on it so that it may fade away. As for Bailey's admonition to stand firm, we encourage strength and persistence in our clients as they strive toward higher levels of being, and nourish within them the faith and belief that the Forces of Light, Love and God will ultimately prevail when we tolerate the pain and grief of our personal vicissitudes.

And finally, let me give you this small clinical excerpt from a session with a patient of mine named Karen. When Karen first came to me, she spoke briefly of fears that had persisted from childhood, but insisted that she didn't want to keep speaking about them because they were evil feelings and frightened her. She was also afraid of some of the meditative and breathing techniques that we use because they made her feel as if there were evil forces around. Undoubtedly, these feelings were expressions of her own hostility and aggressive desires projected outward, but I did not discount the possibly that they were also joined with a sensitivity to outside evil forces, such as those that emanate from evil people or the superordinate powers that surround us. For example, since childhood Karen had been able to see shadowy entities that had vague forms but were not well defined. She saw these entities when it was dark, resulting in her fear of darkness.

Back in the days when I was a traditional psychotherapist, I would have considered such a patient psychotic, but since studying Theosophy and other spiritual instructions, I have taken a different view. For example, as I got to know Karen I realized that she has a very sturdy ego and has surmounted many difficulties in life, including a series of nine operations to restore the use of her hand over the past six to seven years. The added burden of having to deal with an alcoholic husband, raising a son and unemployment all combined to weigh her down mightily. In spite of all this, she managed to conquer these things and to remain stalwart and religious.

Even though I had to treat her for a depression that had caused her progressive withdrawal from society, along with a loss of energy, pride and pleasure in life, she still functioned responsibly, notwithstanding her troubles. In light of all of these factors, there was no question in my mind about the ability of her ego to function and assess reality adequately and well.

Because Karen had such sturdy personal resources, I brought up her visions to the entire group she was in therapy with. I was especially interested in utilizing the abilities of another patient in this group who had psychic powers, could see entities and had accurate precognitions. I began by going into a bit of a lecture designed to try to help Karen and others in the group to confront their fears and to learn something about their essential immortality and spirituality. I told them about the divine spark within them, and the fact that the body is a container for the soul, the spirit and the vital principle. I told them that one could see this easily. When looking upon a dead person or a dead animal, it was clear that the vital principle was gone. I spoke about the fact that people who were quadriplegic remained the same inside as before, as did old people or dwarves. Therefore, the essential person was not the body. I also talked about the etheric body and the aura, which could now be photographed by Kirlean photography, as well as the astral and mental bodies, and even other bodies beyond those.

I spoke of how the first body, the physical body, dies, but how the astral body remains for a time, persistent in its desires to remain close to its physical satisfactions. I went on to explain that if this were the body of someone who had been very devoted to sensuous and selfish pleasures, the astral body would linger as an entity that could be perceived. I also suggested that the way to deal with these entities was not to fear them but to face them and shed light upon them.

Karen argued that she had always tried to deal with these evil entities by calling upon God and not thinking about them. I told her that the dark forces fear the light; that facing them and becoming familiar with them within herself as well as around herself, would throw light upon them. Thereupon, her energies could be freed to become useful. I spoke further about how people ascend in their power as their personality and soul ascends to higher realms, whereby they begin to develop psychic abilities. I pointed out that, whereas she and the other patient had been taught that such psychic powers are to be feared, these powers were actually neutral. They could be used for evil purposes by people who were evilly disposed or for saintly purposes in people who were spiritually elevated.

I thought that this talk was a good and meaningful one, as did a number of other people in the group, but the patient to whom this talk was primarily directed didn't buy it. She remained intransigent in her belief that the things she could sense and see were evil, and would not express anything further about her fears of "dark entities."

Karen's decision saddened me because I thought it would greatly benefit her, and even alleviate some of her depression, to face her fears and vanquish them. When one is working from the orientation of spiritual psychotherapy, the interpretations of things like depression, "seeing things," and neurosis becomes different. The primary difference is that these things are now seen as only aspects of the person. The spiritual psychotherapist is able to see the whole of a person, including the soul and the higher dimensions of human potential that exist within us. This vision leads to a wider and more hopeful vista for a "cure," for ascension and for one's ability to contribute to making a better life for him- or herself and a better world.

A happier ending occurred in Jeremy. I had known him since he was 13. Even then I knew he was a winner, a world-beater. But he had a heavy endowment of self-criticism which was born of his love for his father. His father was a depressive sort of a man, fiercely intelligent, but dissatisfied with himself and his career. He poured his high expectations for himself upon his only son. His pleasure in Jeremy's outstanding accomplishments was hidden behind an unexpressive personality and a wish for his son to do ever better. Thus the carrot was strung in front of the nose, and Jeremy could never catch up. He had an outstandingly successful career, but his love life was unfulfilled. When he married, somewhat late in life, it was to someone who filled his father's shoes, at least in terms of continual criticism and dissatisfaction with Jeremy. After many sessions, and a chipping away at his very clever defenses, we were able to reveal that his holding onto his self-criticism and continual dissatisfaction with himself was a way of staying loyal to and close to his (now deceased) father. When full insight into that mechanism was achieved, Jeremy was able to dissolve an unhappy marriage, and move on to greater appreciation of himself, and move toward the Light, through a lighter approach to life, a lighter approach to himself, and a lighter approach to women. He now is very close to a young woman who fully appreciates him and acknowledges him. His heaviness has given way. He is in the Light, and his own considerable ray shines through.

In Jeremy, we have an example of the Dark Forces finding their way through the neurotic portion which clung to a childish relationship with his father. Insofar as he continued his heavy self-criticism he retarded his own ascension and the considerable contribution he is now making to society. He has single-handedly developed an effort toward the children of the ghetto which teaches them how to make films which are then shown in a Children's Film Festival. This has already caught the attention of the city authorities.

Guidelines and Exercises:

1. How to balance: introspect, write a column of faults; face the things you fear the most to face: don't overestimate them; put light around them, in life by elevating and transcending tendencies to selfishness, greed, separatism, overestimation of power.

2. Attend seminars, self help groups; above all use your "center of Truth."

3. Cultivate idealism, but also be aware of the dark forces and people who would take advantage.

4. Use your intuition to get the "feel" of people. Notice how they talk. The followers of the Light are very clear and honest. Those who obscure and don't feel right are suspect.

5. Know that there are cults which worship Darkness. Take this seriously when people talk about following leaders who promulgate hatred, power and separatism from those who are different. Be aware that there is a Hitler within all of us. He can be defeated by throwing the light of introspection upon him. Be aware of the Hitler in others and protect yourself.

6. Be cautious about any leader who is arrogant, and claims that he/she has the only way. Be cautious about any leader who steals your power by saying that you must listen only to him/her, and not to your own center of truth.

CHAPTER XIII:

The Wisdom of Intuition
And The Realm of Knowing Beyond Knowing

Each Of Us Has An Inborn Intuitive Center; If Suppressed It Withers. If Opened It Enlarges -- Realm Is Related To ESP, Telepathy, Psychokinesis -- Opening The Self -- Open, Receive, Digest, Integrate Into Life -- Thought And Intuitive Thought Create -- Realm Of Knowing Beyond Knowing, Attached To The Intellect, But Beyond Intellect -- The "Aha" Experience -- The Knowing Beyond Intellect, The Omniscient Knowledge Of The Soul -- The Perception By The Witness -- Suspend Doubt -- Dropping Defenses (Relax Into Semi-Sleep, Wait For Signals, Be Courageous About Noting What Comes Up, Record And Remember In Order To Avoid Suppression By Doubt And Forgetting) -- The Witness Hovers Over The Scene -- Meditation As Soul-Knowing -- The Increased Power To Heal Both Within And With Others, That Comes With Soul-Knowing -- The Value Of Prayer -- A **Course In Miracles** *For Transcendence.*

We are taught that the human race is evolving, advancing onto the next level of consciousness. In the future humanity will depend more and more on the use of intuition, replacing the purely rational and intellectual approach to life and its challenges with which we are so familiar today. As we rise in our mental operations to higher levels, we will become more occupied with abstract concepts, aesthetic pursuits, and with the appreciation of the finer arts--all hallmarks of the receptivity called intuition.

It is a strange thing that in our Western science, even in psycho-analysis, which is reputedly the most introspective of the psychological disciplines, intuition is not only ignored but treated with disdain. In Eastern teachings, intuition is spoken of frequently and is recognized not only as the product of a higher mind but as a sensitive receptive apparatus that gathers messages from a higher place.

Each of us is born with an intuitive center, an open-minded mech-anism. Unfortunately, it is often sealed over, dimmed by our adherence to our cultural conditioning, which tells us over and over again that our perceptions are silly, illogical, too subjective, or a product of our imagination.

Insofar as this intuitive center is suppressed, it withers and almost disappears. If we learn to respect our intuitive signals, however, we experience an increasing number of flashes of deep insight, signals that are often validated by later experiences. The more this validation occurs, the more faith we can develop in our intuitive abilities, and the more they will shine as a beacon light, illuminating our knowledge and experience. The more we suspend doubt about these perceptions, the more we will receive.

Nowhere is this increasing receptivity more evident than in the practice of psychotherapy, in those soul-to-soul contacts between therapist and client. When I am in touch with my intuition while working with a client, and am open to receive the signals from my intuition, I experience a kind of resonant thrill. This sensation is frequently accompanied by an expansion of my heart chakra, or an opening in my solar plexus. Not infrequently during such times, I can anticipate what a patient will say, and this perception is beyond anything conveyed by their posture, tone of voice or words.

More and more the evidences of extrasensory perception, telepathy and psychokinesis are being recognized rather than dismissed. For example, it is commonly understood that when two people live together in a loving context, they develop similarities to one another, a close mental and emotional contact, a resonance of signals, and even a similarity in appearance. Perhaps this phenomenon is related to Sheldrake's morphogenic fields, those fields of influence within which knowledge and understanding is communicated within the human and animal world.

Opening the Self

Intuition is based upon an opening of self to the higher Self and to the higher planes that surround us. These insights become especially useful when we experience an intuitive flash, and then are able to withdraw into our accustomed cognitive set to reflect upon the information that has been received. This is the methodology of creation: We dissolve our boundaries to participate in a greater knowledge, and then re-establish our boundaries to taste and reflect upon the new experience. Finally, we integrate the new information into our daily lives. The ascent into a greater reliance upon our intuition is accompanied by a more enlightened orientation toward humanity, a broader participation with our fellow men and women. We find a concomitant desire to serve, a realization of joy in attending to the welfare of those close to us, for those in the community and even for the planet. Gone are the separatist strivings that cause each individual to dominate the other. Cruelty and sadism turn into assertive energy. The pursuit of sensual pleasure moves to a higher and more aesthetic plane.

I remember once seeing a wonderful cartoon movie called Le Planet Sauvage. This was the story of beings who were so far advanced of humanity as we know it today that they used humans as playthings -- not cruelly, but as toys. In one place in the story these beings went into deep meditation, whereupon their heads floated away in a glass sphere and travelled to a distant island. There they met their significant other and, in this spiritual meeting, produced progeny. Then they returned to their bodies.

This is a beautiful analogy of what happens during meditation. We enter into the realm of high mind, travel to other spheres and then create new realities. It is also a possible foreshadowing of what we human beings will become as we advance into yet another plane. As the Tibetan and Alice Bailey have pointed out, we will not need physical sexuality at such a time; we will reproduce by the creative powers of the mind.

This idea of creating with the higher mind is not too far from the creativity that we exercise with our minds now. For instance, an architect can imagine and then create a building, an artist a fully realized sculpture or painting, a composer a symphony. This idea is also not far from the exciting demonstrations of the power of mind that are becoming more and more common in medicine. In many documented cases, deep hypnosis has produced an anesthetic effect sufficient for surgery, someone has stopped the bleeding of a cut by the power of mind alone, and the creative powers of hypnosis and visualization have produced some remarkable remissions and cures in individuals suffering from cancer.

What Do We Mean By Knowing Beyond Knowing?

To fully realize this creative state, the first thing we must get in touch with is our "knowing beyond knowing," a type of intelligence beyond intellect and most of the other mental processes we are familiar with in our daily lives. This state can be experienced in meditation and in other states of mental reflection.

When we reach this state, we begin to understand why intellectual insight is not enough to bring about change. Intuition leads us to a feeling of knowing that seems to come from another realm, a hidden but sensed center of truth within us. Although this facility is actually attached to the intellect, most people have only partial access to it because of social conditioning. I have seen people, however, in which access to the this center of knowing seems automatic, and how they achieve this state is somewhat of a mystery to me. When they speak, they can feel an impact, a sense of realization that accompanies their words. This knowing is missing in the intellectualizer until that important moment when intuitive realization, the dawning of the "aha" insight, arrives on the scene.

I can remember my own struggles with my tendency to intellectualize during my personal training analysis. My analyst often said to me, "Your chief defense is intellectualization." This comment left me puzzled, helpless and despairing until one day, standing on a street corner, I realized that I didn't have to try to understand anything. All I had to do was to wait, for the anxiety was already there and would surely descend. In its train would come understanding and insight. Once I understood this, my whole approach to life and its challenges changed, especially my method of handling anxiety, which had been a real problem for me. Even though anxiety would still come in a crisis, in its wake I could now understand, and with that understanding control and find solution. This was the dawning of insight, of real realization, and relief.

Again, my friend Joy Parker raised an interesting and provocative point. She suggests, following Joseph Chilton Pearce's discussion of the intellect in his book *The Bond of Power,* that our societal conditioning about the limitations of our minds, our abilities, and the reality we inhabit prevents us from using our intellectual insights effectively. She continues by saying that one cannot bootstrap oneself out of that kind of cultural mindset. One cannot experience a higher understanding of reality if one is using only the tools of a much smaller understanding.

In the experience above, when I was trying to fit into the mind-set of my analyst, I experienced a "smallness." When I waited for the knowledge that came automatically, however, I experienced an "aha" that came from a higher place, an intuitive and knowing-beyond-knowing place. I am not the only one who has been "shrunken" and constrained by trying to fit in with accepted scientific and social beliefs. As Joy says, "It does not matter how intelligent one is, or how much will one has, the big picture that we so desperately need to see to reach our greatest potential for living is in the higher Self."

The mystifying anxiety we feel when faced by our inability to get out of our conditioned mindset is very common in our culture. An example of how this limits us can be seen in one of my patients, a thirty-two-year-old named Scott. In spite of the fact that he functioned at a very high level of productivity, Scott was beset by multitudinous fears about everything, especially the fear that his whole world would come to an end if he weren't perfect, in control at all times, and loved by everybody. Scott knew, even as he told me about them, that his fears were silly, yet he was driven by these ideas just as surely as if he were completely unaware of them. The defense mechanism evidenced by this separation between the patient's words and realization is the bane of the insight-seeking psychotherapist. It is also the bane of the insight-seeking patient who really wants to get well, but must find another avenue other than "reason" to do so. He or she cannot "figure things out" because the context they are operating in is too small. They need access to a larger "context" to do so.

There is a knowing within us that is beyond intellect, the knowledge of the soul itself, but this knowing is kept from our conscious realization by several mechanisms, the most powerful of which is our need to cling to the consensus belief system of our society. It is frightening to go upstream; it is frightening to challenge group belief. It is easier to agree.

Even as insightful information is admitted to consciousness, it is often repressed again. One of my patients, a thirty-year-old psychologist named Gerry who came to me for treatment for depression, illustrates this fear well. I was working with Gerry during an era when being homosexual or having homosexual wishes was absolutely destructive to the professional man. In spite of this, when Gerry began telling me about his homosexual attraction toward me, his voice reflected not anxiety but a high state of excitement. I was puzzled because his words didn't seem to fit in with his overall life style. He was happily married, had children, and had never even considered any homosexual adventures before. I was puzzled at why he was able to talk so glibly about what were, to him, reprehensible wishes. Over a period of time, however, I discovered what was behind his comments. Gerry admitted, as I had already intuited, that in saying these things he had only been trying to show me how smart he was, how good a psycho-analytic patient he was and how well he could follow the rule of free association. In this way his ability to truly realize and understand his very real homosexual wishes was lost in the excitement of trying to impress me. In this way, the hidden realization about himself that his soul knew was obscured.

I believe that this type of intervening phantasy--"my therapist will see how smart I am and will admire me"--is often at work in intellectualizers, keeping the true knowing, the soul knowing, the intuitive knowing away so that the individual cannot really be touched or transformed by it.

This dynamic can certainly be seen at work in Scott's case. He wanted so much to be loved, that he felt his world would come to an end if he were not perfectly accepted. In his case, the fantasy that intervened between his being able to hear and accept this deep realization was, "I will say these things to my therapist, he will love me for it, and will take care of changing me."

There is an omniscient knowing that dwells in the soul. It is perceived by the Witness, which is the observing portion of the soul--the high intuitive center. It may be obscured by the armor that results from adhering to consensus thinking, accommodation to the enforced beliefs of society. It may also be submerged by self-doubt, often expressed in such terms as, "When I think about these things I am being silly"; "These things are only my imagination"; or "I am only saying these things because my analyst has told me to say everything, but I don't really believe them." These are some of the mechanisms which keep our inner knowing away.

Dropping Defenses

This type of knowing, this omniscient inner self-knowledge, rises as the patient grapples with his/her defenses against a painful awareness. One way that the understanding of one's defensive maneuvers comes about is through the interpretive suggestions of the therapist, based upon his or her intuitive insights. Psychoanalytic interpretation helps the insight-seeking self to realize and disengage from the defenses. An individual's defensive shields are also automatically lowered in dreaming sleep, in the half-awake state, in hypnosis and in transpersonal breathwork. In all of these deep states, there is an arising of deeply repressed intuitive knowledge.

An example of how these defenses are dropped can be seen in the case of Rita, a thirty-five-year old woman who came to my office in the midst of a depression so severe that she had to be hospitalized. At first I thought that she had such a weak controlling mechanism that we could only support her, rather than to help her to change herself through insight.

Rita progressed beautifully, however, and eventually became quite well-integrated. A tool that helped her a great deal was transpersonal breathwork. In the following passage, Rita described an important break-through that she experienced through this work:

"In the breathing I experienced myself as a `higher being' looking down upon the experiences from my past. I saw myself at each of my parents' funerals standing at their grave-sites crying.

"Also in this session I experienced my `higher self,' looking down and watching myself with my family at a

Dude Ranch when I was twelve years old.

"I have had experiences in the past when I would walk into a house and know the layout of the house, yet be certain that I had never been there in this lifetime.

"I have also had conversations with people that I had never met before, and knew that those same conversations had taken place earlier, yet I knew that they could not have happened in this existence."

During this particular breathwork experience, Rita was finally reconciled with her parents, whom she felt had always neglected her. When alive, they had been so wrapped up in each other that they had little time left for their daughter. Things had gotten better between them as Rita had grown into adulthood, but her parents were suddenly taken away from her in a fatal car accident, preventing a full healing of the wounds she had carried from her childhood. During the breathwork experience, Rita and the souls of her parents were together again, and she felt reconciled and healed. Her depression lifted, and her considerable strength was now able to fully express itself. Afterward, Rita could clearly see that the wound from her childhood, accompanied by its still-alive longings and her concurrent feelings of unworthiness, had been draining her considerable energies and the enjoyment of the blessings in her life. Now she understood and was released from her pain and fear.

Where did this reconciliation come from? Undoubtedly from a meeting of higher minds in higher realms, an exciting consequence of our being lifted into the super-sensible planes.

There were several other things at work in Rita's experience during breathwork. First, there was the Witness, the soul, remembering her past lives. This shows us that whatever "knowing" we experience in this life is certainly related to the experiences we had during our past lives, but this is not surprising since all past-life experiences are stored up in the soul, allowing us access to them. The kind of knowledge that is stored in the soul is a knowing-beyond-knowing in the sense that it is beyond the ordinary intellect we have in this lifetime. In Rita's case, the liberation of this knowledge was created by the special meditative, "altered state" experiences that are created in transpersonal breathwork. Breathwork releases us from the bonds of the material plane and lifts into a higher domain.

Madame Blavatsky wrote that when the physical body and mind are laid aside and the spiritual ego is freed, it finds itself on a higher plane of consciousness in which it can tap into the Universal Mind. Our deepest and most personal knowledge is at one with the greater knowledge of the Universal Mind as it taps into the all-encompassing surround, and probes depths of the inner self. This knowing-beyond-knowing often has a deep connection to our most consuming interests, which often point toward or hint of our greater capacities.

The way in which our interests serve as indicators of our greatest abilities can be seen in the case of Cam, a withdrawn thirty-five-year old who had an all-consuming interest in both computers and creation by numbers, which he explored in his studies of numerology and astrology. These interests, coupled with his fascination with spiritual and psychological matters, eventually pointed him toward his true path. They led him to attend a meeting in which he heard excerpts read from a poetic book, a novel on re-incarnation. This novel resonated strongly within Cam, starting him down the path to many spiritual and poetic quests.

Cam's openness to the spirit was what distinguished him from the ordinary "computer nerd" who is limited by his or her addiction to the computer as a mechanical instrument. He displayed a quick sensitivity and intuitive awareness that is often either shut down or absent in many highly intellectual types who have an addiction to figures. His exceptional mind coupled with an extraordinary creative capacity and sensitivity bespoke an inheritance with which he arrived in this lifetime. We haven't yet explored his past-life experiences, but I strongly sense that he might once have been a Kabbalist, astrologer or astronomer. We shall see.

As Cam illustrates, our true "Self" is really much greater than our present "self." Cam's feeling for the spiritual and parapsychological had only been waiting for a spark to ignite it because it already existed within his soul. Our current life interests reflect the things we have done in past lives because our Selves continue through time, through body after body. Therefore, if we can intuitively trust what we love and what interests us in this life, our passions can become a launching pad for connecting us with greater knowledge of who we really are and what our "mission" in life is.

The question has arisen, "What is Cam's mission in life beyond questing?" The fact is that he is much more integrated now. He is attending to practical matters, making a living instead of simply relying on inheritance, and is using his creativity in the field of computers to create a new business. This is an enormous step forward for someone who had been so fearful of life that he had withdrawn behind the introversion which often surrounds computer activities. He has been very much attracted to spiritu-

themes, but is expressing his spiritual interest in living a love relationship with a woman for the first time in his life. The repressed soul-characteristics and talents cannot be released all at once. In Cam's case, the long period of withdrawal had led to the kind of deprivation in life which had separated him from the fulfillment of business success and the success of a love alliance. I predict that as these essentials are satisfied, his soul-talents and needs will be further expressed in life.

Meditation as a Type of Soul Knowing

When we enter into a real and intuitive communication with ourselves, we experience a certain type of quietude within the mind. Many techniques can help us to find this place within, but one of the most direct and powerful tools is meditation. I often experience soul-knowing during my meditations, at those junctures when my mind is quiet and blank and I simply know that I am there at the center of my most intuitive knowing. This state is accompanied by a sense of quiet bliss and joy, the same kind of bliss that we experience when we enter the dream state. However we achieve it, crossing the wall to the other plane of existence is always accompanied by peacefulness, joy, and bliss. Occasionally, we can achieve these higher states simply by relaxing and being receptive.

When I am able to achieve a state of pure consciousness, I always seem to be beyond thought. I feel as if I inhabit no physical form, and am experiencing no space or time. I simply am what I am.

I have been blessed by the personal and spiritual progress that my work helping to heal others has brought to me. Once I was a very conservative and somewhat snobbish psychoanalyst. I have been broadened since I have entered into the domain of psycho-spirituality--and what joy and power this has brought with it. I no longer feel helpless or despairing when faced with a dying patient, or one with a wasting disease.

I can now see these events from a higher and greater perspective because I know about the immortality of the soul. Initiations into higher and higher knowledge of God's ever-expanding design for the Universe, continually thrill me. I feel as if my life is a never-ending reward-quest that leaves no room for boredom or despair, and I am continually learning more of the wisdom of Intuition, and of an even Higher Mind that I can sense in the shadows not yet penetrated by the light of my individual consciousness. My intuition grows as my faith grows. My belief in our divine nature is constantly validated as I learn to trust the infinity of the mind. Thus, I have a growing conviction that there are no limits to the peace, beauty and creativity that we humans, created in the likeness of God, can achieve. As *A Course in Miracles* has said, "I will be healed, as I let Him teach me to heal."

Jonas Salk, who discovered the vaccine against polio, accomplished this by imagining himself to be a virus, and asking the question, "What would I do if I were a virus?" In so doing, he was tapping into the Universal Mind, dissolving himself into a oneness with the consciousness of the virus and, in this way, finding a way to create a vaccine.

The "eureka" experience of Archimedes was very similar to this. I imagine that he experienced a sudden "click" as he sat in the bath in which he discovered a knowing that had already existed within himself.

The power of the Universal Mind to illuminate our consciousness can also be seen in this story told about Yeats when he was a young man:

"While Russell was studying art he began to write verse and shortly afterwards he was spellbound by a new student who arrived at the Metropolitan School in 1884. This youth, two years older than himself, was slender, dark-haired, and carelessly dressed; he looked and talked like a poet, and it was not long before his conversation was full of stories about Madame Blavatsky and her centuries-old Himalayan Masters.

"The young man was Yeats. A little later, while `waiting for a friend in a lodging house, he fell into conversation with a stranger, Charles Johnston, a recent school fellow of Yeats.' Through this contact he was again drawn to Theosophy.

"A close friend of AE wrote that at this time he was a 'diffident and inarticulate youth', yet that he `assimilated Theosophy with almost miraculous speed, just as though it were a familiar lesson temporarily forgotten, but now recalled with fuller understanding.' Within a week he was taking part in discussions with old students, and giving lectures with his new-old studies.'"[24]

I would imagine that there was a readiness, an inner knowing, within Yeats that was seeking this outer knowledge. When it was found, he then tapped into the Universal Mind and was able to absorb the complicated teachings of Theosophy in short order. It is likely, I believe, that this same tapping into a Universal Mind is the source of the genius composing of Mozart, the genius art of Picasso, the genius choreography of Graham, and the genius mathematics of Einstein.

In my own life, I have often experienced the fruits of that inner readiness and knowing. For example, in 1978 while I was attending a meeting in the offices of the National Institute of Mental Health, the newly published *A Course in Miracles* was offered. I immediately had to buy it, for reasons that were then unknown to me. Upon reading it, I was inwardly compelled to do the one-year course, which was a part of the study in this three-volume set. I was caught in the net of a spiritual calling, and my approach to life and to psychotherapy was forever changed.

By doing this, I had come full circle. The new world that opened for me was a call to the love in my heart, the love that had originally inspired me and so many others to go into medicine. That new world pointed the way to realms of knowledge greater than anything I had ever been taught before, realms beyond the body, showing me how the body and reality could be influenced and changed by Mind, which was something far greater than the brain. That immortality, goodness and unity that I glimpsed within that world was something to which I and my patients could aspire.

In finding this realm, I finally understood myself. I had always been thought of by my colleagues as a little on the fringe--someone who was "different" somehow, in spite of the fact that I was foursquare and solid in my academic training, publishing history, and membership in professional organizations. I had been disappointed over and over again because, even though I had come close to the circles of highest recognition in the psychanalytic field, I had never quite gotten there. There was always something a little too different about me--now I would say a little too "disobedient."

The new opening within myself after discovering *A Course in Miracles* allowed me to transcend this disappointment and even to be glad that I had not been caught in the web of having to agree with my colleagues in order to remain "orthodox." I could now explore the new rooms that intuition had opened. I could become "religious" again, in a new sense of the word, without fearing either the censure of my academic fellows or the too great restrictions of organized religion.

As my new studies captivated me and lifted me, I was able to lift my patients in a new way that was far beyond the simple "curing" of this or that illness. Now we were in the business of creating "better-than-wellness." And many a patient ended by saying that he/she was glad to have experienced their affliction because of the new world that had been opened to them.

Along with intuition, prayer became the partner which accompanied me in my work and my meditations. I pray when I am in a tight spot with a patient and know that I do not understand enough about what is going on--and, sure enough, understanding comes. My clients and I pray at the end of group sessions, and the energy of our prayers fills the room and all of us with quiet joy and a holy feeling. I can be happy trusting my intuition, and having faith that it will continue to grow and come to my rescue. When I am in trouble in therapy, I can use it to get in touch with the subtle vibrations between myself and my patient. More often than not, I will discover a silent and subtle wall that the patient has erected. When I ask him or her to join me in looking at it, the wall comes down and we both move on -- and up!

In this way, intuition and soul-knowing has opened a world of wonder for me and my patients. Again, as the prayer in *A Course in Miracles* says, "I will be healed as I let Him teach me to heal."

Guidelines and Exercises:

1. Quiet the self; await the time of quiet bliss; enjoy; sometimes in a comfortable chair, sometimes in a warm bath, sometimes in contact with nature. Practice achieving this state of quiet bliss.

2. Wait for signals to enter, messages, especially high messages.

3. Look for the "intuitive click" or "intuitive thrill." Become familiar with it. Trust it more and more.

4. Look for hunches -- avoid suppressing them.

5. Make intuitive assessments of those whom you meet. Let experience validate them. Again suspend doubt.

6. In your reading, if new ideas occur to you, value them, especially if there is a click or an "aha."

7. Look for premonitions, record them, honor them. Be not surprised when they are validated.

8. In transaction with someone close to you, settle in, look into the eyes and be silent. Look for intuitive ideas about the feelings in the eyes. Honor them.

9. Settle in with someone with whom you are close. Achieve quietude. Notice your own feelings and response. Honor those feelings. Sift away what are your own feelings of shame or embarrassment in doing this. Record what you have received. Be not surprised when this is validated.

10. Analyze your dreams. Note particularly the feeling in the dream. Note the contact with the day before that triggered the dream. See what the elements of the dream mean to you, being careful not to suppress ideas that you think are "silly" or "crazy." Record and intuitively analyze the dream. Be not surprised if your insights are validated.

11. Look for your contact with the realm of Knowing Beyond Knowing: settle into quietude and quiet bliss. When ideas come in, honor them as coming from on high. See how they fit into your life. Record them. The quiet bliss and the sensing of ideas beyond intellect is entry into the realm of Knowing Beyond Knowing.

12. Resist feelings of shame or fear of inferiority when your ideas do not conform to the commonly accepted beliefs. New ideas come from on high and may be suppressed by what others think. Then apply this to your life. Make it sensible. Remember that too much of our society is stuck on the material beliefs, the accepted beliefs about the mind.

13. In introspection you will notice that the Witness hovers over the scene, watching wherever you are.

14. Locate the point outside of yourself where the self-observing self (the Witness) resides.Notice how the Witness observes you as you talk to someone else as well as observing that someone else.

15. Practice intuition. Notice the part of your body which is the seat of your intuition. Is it in the heart? Is it in the solar plexus? Is it somewhere else within you. Use that response to know when your intuition says, "Yes."

16. Meditation as a "soul-knowing." Quiet the body; quiet the emotions; let the thoughts go as if drifting away; wait for quietude, quiet bliss and know that you are then in contact with your soul. The Hallmark feeling is the feeling of peace.

17. Use the feeling of peace in your close relationships, which will lead to intuitive knowing of each other. Settle down, look at your partner, let peace prevail. Notice the "soul-to-soul" contact, the "heart-to-heart" contact when you are in this envelope together.

CHAPTER XIV:
The Future

When Carl Jung was travelling in Africa, he had the opportunity to visit the Athio Plains, an immense and isolated game preserve at an altitude of eight thousand feet. As Jung gazed out upon the gigantic herds of gnu, antelope, gazelle, zebra, and warthogs that filled the savanna to the horizon, he was struck with a vision -- that this world had not really existed until he had come upon it and given it reality by his conscious attention. In perceiving this, Jung suddenly realized that this kind of objective, creative, enlivening attention was a quality that we usually subscribed only to God. By contrast, human beings perceived reality as a clockwork mechanism.

"...we view life as a machine calculated down to the last detail, which, along with the human psyche, runs on senselessly, obeying foreknown and predetermined rules. In such a cheerless clockwork fantasy there is no drama of man, world, and God; there is no `new day' leading to `new shores,' but only the dreariness of calculated processes. My old Pueblo friend came to my mind. He thought that the *raison d'etre* of his pueblo had been to help their father, the sun, to cross the sky each day. I had envied him for the fullness of meaning in that belief, and had been looking about without hope for a myth of our own. Now I knew what it was, and knew even more: that man is indispensable for the completion of creation; that, in fact, he himself is the second creator of the world, who alone has given to the world its objective existence - without which, unheard, unseen, silently eating, giving birth, dying, heads nodding through hundreds of millions of years, it would have gone on in the profoundest night of non being down to its unknown end. Human consciousness created objective existence and meaning, and man found his indispensable place in the great process of being."[25]

Reading of Jung's experience, we can begin to realize that the great creator is the mind properly used. In viewing the world as a clockwork existence, we disown our power, delegating it to an external machine. By

-239-

so doing, we fail to recognize that we are co-creators with God. We are truly created in God's image, not in form, but in spirit and creative magic.

Theosophy teaches that humanity stands midway on the ladder of ascension. We are above the plants and animals, and below the ascended masters and angels. An individual stands midway because he/she has acquired self-consciousness, and in so doing has acquired the power of the spirit to create.

The creative power of consciousness can be seen clearly in the discoveries of modern physics, which describe what is called the "observer effect." Light, when observed, will either appear as a particle or a wave. In the subatomic world, one can either measure the speed of a particle or its position, not both. Nothing can be observed by a human being without changing it -- a form of creation in itself.

Being conscious of something, being able to imagine it, is often the first step toward bringing this idea forward into reality. The architect places the plans for a building on paper and the construction is carried forward by the crew and the project supervisor. The blueprint manifests concretely. We also know that the mind can influence the body through meditation, hypnosis, and visionary experiences. People are able to cure themselves of cancer and other diseases by visualizing themselves as being well. Sai Baba and Madame Blavatsky were able to produce the manifestation of material objects by employing a larger understanding of the laws of nature. This ability reveals an ascent into the implicate order of things, a realm where the known laws of nature are superseded.

The ability to see into the implicate order is also experienced by those who have had a near-death experience. During these times, people often obtain visions of the other side, as can be seen in the following description by Jung of the knowledge that he received following his own near-death experience:

"Everything around me seemed enchanted. At this hour of the night the nurse brought me some food she had warmed--for only then was I able to take any, and I ate with appetite. For a time it seemed to me that she was an old Jewish woman, much older than she actually was, and that she was preparing ritual kosher dishes for me. When I looked at her, she seemed to have a blue halo around her head. I myself was, so it seemed, in the Pardes Rimmonim, the garden of pomegranates, and the wedding of Tifereth and Malchuth was taking place. Or else I was Rabbi

Simon ben Jochai whose wedding in the afterlife was being celebrated.... I cannot tell you how wonderful it was.... These were ineffable states of joy. Angels were present, and light. I myself was the `Marriage of the Lamb.'...

"All these experiences were glorious. Night after night I floated in a state of purest bliss, `thronged round with images of all creation.' Gradually, the motifs mingled and paled. Usually the visions lasted for about an hour; then I would fall asleep again. By the time morning drew near, I would feel: Now gray morning is coming again; now comes the gray world with its boxes! What idiocy, what hideous nonsense! Those inner states were so fantastically beautiful that by comparison this world appeared downright ridiculous. As I approached closer to life again, they grew fainter, and scarcely three weeks after the first vision they ceased altogether.

"It is impossible to convey the beauty and intensity of emotion during those visions. They were the most tremendous things I have ever experienced. And what a contrast the day was: I was tormented and on edge; everything irritated me; everything was too material, too crude and clumsy, terribly limited both spatially and spiritually.... I had clearly perceived its emptiness. Although my belief in the world returned to me, I have never since entirely freed myself of the impression that this life is a segment of existence which is enacted on a three-dimensional box-like universe especially set up for it."[26]

Reflecting on these pages out of Jung's autobiography *Memories, Dreams, Reflections,* we can see two things. The first is the affiliation that society has with a mechanistic, materialistic, somewhat selfish world. The second is that we can envision a better world. Present-day psychologists and psychiatrists might say that Jung was hallucinating or simply imagining things but again I raise the question, what is imagination? Perhaps there is no such thing, perhaps there is only perception of another plane of reality that we can visit. This idea becomes all the more likely when we realize that we are actually creators of reality.

Consensus opinion once imagined the earth to be a flat surface off of which people could fall and perish. Then it became, despite resistance from the orthodoxy, a sphere. The idea that the universe rotated around the earth was also a reality in its own time.

Descriptions of reality come and go, but there have always been those people sensitive enough to see a greater reality. Interestingly enough, some aspects of this "greater" reality are now being recorded by scientists who utilize various physical instruments for measurement of these subtle energies. In addition to Professor Robert Jahn and Brenda Dunne who are recording the psychokinetic effects of the mind, there is Buryl Paine who has devised instrumentation to detect the biological energies surrounding the body, and Professor Motoyama who can computer record the acupuncture meridians and their points of potential. Rupert Sheldrake's thesis of morphogenic fields, those invisible fields which give form to biological creations and the forms of behavior, are being tested by various experiments across the world. Barbara Brennan, a sensitive who can perceive the auric energies surrounding the body, has developed a training course to help others to perceive the same. And so it goes, at an accelerating pace, we discover more and more about the subtle realms at an ever increasing pace as we approach the millenium.

I contend that we do not have to choose to live in an "either-or" reality. We do have the ability to visit other planes that are as real as this one, but we must also be grounded and sensible enough to function within the reality of our culture. We cannot experience the former at the expense of the latter.

In his book *The Future of the Body* Michael Murphy, one of the two founders of Esalen Institute, has written an exhaustive survey of extraordinary human performance in the athletic and mental realms through which he projects the image of the evolving human. In light of this, why not accept that on the higher planes of the mind we can literally become creators, and in so doing visit and generate other planes of reality?

Many of the Eastern teachers have said that the physical-material plane of reality is the least of all worlds. This is quite a hopeful idea--if this is so, then I believe that things will only get better! Experiences with life after death, which are becoming more commonly reported, teach us that there is a beatific realm up there in which our dear departed appear in their prime, and that this new world is fulfilling, loving and united. Such a view conforms to the teachings of the Ancient Masters who instruct us that after we leave this earthly coil, we linger for a long while in the Devachan, the heaven in which all of our desires are fulfilled according to our earned reward.

If all life is indeed a growing experience converging toward a new truth, why then should we not look forward in the future, as we ascend in personality and mind performance, to a better world in which the increased powers of the mind and spirit are reflected in a better society?

But what, some readers may ask, about the pain, despair and violence that we see every night on the evening news? The cynicism that permeates our present society informs us that, statistically, every year the world is getting worse--more violent and more terrible, and that humanity is becoming more fragmented and alienated from concepts such as compassion and common humanity.

I believe, however, that we do not need to give in to cynicism and lack of hope for the future for the simple reason that what our culture is experiencing at this time is only a part of a larger cycle that we have momentarily lost sight of. World history and cosmic history both indicate that progress occurs and progress recedes. In our world today, there are many hopeful signs of an ongoing elevation and growth in the character and outlook of our people that point to an upswing of the cycle. Currently, we are experiencing an unprecedented renaissance of interest in spiritual and parapsychological matters, subjects that only a few years ago would have been scoffed at. There is also an ongoing radical rebellion against materialism that was very evident in the 1960's and continues today as a counterforce against material and separatist interests.

Secondly, more and more people are becoming aware of how much power they really have to change what is unfair or unjust in our society. I remember not long ago the "Housewife's Rebellion" against the high price of meat. This was a completely unorganized phenomenon, but an effective one nevertheless. At the time, meat prices were just too high--because of this, housewives here and there decided to boycott meat purchase. After a time there was a massive rebellion across the country, and the price of meat came down. Such a rebellion doesn't rest on sheer numbers. The "Hundredth Monkey" phenomenon, which states that one does not need the majority to embrace a new idea to change one's culture, is always ready to work. If a critical mass of opinion is achieved, a complete change in society's attitude will inevitably follow.

In line with this, and as a counterbalance against the academic "establishment," the real work for social change and the real discoveries in science are going on outside of the official institutions. Progress and radical change of belief has always relied on a few outsiders. What better historical example of this is there than that of Jesus and his disciples? Just now, a number of Senators, including Bill Bradley of New Jersey, have resigned their political posts in order to work for society in a freer way. Bradley and other influential congressional voices have said that the real change in government must come from the hue and cry of the people.

There is evidence that many changes desired by the people are already at hand. Recently, for example, a number of state referenda have been passed limiting the amount of campaign contributions that can be made by any individual or organization, including the candidate, to a single campaign. This is something that established government has tried to achieve, but failed to do--clearly a result of the "Hundredth-Monkey" principle.

Finally, we have seen evidence of the power of thought and the power of the word to change reality. In writing about the work of well-respected past-life researchers Helen Wambach and her colleague Chet Snow in *The Holographic Universe,* Michael Talbot reports that when thousands of subjects were hypnotized forward into the future, they all came up with four distinct scenarios, some dreadful and some pleasant. For this reason Wambach and Snow, like many of their colleagues, believe that "we create our own destiny, both individually and collectively, and thus we can glimpse....various potential futures the human race is creating for itself en masse." For this reason Snow recommends that we should spend time believing in and visualizing a positive future rather than in building bomb shelters. I myself have seen this kind of positive thinking work wonders in patients with allegedly hopeless medical conditions, and see no reason why it could it not work en masse as each individual in society is informed and elevated to a level of love that can open the future to the higher planes that are the natural residence of the human soul.

Quoting from the Tibetan in *A Treatise on Cosmic Fire*[27], Bailey and the Tibetan imagine what this new world will be like: "The results of this pranic transmission will be more healthy physical bodies among the sons of men....further that these bodies will have great resilience, great strength, great physical magnetism and `delicacy and refinement of appearance as yet unknown.'" The Tibetan also goes on to say that men will increasingly act on the etheric plane, summoning the electromagnetic energies that now emanate from the mind, and that this will give them an etheric vision. With this etheric vision they will be able to divine more about the electromagnetic field surrounding the body, making medical discoveries and increasing medical cures:

"The centre of attention of medical and scientific students will be focussed on the etheric body, and the dependence of the physical body upon the etheric body will be recognized. This will change the attitude of the medical profession, and magnetic healing and vibratory stimulation will supersede the present methods of surgery and drug assimilation."[28]

In that future time humanity will also recognize its connection with the animal and vegetable kingdoms:

> "The time will come when the attitude of man to the animal kingdom will be revolutionized, and the slaughter, ill-treatment, and that form of cruelty called 'sport' will be done away with.... The unity of life will be a known and a scientific fact with which contact is effected....
>
> "The effect on the mind is direct apprehension of truth and direct understanding of a knowledge which is so wide and synthetic in its grasp that we cover it by the nebulous term, the Universal Mind. This type of knowledge is sometimes called the Intuition, and is one of the main characteristics of illumination."

The Tibetan goes on to speak of the alchemical process, the transmutative process. In contrast to common belief, the true alchemist is not seeking to change base metal into gold; he/she is seeking to change a base personality into a golden one. This is also the task of the psychotherapist, most particularly the spiritual psychotherapist.

This alchemical transformation develops automatically as we help the patient to "house-clean" the emotional residues of past acculturation, of clinging to materialistic fulfillment. The soul rises automatically as this house cleaning takes place, carrying the personality with it. At the same time, however, we need to be wary, for the more we ascend into the Light, the more the Forces of Darkness will seek to obstruct us.

In the end, it is my hope that as these principles are understood, as the path indicated by these visions is followed, and as the new planes of reality that we can co-create arrive, the spiritual psychotherapist will not only participate in this revolution, but be in its vanguard. When that day comes, the world will have seen a true return to the physician-priest who administers not only to the body, but also to the soul of humankind.

THE FUTURE

EPILOGUE

And what would I hope that the message of this book would be? That the soul is easy to seek. It is ever present. It is ourselves at core. The soul is surrounded by layers of repression that we are taught as children to use to hide our selves from our inner Selves. These coverings are further increased by society's admonitions to keep ourselves separate, each from the other, and to practice power rather than love--to seek personal advantage rather than sharing in the joy of bringing advantage to others. The essence of this book's message is that it is easy to find the soul within the self. It is there already, waiting to arise. The soul is the better part of ourselves, the loving part, the giving part, the aesthetic part, and, in fact, the immortal bliss part.

We seek the soul in psychotherapy but, after all, life itself is psychotherapy--often the very best kind. Therefore, it may not be necessary to see a professional in order to release ourselves and our souls, but rather to strive through self-understanding to face the darkness within us, and to dismiss it by throwing the light of understanding and acceptance upon it.

This book is written from the experiences of a traditional psychotherapist who has become a spiritual one. Everything I say has had its source in that transformation. But, I repeat, "We are all therapists to ourselves and to others in life. The most essential teaching that we do is the teaching by virtue of what we are."

Therefore, it is my hope not only that the physician will return to the physician-priest, but that all of us will move forward toward this goal.

ENDNOTES

1. Carl Jung, *Memories, Dreams, Reflections* (New York: Vintage, 1965), page 201.

2. Alice A. Bailey, *From Intellect to Intuition* (New York: Lucis Publishing Co.,1960), pages 79-80:

"Transmutation is the changing, and re-directing of the energies of the mind, of the emotions and of the physical nature so that they serve to reveal the Self, and not simply to reveal the psychical and body natures.

"We are told, for instance, that we have five main instincts, which we share in common with all animals. These, when used with selfish and personal objectives, enhance the body life, strengthen the form or material nature and so serve increasingly to hide the Self, the spiritual man. These must be transmuted into their higher counterparts, for every animal characteristic has its spiritual prototype. The instinct of self-preservation must eventually be superseded by realization of immortality, and `dwelling ever in the Eternal,' man will walk the earth and fulfill his destiny. The instinct which causes the lower self to thrust itself forward, and force its way upward, will eventually be transformed into the domination of the higher or spiritual Self. The assertion of the little or lower self will give way to that of the higher Self. Sex, which is an animal instinct powerfully governing all animal forms, will give place to a higher attraction, and will, in its noblest aspects, bring about conscious attraction and union between the soul and its vehicle; whilst the herd instinct will be transmuted into group consciousness. A fifth instinct, namely the urge to inquire and to investigate which characterizes all minds at a high or a low level, will give place to intuitive perception and understanding, and so the great work will be accomplished and the spiritual man will dominate his creation, the human being, and lift all his attributes and aspects into heaven."

3. Alice A. Bailey, *A Treatise on Cosmic Fire* (New York: Lucis Publishing Co., 1973).

Herein she speaks of transmutation, and the different kinds of transmutation in the hands of the Brothers of Light and those of Darkness:

"First. The white Brother deals with positive electrical energy. The dark Brother deals with the negative electrical energy.

"Second. The white Brother occupies himself with the soul of things. The black Magician centres his attention upon the form.

"Third. The white Magician develops the inherent energy of the sphere concerned (whether human, animal, vegetable or mineral) and produces results through the self-induced activities of the central life, subhuman, human or super-human. The black Magician attains results through the agency of force external to the sphere involved, and produces transmutation through the agency of resolvents... or through the method of the reduction of the form, rather than through radiation, as does the white Magician....

"In the transmutative process as carried on by the Brotherhood, the dinner fire which animates the atom, form or man is stimulated, fanned and strengthened till it (through its own internal potency) burns up its sheaths, and escapes by radiation from within its ring-pass-not.... The fire within burns up all else and the electric fire escapes. The true alchemist therefore in days to come will in every case seek to stimulate the radioactivity of the element or atom with which he is working and will centre his attention upon the positive nucleus. By increasing its vibration, its activity, or its positivity, he will bring about the desired end. The Masters do this in connection with the human spirit and do not concern Themselves at all with his `deva' aspect....

"The process as carried on by the Dark Brotherhood is the reverse of this. They centre the attention upon the form, and seek to shatter and break that form, or the combination of atoms, in order to permit the central electric life to escape. They bring about this result through external agencies .... They burn and destroy the material sheath, seeking to imprison the escaping volatile essence as the form disintegrates. This hinders the evolutionary plan in the case of the life involved, delays the consummation, interferes with the ordered progress of development, and puts all the factors involved in a bad position."

4.   H. P. Blavatsky, *The Key to Theosophy* (Pasadena, CA: Theosophical University Press, 1987), page 29.

5.   Alice A. Bailey, *A Treatise on Cosmic Fire* (New York: Lucis Publishing Co., 1973), pages 475-477.
    Here she speaks of alchemy in the following way:
"The mind of the scientist seeks the universal solvent which will reduce matter to its primordial substance, release energy, and thus reveal the processes of evolution, and enable the seeker to build for himself(from the primordial base) the desired forms. The mind of the alchemist searches for the Philosopher's Stone, that effective transmuting agent which will bring

about revelation, and the power to impose the will of the chemist upon the elemental forces....

"Transmutation is the passage across from one state of being to another through the agency of fire.

"The discovery of the primordial essence of matter, the Philosopher's Stone, has been pursued by seekers from ages long ago. What is the Philosopher's Stone? Webster defines it as, `An imaginary stone, substance, or chemical preparation believed to have the power of transmuting baser metals into gold and sought for by alchemists.' "

6. Michael Talbot, *The Holographic Universe* (New York: Harper Perennial, 1991).

7. Myron Sharaf, *A Fury on Earth* (New York: St. Martin's Press/ Marek,1983).

8. This material is from a lecture called "Pleasure - the Pulsation of Life" delivered by Eva Pierrokos on November 7, 1969.

9. Rodger Kamenetz, *The Jew in the Lotus* (New York: HarperCollins, 1994), pages 204-205.

10. Sri. Aurobindo, *The Synthesis of Yoga* (Pondicheerry, India: Sri Aurobindo Ashram, 1984), pages 484-485.

11. Alice A. Bailey, *From Intellect to Intuition* (New York: Lucis Publishing Co., 1960), page 159.

Bailey speaks of the reception of inspired material from on high through intuition:

"The illumination of the mind by the soul, and the throwing down into the waiting and attentive `mind-stuff1 of that knowledge and wisdom which is the prerogative of the soul produce, in the truly unified and coordinated man, results which differ according to the part of his instrument with which contact is effected....

"The effect on the mind is direct apprehension of truth and direct understanding of a knowledge which is so wide and synthetic in its grasp that we cover it by the nebulous term, the Universal Mind. This type of knowledge is sometimes called the Intuition, and is one of the main characteristics of illumination."

12. Swami Prabhupada, *The Bhagavad-Gita As It Is* (Sydney, Australia: The Bhaktivedanta Book Trust,1986), chapter 8, verse 4.

13. Michael Talbot, *The Holographic Universe* (New York: Harper Collins, 1991), pp. 218-219.

14. H. B. Blavatsky, *The Key To Theosophy* (Pasadena, CA: Theosophical University Press, 1989), pages 29-30.

15. David J. Hufford, *The Terror That Comes In The Night* (University of Pennsylvania Press, 1989), page 10.

16. David J. Hufford, T*he Terror That Comes In The Night* (University of Pennsylvania Press, 1989), page 10.

17. M. P. Pandit, *Dictionary of Sri Aurobindo's Yoga,* (Pondicherry, India: Dipti Publications, 1973), page 233.

18. M. P. Pandit, *Dictionary of Sri Aurobindo's Yoga,* (Pondicherry, India: Dipti Publications, 1973), page 233.

19. Alice A. Bailey, *Letters on Occult Meditation* (New York: Lucis Publishing Co., 1950), page 131.

20. Alice A. Bailey, *Letters on Occult Meditation* (New York: Lucis Publishing Co., 1950), pages 131-134.

21. Alice A. Bailey, *Letters on Occult Meditation* (New York, N.Y., Lucis Publishing Co.1950), page 133.
The Tibetan reminds of the inner divinity which will be a support against despair:
"He should persevere until the end -- the end of what? The end of the enveloping cloud, the point where it merges itself into sunlight.... God is within, no matter what transpires without. We are so apt to look out at surrounding circumstances, whether physical, astral or mental, and to forget that the inmost center of the heart hides our points of contact with the Universal Logos."

22. Alice A. Bailey, *Letters on Occult Meditation* (New York: Lucis Publishing Co., 1950) pages 134-135.

Here she states the dangers of remaining materialistic, shutting out the path to the Light, and being tempted (personality-wise) to fall into the ways of the perverse personality:

"Anyone who overexalts the concrete mind and permits it continuously to shut out the higher, is in danger of straying on the left-hand path. Many so stray.... It is the man who persists in spite of warning and of pain who eventually becomes a brother of darkness....

"The dark brother recognizes no unity with his species, only seeing in them people to be exploited for the furtherance of his own ends.... They respect no person, they regard all men as fair prey, they use everyone to get their own way enforced, and by fair means or foul they seek to break down all opposition and for the personal self acquire that which they desire.

"The dark brother ... cares not what agony of mind he brings upon an opponent; he persists in his intention and desists not from the hurt of any man, woman or child, provided that in the process his own ends are furthered. Expect absolutely no mercy from those opposing the Brotherhood of Light."

23. Alice A. Bailey, *Letters on Occult Meditation* (New York: Lucis Publishing Co., 1950), pages 136-137.

She warns against those who masquerade in the light, and indicates defenses against their lure:

"Oft too the Dark Brother masquerades as an agent of the light, oft he poses as a messenger of the gods....

"At this time their power is ofttimes mighty. Why? Because so much exists as yet in the personalities of all men that respond to their vibration....

"And now what methods may be employed to safeguard the worker in the field of the world? ...

"1- A realization that purity of all the vehicles is the prime essential ... the need of scrupulous cleanliness of the physical body, of clean steady emotion ... in the emotional body, and of purity of thought in the mental body....

"2- The elimination of all fear....

"3- A standing firm and unmoved no matter what occurs....

24. Sylvia Cranston, *HBP: The Extraordinary Life & Influence of Helena Blavatsky* (New York: Tarcher/Putnam, 1993), page 471.

25. Carl Gustav Jung, *Memories, Dreams, Reflections* (New York: Vintage Books, 1965).

26. Carl Gustav Jung, *Memories, Dreams, Reflections* (New York: Vintage Books, 1965), pages 294-295.

27. Alice A. Bailey, *A Treatise on Cosmic Fire* (New York: Lucis Publishing Co.,1973), pages 473-474.

28. Alice A. Bailey, *A Treatise on Cosmic Fire* (New York: Lucis Publishing Co.,1973), page 474.

ENDNOTES

BIBLIOGRAPHY

A Course in Miracles. Farmingdale, NY: The Foundation For Inner Peace, 1983.

Assagioli, Roberto. *Psychosynthesis: A Manual of Principles and Techniques.* New York: Hobbs, Dorman, 1965.

Aurobindo, Sri. *The Synthesis of Yoga.* Pondicheerry, India: Sri Aurobindo Ashram, 1984.

Bailey, Alice A. *A Treatise on Cosmic Fire.* New York: Lucis Publishing Co., 1973.

Bailey, Alice A. *From Intellect to Intuition.* New York: Lucis Publishing Co., 1960.

Bailey, Alice A. *Letters on Occult Meditation.* New York: Lucis Publishing Co., 1950.

Blavatsky, H. P. *Isis Unveiled.* Pasadena, CA: Theosophical University Press, 1988.

Blavatsky, H. P. *The Secret Doctrine.* Pasadena, CA: Theosophical University Press, 1988.

Blavatsky, H. P. *The Key to Theosophy.* Pasadena, CA: Theosophical University Press, 1987.

Castaneda, Carlos. *The Art of Dreaming.* New York: HarperCollins Publishers, 1993.

Chopra, Deepak. *The Path to Love: Renewing the Power of Spirit in your Life.* New York: Harmony Books, 1997.

Cranston, Sylvia. *HPB: The Extraordinary Life & Influence of Helena Blavatsky.* New York: Jeremy P. Tarcher/Putnam, 1993.

De Chardin, Teilhard. *The Future of Man.* New York: Harper Colophon Books, Harper and Row, 1964.

Dossey, Larry. *Space, Time, & Medicine.* Boulder: Shambhala; New York: Distributed in U.S. by Random House, 1982.

Eckhart, Meister. *The Way of Paradox: Spiritual Life as Taught by Meister Eckhart.* London: Darton, Longman and Todd, 1987.

Emerson, Ralph Waldo. *The Oversoul,* in *Emerson: Essays and Lectures.* The Library of America: Viking Press, 1983.

Freud, Sigmund: in Breuer and Freud. *Studies on Hysteria.* New York: Avon Books, 1966.

Freud, Sigmund. *The Interpretation of Dreams.* New York: Gramercy Books, 1996.

Gabbard, Glenn and Twemlow, Stuart. *With the Eyes of the Mind: an Empirical Analysis of Out-of-Body States.* New York: Praeger, 1984.

Grof, Stanislav. *Realms of the Human Unconscious.* New York: Viking Press, 1975.

Houston, Jean. *The Search for the Beloved: Journeys in Sacred Psychology.* Los Angeles: J.P. Tarcher, 1987.

Hufford, David J. *The Terror That Comes In The Night.* Philadelphia: University of Pennsylvania Press, 1989.

Jacobson, Edmund. *Modern Treatment of Tense Patients, Including the Neurotic and Depressed with Case Illustrations, Follow-ups, and EMG Measurements.* Springfield, IL: Thomas, 1970.

Jampolsky, Gerald G. *Love Is Letting Go Of Fear.* Millbrae, CA: Celestial Arts, 1979.

Joudry, Patricia with Pressman, Maurie D. *Twin Souls*. New York: Random House, 1995.

Jung, Carl Gustav. *Memories, Dreams, Reflections*. New York: Vintage Books, 1965.

Kamenetz, Rodger. *The Jew in the Lotus*. New York: HarperCollins, 1994.

Kubler-Ross, Elizabeth. *On Death and Dying*. New York: Macmillan, 1969.

The Mahatma Letters to A. P. Sinnett from the Mahatmas M. & K. H. transcribed, compiled, and with an introduction by A. T. Barker. Pasadena, CA: Theosophical University Press, 1975.

Maslow, Abraham. *Toward A Psychology Of Being*. Reinhold, NY: Van Nostrand, 1968.

Mitchell, Steven. *The Gospel According to Jesus*. New York: HarperCollins, 1991.

Moody, Raymond. *Reflections on Life after Life*. Boston: G. K. Hall, 1978.

Muktananda, Swami. *Siddha Meditation*. Oakland, CA: S.Y.D.A. Foundation, 1975.

Munroe, Robert. *Journeys Out of the Body*. New York: Doubleday, 1971.

Murphy, Michael. *The Future of the Body: Explorations into the Further Evolution of Human Nature*. Los Angeles: J.P. Tarcher, 1992.

Pandit, M. P. *Dictionary of Sri Aurobindo*. Pondicherry, India: Dipti Publications, Sri Aurobindo Ashram, 1973.

Peck, M. Scott. *A Different Drum: Community-Making and Peace*. New York: Simon and Schuster, 1987.

Perls, Frederick, M.D., Ph.D. et al. *Gestalt Therapy.* New York: Bantam Books, 1980.

Pierrokos, Eva. Lecture - *The Pulsation of Life* delivered in Philadelphia November 7, 1969.

Pierrokos, John. *Core Energetics: Developing the Capacity to Love and Heal.* Mendocino, CA: LifeRhythm Publication, 1990.

Prabhupada Swami. *The Bhagavad-Gita As It Is.* Sydney, Australia: The Bhaktivedanta Book Trust,1986.

Ram Dass. *Journey of Awakening: A Meditator's Guidebook.* New York: Bantam Books, 1990.

Ring, Kenneth. *Life at Death: A Scientific Investigation of the Near-Death Experience.* New York: Quill, 1982.

Ryan, Charles. *H. P. Blavatsky and the Theosophical Movement.* Point Loma. CA: Theosophical University Press, 1937.

Sharaf, Myron. *A Fury on Earth.* New York: St. Martin's Press/Marek, 1983.

Sheldrake, Rupert. *A New Science of Life.* London: Blond & Briggs, 1981.

Simonton, O. Carl. *Getting Well Again.* Los Angeles: J. P. Tarcher, 1978; New York: distributed by St. Martin's Press.

Sinetar, Marsha. *Do What You Love and the Money Will Follow.* New York: Paulist Press, 1986.

Singer, June. *Androgyny: Toward a New Theory of Sexuality.* Garden City, NY: Anchor Press, 1976.

Stevenson, Ian. *Studies of Twenty Cases of Reincarnation.* Charlottesville: University Press of Virginia, 1974.

Talbot, Michael. *The Holographic Universe.* New York: HarperCollins Publishers, 1991.

Tart, Charles. *Altered States of Consciousness.* San Francisco: Harper, 1990.

Vaughn, Frances. *Awakening Intuition.* Garden City, NY: Anchor Press, 1979.

Verney, Thomas. *The Secret Life of the Unborn Child.* New York: Delta Books, 1981.

Watts, Alan. *The Way of Zen.* NewYork: Pantheon, 1957.

Weiss, Brian. *Many Lives, Many Masters.* New York: Simon & Schuster, 1988.

Wilber, Ken. *A Brief History of Everything.* Boston: Shambhala, 1996.

Young, Arthur. *The Reflexive Universe: Evolution of Consciousness.* New York: Delacorte Press, 1976.

Zukav, Gary. *Seat of the Soul.* New York: Simon and Schuster, 1989.

Dr. Pressman is available for seminars, workshops, and classes.
For more information contact:

Maurie D. Pressman, M.D.
Pressman Center for Mind/Body Wellness
200 Locust Street
Philadelphia, PA 19106

Telephone: 215-922-0204
Fax: 215-922-3008
E-mail: mauriedavid@spirituali.com

Website: http://www.mauriepressman.com/

To order this and other works by Maurie D. Pressman, M.D., contact him at
200 Locust Street, Philadelphia, PA 19106
or
Inkwell Productions
3370 N. Hayden Road #123-276, Scottsdale, AZ 85251
Phone 480-315-9636
Fax 480-315-9641
Toll-Free 1-800-214-3550
E-mail: info@selfpublishersgroup.com
Website: www.selfpublishersgroup.com